The One Year®
Daily Moments of Strength

THE ONE YEAR®

DAILY MOMENTS OF

STRENGTH

INSPIRATION FOR MEN

WALK THRU THE BIBLE®

TYNDALE
MOMENTUM™

The nonfiction imprint of
Tyndale House Publishers, Inc.

Visit Tyndale online at www.tyndale.com.

Visit Tyndale Momentum online at www.tyndalemomentum.com.

TYNDALE, *Tyndale Momentum*, Tyndale's quill logo, *One Year*, and *The One Year* are registered trademarks of Tyndale House Publishers, Inc. The Tyndale Momentum logo is a trademark of Tyndale House Publishers, Inc. Tyndale Momentum is the nonfiction imprint of Tyndale House Publishers, Inc., Carol Stream, Illinois.

Walk Thru the Bible is a registered trademark of Walk Thru the Bible Ministries, Inc.

The One Year® Daily Moments of Strength: Inspiration for Men

Designed by Mark Anthony Lane II

Some of these devotions were previously published by Walk Thru the Bible in Stand Firm magazine, September 2013.

For information about special discounts for bulk purchases, please contact Tyndale House Publishers at csresponse@tyndale.com or call 1-800-323-9400.

ISBN 978-1-4964-0606-4

Printed in the United States of America

23   22   21   20   19
7   6   5   4

INTRODUCTION

As MEN, WE OFTEN FEEL challenged to prove our worth to the people around us, whether it's at home (perhaps as husbands and fathers), at work (as employees or supervisors), or on the basketball court or golf course with our friends. But with all the demands on our time, energy, and resources—not to mention our relationships—we can feel weak, overwhelmed, and exhausted. Thankfully, God never intended for us to go it alone, in our own power. He designed us to draw our strength and direction from Him, and to find encouragement and inspiration in community with our families and with other men. In fact, God tells us, "My grace is sufficient for you, for power is perfected in weakness" (2 Corinthians 12:9, HCSB) and "[we] can do everything through Christ, who gives [us] strength" (Philippians 4:13).

This book of daily devotions is an invitation for you to spend a few minutes each day in quiet conversation with God—whether it's first thing in the morning, during your lunch break, or just before bed. God designed us to function best (and be strongest) when we regularly take time to connect with Him through His Word and in prayer. As God told the Israelites, "Only in returning to me and resting in me will you be saved. In quietness and confidence is your strength" (Isaiah 30:15).

The One Year Daily Moments of Strength devotional can be your means of connecting with God for a few minutes each day throughout the coming year. It will also serve as a daily reminder that all our strength comes from God, and that He uses His strength to work through the weakness of our lives to accomplish His purpose and plan on earth. Written from a variety of perspectives and in a variety of styles, each devotion will encourage you to place your trust in the hands of the all-powerful God of the universe, in whom is found all we need to live our lives for Him.

You can use the Moment of Strength Scripture passage at the end of each reading to take a deeper look at what God's Word says about that day's topic, and to initiate a conversation with God about the situations and people you encounter in your day-to-day life.

This resource from Walk Thru the Bible is designed to inspire you to fully embrace your relationship with God and to walk in the strength of His love, mercy, and grace. For "His divine power has given us everything required for life and godliness through the knowledge of Him who called us by His own glory and goodness" (2 Peter 1:3, HCSB).

GOOD GRIEF

For the kind of sorrow God wants us to experience leads us away from
sin and results in salvation. There's no regret for that kind of sorrow.
But worldly sorrow, which lacks repentance, results in spiritual death.
2 Corinthians 7:10

AT THE BEGINNING OF A NEW YEAR, many people look back at the previous twelve months with some regrets. A relationship that went bad. Words that should—or shouldn't—have been said. A risk not taken. These regrets may turn into grief and affect the way we live.

Grief is a common emotion as we face the difficulties of life. But grief can either be *helpful* or *harmful*.

Godly grief, as the apostle Paul calls it, brings about repentance and change for the better as we live for God. Godly grief doesn't last long, but its impact can be life changing. Grappling with godly sorrow can help to deepen our resolve to live right and give us a greater appreciation for God's grace.

Feelings of guilt induced by Satan last longer and only bring us down. We know that our sorrow is "worldly" when we struggle to move out of it. When you just feel like you're in a slump or like you're worthless, that's a sign that your enemy the devil is at work.

Paul puts it this way in 2 Corinthians 7:10: "For the kind of sorrow God wants us to experience leads us away from sin and results in salvation. There's no regret for that kind of sorrow. But worldly sorrow, which lacks repentance, results in spiritual death." God doesn't want us to get caught up in guilt and regrets. Sure, we need to learn from the past. But instead of dwelling on past failures, we should look forward to godly successes. God doesn't hold a grudge against us.

BOTTOM LINE

What regrets are bogging you down? Ask God to help you learn from those
mistakes and serve Him with renewed energy and confidence.

Moment of Strength: Philippians 3:12-14

IN AND OUT OF SEASON

He never left them without evidence of himself and his goodness. For instance,
he sends you rain and good crops and gives you food and joyful hearts.

Acts 14:17

So the Christmas season is over, and though you may be glad that the world can get back to normal, you at least have to admit that there is an increase of spiritual awareness or openness during December. It's easy to invite a coworker to church for the special music, or to a Christmas Eve service. But now that it's January, are there no more opportunities to witness to people?

All times are God's seasons. A discerning Christian can learn many ways to sow seeds of God's love. But like good farmers, we need to know whether it's time to plant, whether the crop needs some watering or sunshine, whether it needs to be weeded a little, or whether it is ripe for harvest. All of these are critical points in the timeline of someone's journey toward Christ. So, what seasons of opportunity are coming up soon?

- *Super Bowl.* Though it's great to be a champion on the field, it can sometimes be a struggle to be a champion off the field. Start a conversation with a coworker or a friend about the importance of being consistent in all areas of our lives.
- *Daytona 500.* Reflect with a colleague about the endurance that NASCAR drivers must have and how the real-life race can be even tougher.
- *March Madness.* Google the story of basketball stars Jack Twyman and Maurice Stokes, and discuss with a friend the kind of love it took for Jack to adopt Maurice.

BOTTOM LINE

Ask God to give you the words and the heart to share His love with others.

Moment of Strength: 1 Peter 3:15

KNOW YOUR NEIGHBOR

Do not seek revenge or bear a grudge against a fellow Israelite,
but love your neighbor as yourself. I am the LORD.
Leviticus 19:18

THE WORD NEIGHBOR IS mentioned more than 130 times in the Bible. Among other things, we're told not to give false witness against our neighbors (Exodus 20:16) or covet our neighbor's house or wife (Deuteronomy 5:21), and we're instructed to build up our neighbors for their good (Romans 15:2) and love our neighbors as ourselves (Leviticus 19:18). That last one is probably the most famous. Jesus even used those words when He was asked about the greatest command in all of the Old Testament law (Matthew 22:39).

Yet despite the importance the Bible places on how we treat our neighbors, research shows that many of us don't really know our neighbors. How can we love our neighbors if we don't even know them?

The Bible describes a neighbor in broad terms—including people in need whom we come across—not just people who live on our street. When we concentrate on knowing and loving the people in our community, we, too, are blessed. Studies show that when we know our neighbors, we build a safer, stronger, healthier environment to live in. And the best part is that it doesn't take a lot of effort to get to know our neighbors. We just need to be friendly and say hello. Taking the initiative may stretch our comfort level a little, but it's the right thing to do. We may even make some new friends and find opportunities to share the gospel in the process.

BOTTOM LINE

Make it one of your resolutions this year to know your neighbors better. It's not complicated; it just takes a little intentional effort.

Moment of Strength: Matthew 22:36-40

FUNERAL FINANCES

Then he said, "Beware! Guard against every kind of greed.
Life is not measured by how much you own."
Luke 12:15

IT'S INTERESTING what nobody ever says at a funeral. You rarely hear statements like these: "But most of all, he had an airtight 401(k)" or "I just can't get over how awesome his pool was" or "Can you believe this guy's car?"

At a funeral, people don't comment on the deceased's possessions, because when someone dies, what remains of his life is what he invested—not in stocks or mutual funds or real estate but in the eternal and precious commodity of people. Some of the most well-attended funerals memorialize people with few earthly possessions. And yet their lives touched many other lives. They served the Lord by giving all they had and all they could to the people God called them to serve.

Whether you realize it or not, you have already begun to plan your funeral. The statement of your life—what will be remembered—is being written today in the choices you make. Will you abandon yourself and live for your Creator, or will you live for yourself? Will you build up a nest egg of temporary treasures, or will you send your wealth on ahead to the Bank of Heaven?

God has gifted you with one life, one chance to display His glory in the circle of influence you have today. What are you doing with this chance? Are you making "the most of every opportunity in these evil days" (Ephesians 5:16)? Every day counts. Every choice matters. Choose wisely.

BOTTOM LINE

Financial security is important, but eternal reward is much, much more important.

Moment of Strength: Matthew 6:19-20

TELEPHONE GAME

*Discipline your children, and they will give you peace of
mind and will make your heart glad.*
Proverbs 29:17

REMEMBER THE GAME you played in school where everybody formed a line and the teacher whispered a message into the first person's ear? As the message was passed along, it usually got messed up and garbled before it reached the last person.

That same thing is true today with kids and cell phones—the message is getting garbled. Trends show that parents are buying their children cell phones at younger and younger ages. However, many parents aren't united in how to handle the challenges that a cell phone brings into their home.

As parents, it's our responsibility to establish boundaries. When our children hit different milestones (first cell phone, first date, getting a driver's license), we should already have a plan worked out about the rules. Some parents even come up with a contract that everybody signs before allowing their children certain privileges, such as a cell phone.

The Bible tells us to "discipline your children, and they will bring you peace of mind and will make your heart glad" (Proverbs 29:17). Discipline, whether in the sense of punishment or in a careful and deliberate approach to a situation, brings stability. Our children need to know where the boundaries are and what the consequences will be for stepping over the line. Make sure your children get the message loud and clear—not like kids at the end of the line in the telephone game.

BOTTOM LINE

*Having discipline in your home brings peace of mind for you and your child.
Are there areas where you need to provide better boundaries?*

Moment of Strength: Proverbs 16:21

THE VALUE OF MARRIAGE

Guard your heart; remain loyal to the wife of your youth.
Malachi 2:15

YOU CAN'T BUY HAPPINESS. But happiness can pay dividends, especially in your marriage. Economists David Blanchflower and Andrew Oswald calculated the "compensation value" of marriage by surveying 100,000 American and British couples from the 1970s to the 1990s. After compiling mounds of data and working through complex equations, they found that a happy marriage was worth $100,000 annually. As you can see, working toward a happy marriage makes a lot of sense (and cents)!

God doesn't mince words when it comes to marriage. He wants you to love and honor your wife in a lifelong covenant relationship. Yet many times we find ourselves frustrated in our most important relationship. Those frustrations can bubble over into hurtful words or neglectful actions.

Being in a marriage isn't easy. We must watch ourselves carefully so that we "do not act treacherously against the wife of [our] youth" (Malachi 2:15, HCSB). "Acting treacherously" doesn't necessarily mean having an affair or emotionally checking out of the marriage. A treacherous act is anything that undermines the relationship, and it can be as simple **as** not honoring your wife's opinion. Instead of taking little bits out of your wife's heart, invest in building her up. God urges men to treat their wives well for many reasons. Happiness is just one of them.

BOTTOM LINE

Watch yourself carefully so that you treat your wife the way God wants you to. It's not always easy, but it's always the right thing to do.

Moment of Strength: Ephesians 5:25

DAD: TEACHER, MENTOR, TRAINER

Teach a youth about the way he should go;
even when he is old he will not depart from it.
Proverbs 22:6, HCSB

IT'S EASY TO READ the principles and adages expressed in Proverbs—especially one like today's verse—and assume they're promises that God will always fulfill. But more often than not, proverbs and principles are just that—principles that *usually* work out that way in our lives.

Many a dad has viewed today's verse as God's promise that even if his children rebel and abandon their faith, it's a certainty that they will return. We need to understand that it's a *principle*, not an absolute promise. The Bible is filled with both promises and principles; and it's crucial to understand the difference, or we could experience great disappointment.

So what's a dad to do? One thing is to always try to be moving ahead, encouraging your children in their faith and setting a good example.

One couple who had three boys agreed on four godly principles to instill in their sons. First, they would prepare their sons for the path, not prepare the path for their sons. Second, they would prepare their sons to do their best. Third, they would train them to be leaders. And fourth, they would teach them to deal with both open and closed doors. A boy who learns those principles is likely to hang on to his faith, even through tough times.

BOTTOM LINE

Prayerfully decide what principles you want to teach your children, and implement a plan that will help them stay strong in their faith.

Moment of Strength: Ephesians 6:1-4

A GOD ENCOUNTER

[Jacob] reached a certain place and spent the night there
because the sun had set. He took one of the stones from the
place, put it there at his head, and lay down in that place.
Genesis 28:11, HCSB

WALKING ACROSS THE university graduation stage. Standing at the church altar on your wedding day. Pacing in a hospital birthing suite. Receiving a court summons. Strolling a Maui beach. Waiting in an emergency room. Looking down at a loved one in a casket. Certain places have significant meaning. In fact, certain sights, certain smells, or even a glimpse of someone who looks familiar can flood our minds with memories and escalate our emotions. Some of the events we recall are filled with great happiness and others with profound sorrow. Yet each holds a special place in our hearts.

In Genesis 28:11, we are told that Jacob reached "a certain place." The underlying Hebrew phrase may simply describe a locale, but it often refers to a sanctuary. This "certain place" was a particular sacred spot—a transforming place—and it was sacred because God was there. Jacob was not expecting to see God in this place, but he did.

God is not absent. He is involved and at work in our lives. If we are His children, we can be certain that He hasn't forgotten us. Just because we may not see what He is doing doesn't mean He isn't doing anything. God often works behind the scenes and in ways we will never know on this side of eternity. Are you awake to His presence and activity?

BOTTOM LINE

God doesn't always change the circumstances of our lives, but He can use our circumstances to change us. If we look and listen, we just might encounter God.

Moment of Strength: Psalm 59:10

MISSING GOD

Jacob awoke from his sleep and said,
"Surely the LORD is in this place, and I wasn't even aware of it!"
Genesis 28:16

A SCENE FROM THE 1999 MOVIE *October Sky* depicts high school student Homer Hickam winning the national science fair. Following the presentation, people rush to congratulate him. One is Wernher von Braun, Homer's scientific hero and the man heading up the rocket team at NASA at the time. But Homer doesn't recognize von Braun or know that the man who shook his hand was the great scientist. He misses his hero.

God was in Haran—far from Beersheba—and Jacob almost missed Him. In those days, people believed in territorial gods, who were present only in certain locales, so a person could move beyond a god's reach. Jacob thought that because he had traveled to Haran, he had left God in Beersheba. Jacob was wrong. God was in Haran, too.

Like those people who missed their chance to board the *Titanic*, we will never know how many times God has been watching over us, protecting us, and we didn't even recognize Him. Sometimes we drown out God's voice with our complaining. Other times we are so caught up in busyness and personal pursuits that we don't notice God's gracious acts of love. And then there can be times of suffering when we grow despondent and cold, faithlessly giving up on God and forgetting that it takes the fallow ground of winter for the bright blooms of spring to unfold. In our loneliness and despair, God is trying to break through. Look for Him. Listen for Him. Don't miss Him.

BOTTOM LINE

God is always watching, always working, always preparing, and always communicating. We need to learn to pay attention. We need expectant faith.

Moment of Strength: Exodus 33:14

MARK THE PLACE

The next morning Jacob got up very early. He took the stone he
had rested his head against, and he set it upright as a memorial
pillar. Then he poured olive oil over it. He named that place Bethel
(which means "house of God"), although it was previously called Luz.
Genesis 28:18-19

WE UNDERLINE KEY QUOTES IN BOOKS. We use pushpins on maps of places we've visited. We take pictures of people who are important to us. We record significant events in scrapbooks. We hang our diplomas on the wall. If it matters, we mark it or commemorate it.

It was no different with Jacob and his "certain place" in the wilderness. Though barren and desolate, this place had special meaning and significance to him. He placed a stone, a marker, like we do with monuments or markers at national historical sites, as a reminder of his encounter with God. He renamed the place *Bethel*, meaning "God's house." In renaming the site formerly known as Luz, Jacob made a lasting statement about the meeting he'd had there with the living God. This place was a sanctuary—a place where he met God, and he marked it for future generations to see.

That's not a bad idea. We can't erect Stonehenge in our backyards, but we could place a small rock on our desk or coffee table to remind us of a time when God's presence and protection were tangible. Drawing a picture or writing a poem could remind us that God is never more than a prayer away. A plaque with a meaningful Scripture passage placed in a prominent place can serve as a reminder of God's promises to us. Reminders of the Lord's presence can be helpful because it's easy to get caught up with everyday tasks and responsibilities and forget that He is with us to help us and work through us.

BOTTOM LINE

The next time you have an encounter with God, mark that place. Every time you see that marker, it will remind you of God's faithfulness.

Moment of Strength: Psalm 89:1

THE SOIL OF HUMILITY

All around him was a glowing halo, like a rainbow shining in the clouds on a
rainy day. This is what the glory of the LORD *looked like to me. When I saw it,*
I fell face down on the ground, and I heard someone's voice speaking to me.
Ezekiel 1:28

IN A COLLECTION OF children's letters to God, Wayne, age eleven, wrote: "Dear God, my dad thinks he is You. Please straighten him out." When we come before God, we must remember who we are talking to. We need to come to Him in an attitude of humility, recognizing His greatness.

A humble attitude reflects our understanding that we come to God on *His* terms. We come down from our lofty perch of self-importance and meet God on the soil of humility. It is worth remembering the root of the word *humility* is *humus*, meaning dirt or soil. Humbling ourselves before God doesn't mean we become dirt; rather, it means we recognize our place as created beings who are completely dependent on God for everything.

When Ezekiel experienced the presence of God, he understood his place and the appropriate posture he should take. In humility, he fell facedown before God. It is interesting that God called Ezekiel "son of man" or "son of dust." Ezekiel recognized the difference between himself and God, and he responded with appropriate awe and humility.

When we experience God, we will often be overwhelmed by His holiness and aware of our own sinfulness and insignificance. We, too, will often fall before Him in reverence and deep humility. He is a loving heavenly Father *and* an awesome God.

BOTTOM LINE

Have you taken a posture of humility before the holy God? It's a natural response to His greatness.

Moment of Strength: Zephaniah 2:3

SIZING UP THE BODY OF CHRIST

The human body has many parts, but
the many parts make up one whole body.
So it is with the body of Christ.
1 Corinthians 12:12

HAVE YOU EVER THOUGHT about how huge the church is worldwide? China Petrochemical, one of the world's largest corporations, has a labor force of 1,190,000. How does that compare to the church? The body of Christ is at least a thousand times larger—numbering three million churches and hundreds of millions of Christians. Furthermore, a 2006 Gallup poll conducted in nineteen African nations revealed that the church was the most trusted institution in African society.

The numbers above come from Scott Todd's book *Hope Rising: How Christians Can End Extreme Poverty in This Generation*. Todd is an executive with Compassion International, and his ministry assignment is to challenge men to go boldly where, historically, the church has often not been bold enough. Todd sees the church as the avenue through which God can meet both the spiritual and physical needs of the world.

As men, we can do that when we understand two things: first, that we are part of a muscle, a bone, an organ, a corpuscle, or a cell—a critical and unique part of the body of Christ; and second, that we are called to minister in the name of Christ and in connection with other believers.

BOTTOM LINE

How are you using the abilities, talents, and resources you have to help meet the physical and spiritual needs of the world?

Moment of Strength: Ezekiel 37:1-10

THE WISDOM OF MAN

He showed me another vision. I saw the Lord standing beside a
wall that had been built using a plumb line.
Amos 7:7

THERE ARE A LOT OF HELPFUL Christian books available, and we encourage you to read as many of them as you can. A reliable Christian author can offer valuable insights about the life of faith that God can use to help grow your faith.

But is there any danger in reading how other men interpret and apply Scripture? Possibly. We need to measure a man's words against the Word of God, just as we would use the builder's plumb line, mentioned by the prophet Amos, to build a wall.

In his classic *The Pursuit of God*, A. W. Tozer uses a similar illustration from music. A piano tuner doesn't tune one piano to another piano, because differences in tone would still occur and both pianos would still be a little bit out of tune. Instead, he tunes each piano to a tuning fork—a reliable and consistent standard—and thus even a hundred pianos, all tuned to the same tuning fork, will be perfectly tuned to each other.

What can we learn from that example? When we read our favorite, trusted authors, we shouldn't automatically take their interpretation of Scripture as the final word on the subject. Rather, we must apply God's "tuning fork"— His inspired and holy Word—to find His truth, measuring all things against Scripture. At the same time, we should recognize that our own interpretations are fallible as well, and it is wise to prayerfully study the Bible with other Christians.

BOTTOM LINE

Read your favorite authors, but look up the Scriptures they cite and see
whether their ideas line up clearly with the Word of God.

Moment of Strength: Amos 7:7-9

SHE LOOKS GOOD!

How beautiful you are, my darling, how beautiful!
Song of Songs 1:15

REMEMBER THAT FIRST DATE with your future wife and how good she looked? After all you've been through together, she looks even better now. Your heart still skips a beat when she comes into the room or gives you a certain look. She's got it going on, so don't be shy about letting her know it. Despite the challenges we all face in marriage, God knew what He was doing when He designed men and women to walk through life together. During the hard times you experience together, just a touch of her hand or a whisper of support can help to make things better. It's that kind of love between a husband and wife that defies description.

They say that beauty is only skin-deep, but that couldn't be further from the truth. Yes, your wife is gorgeous on the outside, but it's her heart that makes her the very best mate you could imagine. When you watch her interact with others, you wonder what in the world you did to be so blessed by having her as your wife.

As time passes, gray hairs will start cropping up. Gravity will take over, and things will sag. It happens to everyone, but the cool thing about marriage is that it happens to husbands and wives together. She is, and always has been, your best friend, your partner in fun, and your lover. She is God's gift to you. So give thanks to God for her. And let her know how much she means to you.

BOTTOM LINE

Your wife is not only beautiful on the outside, but she's got it going on in her heart as well!

Moment of Strength: Song of Songs 4:9-11

GRACE FOR THE CHURCHED

*Therefore, whenever we have the opportunity, we should do good
to everyone—especially to those in the family of faith.*
Galatians 6:10

ISN'T IT AMAZING HOW hardened we can become toward our longtime Christian friends? When one of them offends us or slips into a pattern of sin, we often treat them with less grace than we would treat someone who is unchurched. Granted, a veteran believer should know better, but that doesn't make the battle against sin any easier.

Scripture tells us that we should care for our fellow believers. As much as we should exhibit patience, kindness, and grace toward those who do not know Christ, we should also demonstrate these same qualities to those in the family of God. In fact, Jesus Himself said that our love for our fellow Christians would be a beautiful image for unchurched people to see (John 13:35). How Christians treat one another is a huge witness to a watching world. Love and grace are attractive—and unusual.

Perhaps our stingy expressions of grace stem from unhealthy expectations we have for our Christian friends. We may demand a level of perfection and sanctification from them that we don't even demand from ourselves. We act surprised when they display human weaknesses. We may forget that (just like us) they need the gospel as much today as when they were first converted. No Christian ever advances to a state of perfect holiness in this life. It's a struggle all the way through, but it's a struggle made better in the presence of grace.

BOTTOM LINE

Don't be stingy with the grace you show to fellow believers.

Moment of Strength: 1 John 3:18-20

READ, CHRISTIAN, READ

When you come, bring the cloak I left in Troas with Carpus,
as well as the scrolls, especially the parchments.
2 Timothy 4:13, HCSB

"THE AVERAGE CHRISTIAN MAN DOESN'T READ BOOKS." This is a well-worn axiom among some Christian publishers. Some blame the shortage of good materials that interest and challenge men. Others blame the demands of career and family. Neither explanation holds much water.

The pursuit of knowledge and truth is one way we can demonstrate our love for God. If we are to love God with all our minds, as Jesus instructs us in Matthew 22:37, one of the best ways we can do that is by reading. Consider the apostle Paul's request to Timothy to bring him his scrolls and parchments. The man who wrote more than half of the New Testament and planted numerous churches still felt the need to stimulate his mind by reading.

Some consider the reading of good books to be optional, but the Bible itself comes to us in the form of a book, and Christians have often been known as "people of the Book." Reading is an acknowledgment of our need to learn and grow and of the fact that we don't know everything. It requires a posture of humility.

Reading isn't the only tool for spiritual growth, of course, and on its own it cannot guarantee spiritual wisdom. But every Christian man should prayerfully pursue a disciplined life of the mind, and for that, reading is essential. Thankfully, it's not just a duty but also a great pleasure. So, guys, make reading a priority.

BOTTOM LINE

Many Christian men pursue the reading of good books. And they enjoy it! Have you read any good books lately that have stretched your faith?

Moment of Strength: Matthew 22:37

EXPLORING GOD'S OMNIPOTENCE

A final word: Be strong in the Lord and in his mighty power.
Ephesians 6:10

GOD IS ALL-POWERFUL. He alone possesses the "vast strength" of omnipotence. Nothing is too difficult for God. He can do everything except contradict His own character.

God can create the galaxies with a word, and He can roll them all up again like a scroll. He rides forth in majesty and grandeur, never flustered, never at a loss. He depends on nothing, seeks help from nobody, and finds counsel nowhere but in Himself. He can do anything but fail.

God's vast strength can strengthen you, as well. His omnipotence can calm every crisis, provide for every need, and help you overcome every obstacle in your life. Whatever your struggles, you can face them all with the power of God.

You can boldly face that illness, that court appearance, or that mountain of debt. With God's help, you can handle a shattered relationship, comfort a heartbroken child, and ace a job interview. He'll help you start a new business, patent an invention, or translate the Bible into a tribal tongue. God's power is present to finish your degree, to reconcile your marriage, to lose extra weight, and to resist temptation. When He calls you, He strengthens you to fulfill every calling He places on your life. Nothing depends on you and your strength, but everything depends on God and His strength.

BOTTOM LINE

When the voice inside your head says, "I can't," turn to God, who says, "I can, and I will, give you all the strength you need."

Moment of Strength: Joshua 1:6-9

WEARING GOD'S ARMOR

*Therefore, put on every piece of God's armor so
you will be able to resist the enemy in the time of evil.
Then after the battle you will still be standing firm.*
Ephesians 6:13

EVERY CHRISTIAN IS a soldier in an all-out war against Satan. Scripture commands us to take up the full armor of God. Leave no place unguarded. The enemy prowls around like a roaring lion (1 Peter 5:8), seeking to kill your joy and neutralize your testimony. Be alert; the enemy will exploit any opening you give him.

A Christian in complete armor is invincible. We can resist the devil. We can take our stand against the darkness of deception. In our own strength, we may be weary, weak, and worn. But what matters is the armor of God and our faith to wear it.

The apostle Paul identifies six pieces of armor: the belt of truth; the breastplate of righteousness; the boots of the gospel of peace; the shield of faith; the helmet of salvation; and the sword of the Spirit, God's Word. He wraps up this inventory by reminding us to be persistent in our prayers for one another (Ephesians 6:18).

If you're looking for instructions on how to use the armor, you will be disappointed. Scripture is not about methods and techniques; it is about Jesus. He is your truth, your righteousness, your shield, your peace, and your salvation. God tells you to "put on the shining armor of right living" and to "clothe yourself with the presence of the Lord Jesus Christ" (Romans 13:12, 14). The open secret of effectively wearing God's armor is a maturing walk with Christ. When we abide in Him, we're able to fight off the attacks of the enemy.

BOTTOM LINE

Spiritual warfare is Christ-dependent. He has given us what we need, and He is with us by His Spirit. Walk confidently in His truth and power.

Moment of Strength: Isaiah 59:16-20

ALL FOR NOTHING

Don't receive God's grace in vain.
2 Corinthians 6:1, HCSB

WHY DO SOME PEOPLE SEEM TO make great strides in their faith, while others seem to be stuck in neutral? In 2 Corinthians, the apostle Paul writes to a church that has gotten off track, a church in name but not in deed.

Where did your ideas about faith in God come from? If they came from the Bible, all is well. But if they came simply from the world around you . . . well . . . your faith may be all for naught. The Greek word for *vain* means "having nothing" or "containing nothing." It's easy to look righteous on the outside but to be living an empty life of moral compromise on the inside.

If you have received the gospel of Jesus Christ, God is working in you to make you more like His Son. As Jesus said, "My purpose is to give them a rich and satisfying life" (John 10:10). Rich and satisfying. Abundant, not skimpy. Full, not empty. The very opposite of grace received in vain.

God wants us to show others this abundance of His life, this fullness of His grace. When we live in the lavishness of His love, mercy, and grace, we will want to share that with others. We are meant to be conduits of grace. So ask God to continue to change you by His grace. And ask Him to help you love others in Jesus' name and by the power of His Spirit. He will surely answer that prayer.

BOTTOM LINE

God's grace changes us. It makes us more like Jesus. We are more loving, more joyful, more alive. Ask God to help you experience more of His grace.

Moment of Strength: Romans 6:1-4

DEALING WITH ANGER

Don't sin by letting anger control you.
Don't let the sun go down while you are still angry.
Ephesians 4:26

"You are just like your mother!" Carl roared through the bedroom door. As soon as the words left his mouth, he wished he could take them back. What started as an innocent conversation about weekend plans had quickly digressed into shouting and door slamming. Although he had made progress in recent weeks in controlling his anger, Carl had once again lost control and let his anger get the best of him.

Anger is a real and normal human emotion and an unavoidable ingredient in any marriage. It is unhealthy to deny or otherwise suppress our anger. Unfortunately, for many of us anger has become a problem because we have allowed it to lead to destructive behaviors. But notice that the above passage does not say "Don't be angry" or "If you get angry," but rather, "Don't let anger control you." Paul acknowledges that we will get angry, yet he tells us to be responsible when we do.

Anger does not have to be destructive. We can be angry without harming those around us. In fact, anger can serve as a constructive force in our lives. Anger alerts us when something is wrong; as a result, it can protect us. A conflict-free marriage is rare. Our responsibility is to deal with our anger in constructive, godly ways rather than blowing up and causing hurt.

BOTTOM LINE

We must acknowledge our anger rather than hide from it. But acknowledging it doesn't mean that we can release it in destructive ways.

Moment of Strength: Proverbs 29:11

WALK IN LOVE

Live a life filled with love, following the example of Christ. He loved us and offered himself as a sacrifice for us, a pleasing aroma to God.

Ephesians 5:2

ASK ANY MAN ABOUT the word *commitment*, and he can tell you right away what he's committed to. A job. A wife. A team. Kids. The church. Jesus. But linguists say that the word *commitment* was not used as much fifty years ago as it is today.

When you make a commitment, you are still in the driver's seat, no matter how noble the cause to which you are committed. You can commit to make car payments, pray, memorize Scripture, lose weight, give money. Whatever you choose to do, you remain accountable.

Remember that moment in Matthew 26:39 when Jesus is in the garden? "My Father!" He says. "If it is possible, let this cup of suffering be taken away from me. Yet I want your will to be done, not mine." He surrendered to His Father's plan, even if His flesh was tempted to waver for a moment.

When you remain in control of everything as a husband, your flesh will be tempted to waver from your commitment. But a husband who is surrendered to walking in love gives himself up daily, sacrificing his own wants for the sake of the marriage. He gives up trying to control every situation and simply surrenders every part of his marriage to the Lord. That isn't weakness. It's really the beginning of great strength. And what relief it brings—both to you and to those around you. You don't have to try to control outcomes anymore; you can leave things to God.

BOTTOM LINE

Wave a white flag to God's plan for your marriage today. It may sound like defeat, but it's actually the path to lasting victory.

Moment of Strength: Matthew 26:36-46

THE ART OF LISTENING WELL

Spouting off before listening to the facts is both shameful and foolish.
Proverbs 18:13

IT SEEMS THAT LISTENING should be easy, but it's not. Listening means we have to be quiet, and this is often the difficult part. We may prefer talking over listening because it gives us the illusion of control. We can even control the silences between words by choosing when to talk. Silence can cause our anxiety to increase, so we talk—even when we have nothing to say. Good listeners are relatively rare.

It is a tremendous experience to have someone really listen to us—to have someone's complete and undivided attention. When someone listens to us, it communicates at a very deep level that we have value and that we are worthy. Over time, being listened to can begin to convince us that we are worth someone's attention and that we are worth being loved. Being listened to breaks into our isolation and loneliness.

To be good listeners, we must be secure in who we are. Worrying about how we are being received by another individual or thinking about what we will say next while someone else is talking sends the message that what we have to say is more important than what anyone else has to say.

When was the last time you really listened to a friend? What about the last time you felt that someone really listened to you? What was the experience like?

BOTTOM LINE

Listening is difficult work, but it's worth the investment. It's something we can improve on with intentionality and God's help.

Moment of Strength: Proverbs 1:5

NOTHING'S GOING RIGHT

I pour out my complaints before him and tell him all my troubles.
Psalm 142:2

WE'VE ALL EXPERIENCED those times when nothing seems to go right. We might have a major, life-changing issue thrown at us—such as an illness or a change in a relationship—or just a bunch of minor, everyday annoyances. Whatever the case may be, it's sometimes easy to get the feeling that there's no way out of the difficulty we're in.

For those who have never been through the kind of agony caused by the death of a child or a cancer diagnosis, it's almost impossible to comprehend such a thing. But we all know what it's like to experience one crazy irritation after another. A flat tire. A leaky roof. An annoying headache. We almost can't help but feel sorry for ourselves.

We're certainly not alone. Check out Psalm 142, which describes David's experience while seeking refuge from Saul in a cave, cut off from the rest of the world. His words of praise in such a difficult time serve as an inspiration during our own times of difficulty. In verse 5, David says, "I pray to you, O LORD. I say, 'You are my place of refuge. You are all I really want in life.'"

When it seems as if our world has spun completely out of control, that's precisely the time to turn control over to God. That might sound like a cliché or a Sunday school kind of answer, but it's the right answer. And sometimes it's all we can do. Jesus is far bigger than our biggest problems.

BOTTOM LINE

Forget about the old saying, "When the going gets tough, the tough get going." When the going gets tough, the tough call on God for strength and protection.

Moment of Strength: Psalm 142

OUTRAGEOUS BEHAVIOR

Now is the time to get rid of anger, rage, malicious behavior,
slander, and dirty language. . . . For you have stripped
off your old sinful nature and all its wicked deeds.
Put on your new nature, and be renewed.
Colossians 3:8-10

OUTRAGE WAS SPARKED several years ago when a video surfaced online of a group of middle school students verbally berating a school bus monitor. These weren't your average back-of-the-bus shenanigans, either. They weren't making faces at passing vehicles. Their insults were merciless and vile.

How could they have been so completely cruel? Many people were so upset by the episode that a fund was started to send the monitor on a nice vacation—a fund that eventually exceeded $700,000. It's quite possible that the fund became so large precisely because a lot of people know what it feels like to get picked on.

The school bus incident serves as a teachable moment if ever there was one. Obviously, it's a prime example of how kids should *not* act—not because they might get caught but because being cruel to others is simply wrong. Who would want to be on the receiving end of a verbal barrage like that?

It's not just children who can learn from this. Dads, how do you treat others in the presence of your children? Do you talk about other people behind their backs or maybe even insult them to their faces? Your kids are watching and listening. What kind of example are you setting for them?

BOTTOM LINE

Model and teach your kids to stand up for others who are being abused and to ask for help if they're being bullied. It's the right thing to do.

Moment of Strength: Deuteronomy 4:9

THE LORD IS GRACIOUS

*The LORD is merciful and compassionate, slow to get angry
and filled with unfailing love. The LORD is good to everyone.
He showers compassion on all his creation.*

Psalm 145:8-9

A. W. TOZER WRITES IN his spiritual classic *The Knowledge of the Holy*:

> What comes into our minds when we think about God is the most important thing about us.
>
> The history of mankind will probably show that no people has ever risen above its religion, and man's spiritual history will positively demonstrate that no religion has ever been greater than its idea of God. Worship is pure or base as the worshiper entertains high or low thoughts of God.

Unless we have an accurate idea of who God is and how He relates to us, everything else in our Christian life will be off-kilter. Psalm 145:8 says that God is "merciful and compassionate, slow to get angry and filled with unfailing love." Is that how you see God?

Tozer continues:

> For this reason the gravest question before the Church is always God Himself, and the most portentous fact about any man is not what he at a given time may say or do, but what he in his deep heart conceives God to be like. *We tend by a secret law of the soul to move toward our mental image of God.* This is true not only of the individual Christian, but of the company of Christians that composes the Church. Always the most revealing thing about the Church is her idea of God.

We become what we behold. When we behold God's grace and goodness, we become more like Him. Make sure you have an accurate view of God.

BOTTOM LINE

What we believe about God affects everything! Read Psalm 145 slowly, asking God to help you see Him more clearly and believe Him more deeply.

Moment of Strength: Psalm 145

GOOD GUIDANCE

You are my rock and my fortress.
For the honor of your name, lead me out of this danger.
Psalm 31:3

MANY DADS FEEL THAT the most difficult part of fathering is behind them after diaper changes and late-night crying sessions are over. But once your children enter the final years of high school, a whole new challenge presents itself: helping your kids decide what they want to do with their lives.

For many of us, our college years are a distant memory. And the truth is, a four-year university may not be the right choice for every child. Junior college, trade schools, or career colleges can be good options. As fathers, we need to step up and guide our children through this transition.

Just as God knows us and guides us with His Holy Spirit, we need to nudge our older children to follow their God-given passions and talents. We can't leave this important stage of life to somebody else. According to the American School Counselor Association, the ratio of high school students to counselors is 491:1. As dads, we can get one-on-one with our children to provide loving guidance.

The promise of Psalm 31:3 is that God will lead us and guide us. His name—His character as a good heavenly Father—requires it. We need to lead our children in God's name, as well. We must encourage them to follow Him on their own in their next stage of life. When they do, they'll discover that life can be an exciting adventure.

BOTTOM LINE

The transition from high school to college isn't easy. We need to be there for our kids.

Moment of Strength: Psalm 78:70-72

GOD'S BEST COMMERCIAL

If someone asks about your hope as a believer,
always be ready to explain it.
1 Peter 3:15

FOR A THIRTY-SECOND COMMERCIAL during the 2017 Super Bowl, companies paid as much as $5.02 million. That sounds like a lot of money, but advertisers know they're getting a big bang for their buck. Many people watch the Super Bowl just to see the ads. During normal games, TVs are often muted during commercials; however, fans actually turn up their sets to see Super Bowl advertisements.

Super Bowl ads even have a life beyond the big game. *Time* magazine, reporting on "the twenty-five most influential Super Bowl ads of all time" identified the 2011 Volkswagen commercial with the little boy dressed as Darth Vader who "started" the car as the "most-shared Super Bowl ad of all time and second most-shared TV commercial ever."

Companies know the power of a good advertisement. In 2012, a Christian ministry took out a commercial during a playoff game between the Denver Broncos and the New England Patriots, featuring children reciting John 3:16. But commercials to promote Christianity aren't limited to the airwaves. God wants you to be a walking commercial for Him. First Peter 3:15 says, "If someone asks about your hope as a believer, always be ready to explain it." Commercials effectively tell a message in a little bit of time. When people spend time with you, what message are they getting?

BOTTOM LINE

You're always being watched. Are you a powerful walking commercial for God? What can you do to be more effective?

Moment of Strength: Mark 16:15

RETIREMENT?

Gray hair is a crown of glory; it is gained by living a godly life.
Proverbs 16:31

RETIREMENT: It's a time in our lives that all of us dream about. We're going to trade in our work clothes for a comfy Hawaiian shirt, shorts, and sandals, and we're going to hit the road for a cross-country RV trip. We may drive five miles one day and five hundred the next—it just depends on how we're feeling!

Isn't it a blast to daydream about how you're going to spend your retirement? You've worked very hard for all these years, and when the time is right, you're going to go from employment to enjoyment. Your career may or may not have been fulfilling, and maybe for most of it you were on somebody else's schedule. No more!

There's no mention in the Bible of an easy, post-career life completely free of responsibility. When we hit that long-awaited point in our lives, it doesn't necessarily mean we can do whatever we want, whenever we want, however we want. There's still work to be done for God's Kingdom.

You've got some years under your belt, and you may have a few gray hairs here and there to prove it. Why not take a young friend from church under your wing and be a mentor? You're not too old to teach a youth Sunday school class. One thing's for sure: You've got too many gifts to let them waste away in retirement. The Lord will provide all the opportunities you need to continue to contribute.

BOTTOM LINE

You've earned a chance to relax a little in your retirement, but God isn't finished with you yet!

Moment of Strength: Isaiah 46:4

CONFIDENCE IN THE LORD

O Lord, I give my life to you. I trust in you, my God!
Do not let me be disgraced, or let my enemies rejoice in my defeat.
No one who trusts in you will ever be disgraced, but
disgrace comes to those who try to deceive others.
Psalm 25:1-3

Biblical scholars categorize Psalm 25 as a "psalm of lament," which is to say it's a prayer to God while in distress. Let's be honest, many (most?) of our prayers take the form of a lament—they are complaints to God about our situation. This is okay, because life in this world is full of troubles and problems that collectively (or even individually) are too much for us to handle on our own. God is not in favor of our pretending that everything is okay when it isn't.

So both the Bible and Psalms in particular allow us to voice our complaints to God in healthy ways. We can be honest with God without being irreverent. Psalms of lament are grounded in faith and hope (rather than being just an exercise in whining) because we believe that the God we pray to is willing and able to help us.

In this particular lament, David (the psalmist) starts off by declaring his dependence and trust in the Lord: "Lord, I give my life to you. I trust in you, my God!" He starts with a foundation of faith—a bedrock of belief—despite how things look on the outside. His fear, apparently, is of being disgraced (or *ashamed*, as some translations put it): "Do not let me be disgraced, or let my enemies rejoice in my defeat." Every man knows this fear very well. The fear of failure can haunt our every step, which means our need for the Lord's help is ever present.

BOTTOM LINE

When you're tempted to give in to fear and worry, express your confidence in God out loud. He promises to come to your aid.

Moment of Strength: Isaiah 54:4

TEACH ME YOUR PATHS

Show me the right path, O LORD; point out the road for me to follow.
Lead me by your truth and teach me, for you are the God who saves me.
All day long I put my hope in you.
Psalm 25:4-5

AFTER BEGINNING PSALM 25 with a confident declaration of trust in God (despite the presence of dangerous enemies and a potentially crippling fear of disgrace), the psalmist shifts gears and asks God for help in knowing what to do. The fact that God rescues us doesn't mean we have no part to play in the rescue. God often rescues us by guiding us and strengthening us to do what we ought to do and go where we ought to go. We are, after all, following Christ, not just some vague notion of morality. That being said, God's ways—such as telling the truth and being generous—are not mysterious but are revealed in His Word. Christ and the Scriptures are of one mind. The *person* and the *principles* point down the same path.

Ever notice how many of the Psalms talk about waiting? (A lot.) Waiting seems to be almost synonymous with trust—the very opposite of "taking things into our own hands." It comes down to this: Are you going to panic and try to solve things your own way? Or are you going to surrender to the love and wisdom of your heavenly Father and trust Him to guide you where you need to go? When you think of it that way, it's easy to understand why the Bible says that "it is impossible to please God without faith" (Hebrews 11:6). God wants us to trust Him.

BOTTOM LINE

We follow a Good Shepherd who cares about His sheep. Knowing that, we can relax and listen rather than panic and rush ahead.

Moment of Strength: John 10:1-3

THE NECESSITY OF FORGIVENESS

Remember, O LORD, your compassion and unfailing love, which you have shown from long ages past. Do not remember the rebellious sins of my youth. Remember me in the light of your unfailing love, for you are merciful, O LORD.

Psalm 25:6-7

MOST OF US ARE FAMILIAR WITH the prayer acronym ACTS, which stands for Adoration, Confession, Thanksgiving, and Supplication. It's meant to guide our prayers so that we don't just jump right into asking God for things. That's not a bad idea, though the Bible also talks about coming to God like a child (Matthew 19:14), and children feel no shame in immediately asking for what they want. In any case, one absolutely indispensable part of prayer is confession, and one absolutely indispensable answer to prayer is forgiveness. Yes, we need to trust God, and yes, we need guidance; but we also need to be right with God before any of that. We need His forgiveness. Otherwise, guilt and shame will overwhelm us.

Reminding God of His promises can almost seem a little manipulative, like a boy bugging his dad about his dad's promise to play catch with him after work, even though his dad may be exhausted after a really long day. But God is different from a tired dad. He delights to honor His promises. Honoring His promises gives Him glory.

Like most of us, the psalmist considers the possibility that the trouble he's in now is due (at least in part) to mistakes he's made in the past: "Do not remember the rebellious sins of my youth," he prays. But he also remembers that God is good and merciful and willing to forgive. That's key.

BOTTOM LINE

It's so hard to believe that we're forgiven, because we need forgiveness so often. This fact hurts our pride, yet God graciously gives us what we need.

Moment of Strength: Psalm 130:4

GOD IS GOOD

The LORD is good and does what is right; he shows the proper path to those who go astray. He leads the humble in doing right, teaching them his way. The LORD leads with unfailing love and faithfulness all who keep his covenant and obey his demands.

Psalm 25:8-10

MANY OF US COULD PASS a theology test about God's character, but there's a huge difference between knowing what we're supposed to believe about God and actually believing in Him at a true heart level. The true test of our faith is how it affects the way we live our lives, especially when things go wrong.

Psalm 25:8 declares in no uncertain terms that God "is good and does what is right." Do you believe that? Really believe that? Has anything ever happened in your life that has caused you to seriously doubt God's goodness? Sooner or later (and probably multiple times) most of us will be tested at this very point: Is the Lord good despite what has happened? The answer according to Scripture is yes. "All the LORD's ways show faithful love and truth" (Psalm 25:10, HCSB).

Notice the connection between the first half of verse 8—"The LORD is good and does what is right"—and the second half: "He shows the proper path to those who go astray." Verse 9 adds, "He leads the humble in doing right, teaching them his way." The Lord's goodness is demonstrated in how He treats sinners—which is *well.* Moreover, He "leads with unfailing love and faithfulness all who keep his covenant and obey his demands." As creatures who still struggle with sin (and a lack of humility), we are not in a good position to judge God. We don't actually know what *good* is. Instead, we're told to trust God because *He* is good.

BOTTOM LINE

God's goodness cannot be rightly judged by our circumstances, which aren't always good. He is good no matter how things look on the outside.

Moment of Strength: Psalm 119:68

THE WAY OF RESCUE

The secret counsel of the LORD is for those who fear Him, and
He reveals His covenant to them. My eyes are always on the LORD,
for He will pull my feet out of the net.
Psalm 25:14-15, HCSB

FRIENDS SHARE THEIR hearts with one another. And Jesus calls us His friends: "I no longer call you slaves, because a master doesn't confide in his slaves. Now you are my friends, since I have told you everything the Father told me" (John 15:15). That might be one of the most encouraging verses in all of the Bible. We can count the Lord Jesus among our friends—we're not just His servants, but His friends. Remarkable.

We see the same thing in Psalm 25:14: "The secret counsel of the LORD is for those who fear Him" (HCSB). God reveals His heart and ways to those who fear Him, to those who want to know Him and walk with Him, and He is their friend. This is really what the Christian life is all about—knowing God, walking with Him, and sharing His love with others. That's what love looks like, and that's the sum of the law and what God desires of us.

Practically speaking, the way to stay close to God is to constantly look to Him for help, counsel, encouragement, fellowship—whatever we need. Jesus puts it like this in John 15:5: "I am the vine; you are the branches. Those who remain in me, and I in them, will produce much fruit. For apart from me you can do nothing." So in this Old Testament psalm, we see essentially the same thing that Jesus teaches in John 15—that we should look to Him and walk with Him.

BOTTOM LINE

God desires that we walk with Him as friends, listening and sharing life together. Our focus should be on Him rather than on ourselves.

Moment of Strength: John 15:1-17

A CRY FOR GRACE AND MERCY

Turn to me and have mercy, for I am alone and in deep distress.
My problems go from bad to worse. Oh, save me from them all!
Feel my pain and see my trouble. Forgive all my sins.
Psalm 25:16-18

EUGENE GLADSTONE O'NEILL DESCRIBED the human condition as follows: "Man is born broken. He lives by mending. The grace of God is glue." That's about right. We're all sufferers in need of God's grace and mercy. Thus, the prayer offered in Psalm 25:16-18 is one we all can relate to, having experienced loneliness and affliction, as well as the crushing burden of sin, at one time or another.

Sometimes all we can do is cry out to God for grace and mercy. We don't have any solutions of our own. We are in a position of complete dependence on Him. His grace (giving us what we don't deserve) and His mercy (not giving us what we do deserve) are our only hope.

Though the psalmist is obviously distressed, he is not without hope (and neither should we be). His instinct is to turn to God for help, to plead with the Lord for forgiveness and deliverance. He knows God's character. He knows that God's faithfulness is not dependent on his own. So he prays.

Life has a way of humbling even the proudest, most self-sufficient among us. Though no one enjoys suffering, it does produce endurance, character, and hope, as Paul details in Romans 5:3-4. Don't be surprised if you can't handle things on your own. You're not supposed to be able to. God wants us to learn to trust Him.

BOTTOM LINE

Prayer is our lifeline to God. Ask Him for help. Ask Him for forgiveness. Ask Him to provide what you need. He delights to come through for His children.

Moment of Strength: Psalm 32:6

BEAUTIFUL THINGS

*The heavens declare the glory of God, and
the sky proclaims the work of His hands.*
Psalm 19:1, HCSB

THERE IS BEAUTY IN THE touch of your wife's hand and the all-out belly laughs of your children. It's there in the chill in the air on a sunny morning and in a soft afternoon rain shower. Beauty is a snow-covered field on a quiet moonlit night. Beauty is the leaves changing colors in the Appalachian Mountains and the muted browns of the Arizona desert.

How would you like to hear beauty? Listen to your favorite music with the car windows rolled down. Want to feel beauty? Wiggle your bare toes in the not-too-hot sand of the beach. How about smelling beauty? Visit a bakery. Want to experience beauty? Cross the finish line of a 5K race with friends and family cheering you on.

In the book of Genesis, when the floodwaters finally receded, God signified His covenant with Noah by placing a rainbow in the sky. The array of colors was His signature, and to this day, they remind us of His beautiful faithfulness. He's the ultimate artist.

All we have to do is take the time to look around and appreciate the magnificence of what God has created. There is beauty to be found around every corner, in both everyday circumstances and once-in-a-lifetime events. Don't stop to just smell the roses and then move on without a second thought. Smell them, and then give thanks for them!

BOTTOM LINE

Only God could create the kind of beauty that we see and experience all around us. Take notice and give thanks!

Moment of Strength: Genesis 9:12-17

HANDLING DISAPPOINTMENT

*You rejoice in this, though now for a short time you
have had to struggle in various trials.*
1 Peter 1:6, HCSB

YOU HAVE A GOOD JOB, but you've applied for what appears to be a dream gig. If only your potential employers would see the light of day and hire you, this is a job that you could absolutely knock out of the park. The more you think about this new opportunity, the more excited you get.

The job seems to be perfect for you, and you seem to be perfect for it. The company, however, hires someone else. Your application was one of maybe hundreds that flooded the human resources department, and this time around, yours didn't make it to the top of the heap. The disappointment you feel is very real.

After some prayerful consideration, you're able to put the episode into perspective. As nice as the new job would have been, life is great as it is right now. You're more than able to make ends meet with the job you have, and that's a lot more than many people can say these days.

Think about what a potential relocation would have meant. You and your wife have extensive roots where you live now—you attend a great church and your kids go to an awesome school. What other costs might have been involved? You didn't get this job, but in the end, you can be thankful. God knows what He's doing. The important thing is to keep praying and to trust Him no matter what.

BOTTOM LINE

*You know that job you really, really want? It may not be so perfect after all.
Surrender to God's will, and be thankful for what you have and where you are.*

Moment of Strength: Philippians 4:4-7

EXHAUSTED

*Those who trust in the LORD will renew their strength; they will soar on wings
like eagles; they will run and not grow weary; they will walk and not faint.*
Isaiah 40:31, HCSB

FOR THOSE WHO HAVE never worked the overnight shift, it's hard to comprehend the sacrifices that such a job requires. When everybody else in the world seems to be asleep, those working graveyard hours must be awake and alert. When the sun rises, just the opposite is true. Heavy drapes go over the bedroom windows as we attempt to get some rest.

It might not be an overnight job, but millions start work well before daylight. Others are on the clock for up to eighty hours a week, and they sometimes get so tired that they can barely see straight. Many of us can't help but wonder, *What's the point?* Plain and simple, some of us are exhausted.

Perhaps you're one of the exhausted ones. Maybe you're going through a particularly challenging time at work right now. As hard as it may be to see the light at the end of the tunnel, it's there. Working hard to support your family is something you can be proud of. You've got responsibilities, and you're doing everything you possibly can to meet them.

The Bible promises us the ultimate rest, and those who have worked hard for so long can no doubt take special comfort in that fact. Consider God's promise in Isaiah 40:31 to renew your strength, and take heart. One day it will be renewed and never wane. In the meantime, keep plugging away, trusting the Lord to strengthen you.

BOTTOM LINE

Work is often difficult and exhausting, but God sustains His people. Trust Him to renew your strength.

Moment of Strength: 2 Corinthians 4:8-10

FOXHOLE MARRIAGE

Let your wife be a fountain of blessing for you. Rejoice in the wife of your youth.
Proverbs 5:18

IF YOU'VE BEEN MARRIED TO your wife for a long, long time, there may be times when you can't remember what life was like before she came along. You've been through a lot together. When the preacher at your wedding got to the part about "for better or worse," he really knew what he was talking about, didn't he?

You've struggled to get the bills paid on time, and just when you think you've got it made, your car needs a transmission overhaul. Together you have juggled jobs, kids, church, sports practices, and music and dance recitals. Over the years, you've become quite the tag team, haven't you?

There have been plenty of times over the course of your marriage when it seemed as if you were in a foxhole together, trying desperately to fend off any number of oncoming attacks. That's the key. When you have faced difficulties, you've done it together as partners and friends. You wouldn't have it any other way, would you?

You look at her, and you still see the beautiful woman you married all those years ago; but somehow, she means even more to you now. She's had your back and has been your counselor, prayer warrior, and most enthusiastic cheerleader. When times are tough, stop a moment and tell your wife how much she really means to you.

BOTTOM LINE

You and your wife are partners in this thing called life. Thank God today that you have a mate who stands by your side through thick and thin.

Moment of Strength: 1 Corinthians 13:4-7

TIGHTROPE PARENTING

Fathers, do not exasperate your children, so they won't become discouraged.
Colossians 3:21, HCSB

BEING A FATHER MEANS walking a tightrope of responsibility. You have to work hard to provide for your family, but you can't make your job your life and neglect spending time with your wife and children. You want to encourage your kids, but you need to have realistic expectations for them.

You need to get along with your children, but trying to be best buddies with them has its pitfalls as well. You have to discipline them, but you can't be a cruel dictator. Being a father is an endless cycle of challenges, but how you handle things could have a long-lasting impact on your children's lives. (No pressure!)

Have there been times when your kids had you so confused, angry, disappointed, or terrified that you could hardly see straight? Of course. Every father is going to make mistakes when it comes to handling such situations, but it's how you bounce back that truly matters.

Nobody said fatherhood was a job for the faint of heart, but guess what? It's worth it. It's incredibly challenging and incredibly rewarding. Your kids are a gift from God. He's given them to you as a sacred trust, and He will help you parent them. There's nothing like seeing your kids build on the foundation you've given them in the Lord.

BOTTOM LINE

Being a father can be difficult, but it's one of your greatest legacies. So, with much prayer and reliance on God's grace, aim to be a great dad.

Moment of Strength: Psalm 127:3-5

DON'T STRESS ABOUT IT

*Peace I leave with you. My peace I give to you. I do not give to you
as the world gives. Your heart must not be troubled or fearful.*

John 14:27, HCSB

JACK COULDN'T SHAKE the feelings of lethargy. That "afternoon drowsiness" now seemed to stretch from morning till night. He didn't sleep well, and his supervisor had started to notice that his production at work had dropped off. Plus, he'd put on a few pounds that he couldn't lose. Jack didn't know what was wrong. *Maybe I should start taking vitamins or exercising more,* he thought.

The real problem could have been stress. Stress can manifest itself in a myriad of symptoms such as the ones above or cause angry outbursts, sadness, and irritability. Left unchecked, stress can lead to high blood pressure, heart disease, and diabetes.

All those symptoms may sound scary, especially since you can't always avoid stress. Life is filled with it: work deadlines, discipline issues with children, marital conflicts, and family issues. Though stress may be unavoidable, you can work with your doctor to make a plan to manage stress through physical activity, times of relaxation, and getting into God's Word. Plus, you have the ultimate stress buster in your life—the peace of the Lord.

In John 14:27, Jesus says, "I am leaving you with a gift—peace of mind and heart. And the peace I give is a gift the world cannot give. So don't be troubled or afraid." God doesn't want us to be overly stressed. Instead, He wants us to find our rest in Him.

BOTTOM LINE

Too much stress doesn't help anything. If anything, it hurts us physically. Be sure to schedule regular checkups with your doctor. Seek to rest in God.

Moment of Strength: Matthew 11:28-29

WORK AT IT

Whatever you do, do it enthusiastically,
as something done for the Lord and not for men.
Colossians 3:23, HCSB

IN 2001, JIM COLLINS AND a twenty-one-person research team looked into the question of how good companies become great. They focused on eleven companies and reported the findings in the book *Good to Great*.

We all want to be great. Maybe you're one of the more than 3 million people who bought *Good to Great*, hoping to help yourself and your company take that step into greatness. Among other insights, Collins discovered that great companies pinpointed and promoted disciplined workers who acted in a disciplined manner.

More recently, *Inc.* magazine published an article noting that great employees were diligent, reliable, and dependable. That sounds good, not great. On the other hand, remarkable employees stand out. They aren't afraid to be different, stretch the boundaries, and improve processes. Remarkable employees inject their God-given creativity and personality into their work.

Colossians 3:23 reminds us to do everything—including our work—enthusiastically, as if we're doing it for the Lord. As you go about your daily responsibilities at your job, prayerfully look for ways to improve the process. How can you make things better? Don't be afraid to take chances and stand out remarkably for God at work.

BOTTOM LINE

Good doesn't cut it at work or in our spiritual lives. Strive to be remarkable!

Moment of Strength: Matthew 5:16

HELP BY HELPING

Based on the gift each one has received, use it to serve others,
as good managers of the varied grace of God.
1 Peter 4:10, HCSB

WE ALL WANT OUR KIDS TO BE HELPFUL. When they demonstrate a helpful spirit, they show that they're following God's command to use the gifts they've received to serve others.

God wants His followers to serve the people around them. But have you ever thought that there may be more to God's plan? Sure, He wants us to serve others to benefit His Kingdom and those being helped. But what about the person doing the helping?

It turns out the helper benefits greatly as well. A study at the University of Missouri found that kids who engaged in positive social behaviors—such as volunteering and helping others—were less likely to take part in risky behaviors as young adults. In other words, when your kids help others, they help themselves live godlier lives and build their own moral character.

As parents, we want our kids to be kind, considerate, selfless, and respectful. We can preach those character traits to our kids and model them in our own actions, but one of the most effective ways to build those values may be to encourage our kids to serve.

When our kids serve others, we can also look forward to the benefit of seeing them make healthier choices and display godlier values. Talk about a win-win!

BOTTOM LINE

Encourage your kids to serve. It'll help your community . . . and your children.

Moment of Strength: Isaiah 58:10-11

IN HIS HOUSE

[Jesus] came to Nazareth, where He had been brought up. As usual,
He entered the synagogue on the Sabbath day and stood up to read.
Luke 4:16, HCSB

IN HIS BOOK *Just Like Jesus*, Max Lucado writes, "God loves you just the way you are, but he refuses to leave you that way. He wants you to be just like Jesus." Becoming more Christlike takes understanding, encouragement, and time. Some transformation can be worked out through personal Bible study and prayer. However, a key element of true life change can come only through participation in the church.

The teaching of a godly pastor and the accountability found in relationships with other Christians help us move forward in our journey to become more like Jesus. If you don't feel as if your life is being changed by attending church, pray about how God might want you to become more involved in the church by investing in the lives of others. But don't stop attending. God's Word instructs us numerous times to gather with other believers. It benefits us and is also good for the body of Christ.

Luke 4:16 tells us that Jesus regularly went to the synagogue. He understood everything about God and His Word, yet He still went to synagogue. If Jesus thought it necessary to worship with God's people each week, then so should we. And we should not be afraid to invite others to come with us.

BOTTOM LINE

We should attend church with anticipation, expecting that it will change us to be more like Jesus.

Moment of Strength: 1 Corinthians 12:27-28

THE REALITY OF MARRIAGE

*For we all stumble in many ways. If anyone does not stumble in what he says,
he is a mature man who is also able to control his whole body.*

James 3:2, HCSB

NOBODY'S PERFECT, RIGHT? How often have you said that? You don't have to be a seminary professor to understand that every human being is a sinner. But the problem, when it comes to our relationships, is that we often expect others to live perfectly while expecting grace for our own failures. This is why so many marriages, even Christian marriages, struggle to develop a growing intimacy.

James, pastor of the church at Jerusalem, says, "We all stumble in many ways." The apostle Paul personalized this truth by declaring himself to be the chief of sinners (1 Timothy 1:15). Both men understood the need for honesty about their own faults and failings. For a husband, this can be a powerful principle. It enables him to stop seeing his wife as the chief problem in their marriage. He is angered first by his own sins, not hers. He weeps first over his own failings, not hers. He is also able to apply forgiveness and grace toward the sins of his wife, rather than hold a grudge.

We redeem the reality of marriage when we stop looking for something in our wives that we can find only in Christ. Only God is worthy of worship, and only God can give ultimate satisfaction. This allows a man to see his wife as who she really is: an heir of the grace of life and a gift to him. In the gospel, he finds the grace to forgive and be forgiven.

BOTTOM LINE

Biblical expectations are the foundation of a God-honoring marriage. Are you expecting too much from another imperfect person?

Moment of Strength: 1 Peter 3:7

A LOVE THAT WORKS

Love never gives up, never loses faith, is always hopeful, and
endures through every circumstance.
1 Corinthians 13:7

WHEN A MAN FIRST GETS MARRIED, he usually describes it as something that has happened to him. And of course there is something powerful about romantic attraction, discovered compatibility, and linking your life to another person's. But there is a next level of love, a kind of love that endures and forms the basis of a lifelong, joyful union. This kind of love does not come in the form of a passive noun—something that happens to us. Instead, real, lasting, biblical love is more like a verb—something we choose to do.

Listen to the language of Paul's famous discourse on love in 1 Corinthians 13, particularly verse 7. You will notice how love is not a state of fuzzy romantic feelings but is a series of actions. It never gives up, never loses faith, never loses hope. In other words, you cannot achieve a strong and powerful and unbreakable love if you do not actively pursue it. As the husband, at times you must bear the unbearable. You must believe the unbelievable. You must hope even when life seems hopeless.

Active, pursuing love is not generated simply by goodwill. Our willpower is quite limited. Rather, our ability to love must be fueled by the love we've been shown by God in Christ. We endure, believe, and hope because God's love toward us is not passive, but active on our behalf. We love out of the abundance of love we have received from God.

BOTTOM LINE

Love is not something we simply experience; it's also something we share as we receive God's love moment by moment.

Moment of Strength: 1 Corinthians 13

RISKY BUSINESSES

*Husbands, love your wives, just as Christ loved the church
and gave Himself for her.*
Ephesians 5:25, HCSB

DOES YOUR JOB AFFECT YOUR MARRIAGE? Many men would answer in the affirmative. Whether they involve long hours or high stress, careers can naturally spill over into our personal lives. When Michael Aamodt published a study that broke down the divorce rates of 449 occupations, he created more questions than he answered. Why do dancers divorce so frequently, especially compared to engineers? Why do optometrists have the lowest divorce rate? Do they just see things more clearly?

The answer could be that certain careers attract certain personality types. Or maybe some jobs are filled with marital pitfalls. Working late hours in a bar could naturally detract from marital bliss.

No matter what career choice you've made, commit to working on your marriage with the same (or more) dedication you put into your job. Any relationship takes effort. And your marriage is your most important earthly relationship.

In Ephesians 5:25, the apostle Paul encourages husbands to "love your wives, just as Christ loved the church and gave Himself for her" (HCSB). Jesus showed His love for the church by giving everything. We have to be willing to do the same. Our wives must feel loved—not only by our words, but also through our actions. Give the time and effort at home that earns you a promotion that really matters.

BOTTOM LINE

Any job can lead to divorce if you put it above your relationship with your wife. Show your wife the love she needs.

Moment of Strength: 1 Peter 3:7

SHARP AS A RAZOR'S EDGE

Using a dull ax requires great strength, so sharpen the blade.
Ecclesiastes 10:10

AN AX HAS TO BE SHARPENED often if its user is to experience its maximum utility. Whatever your occupation or hobby or interests, you know that your tools have to be maintained to get the best results. A knife must be sharpened, and a gun must be cleaned. A uniform must be laundered. A motor must have oil, and a baseball glove must be oiled. Computer software has to be updated.

Whatever you're doing, the tools you're using have to be kept in prime condition if you expect to achieve the best results for the task at hand.

When it comes to a vibrant, effective Christian faith, it's also imperative that your "tools" be sharp, always ready for whatever situation you face. If you want your faith to be strong, regularly sharpen the tools that make it possible. Some of those tools are study, prayer, fellowship, serving, and worship.

Spend time reading the Bible, participate with an accountability partner or a small group of men you trust, find ways to serve others selflessly (through your church or community groups), and never forget the critical role of worship in maintaining a strong faith. When, by the grace of God, you keep your faith tools sharp, you're well on your way to becoming a master faith builder. But if you don't, you may find your faith becoming less and less enjoyable and less and less effective. Build your faith to last.

BOTTOM LINE

Make a list of the faith tools you need to sharpen, get out the sandpaper or the file, and go to work.

Moment of Strength: Romans 12

RESPECT ONE ANOTHER

If you are always biting and devouring one another, watch out!
Beware of destroying one another.
Galatians 5:15

WHEN GOD HANDED DOWN HIS LAWS, He commanded His people again and again not to eat blood (Genesis 9:4; Leviticus 7:26; 17:10; Deuteronomy 12:16; Acts 15:29). Before they butchered an animal, they were to drain its blood. The blood was poured out on the ground (Deuteronomy 15:23). Moses explained, "For the life of the body is in its blood" (Leviticus 17:11). He wasn't making a medical statement but a theological one. The animal's life was symbolized by the blood, and because life is sacred, the people couldn't eat the blood.

Life is precious. Life is sacred, and it all belongs to God. Human beings, however, are made in the image of God and are especially valuable to Him (Psalm 8). Human life is sacred in a way no other life is sacred.

You are valuable. You are a sacred person, precious in the eyes of God, made for dignity and love. No one has the right to diminish, demean, or damage you.

Neither do you have the right to suck the life out of other people. Abuse, labeling, sarcastic jabs, cruel teasing, slander, exploitation, and violence have no place in a Christian's life. Don't "bite and devour one another," draining the life out of the people around you. Instead, build others up, treating them with the honor and dignity they deserve.

BOTTOM LINE

We are to build a wall of protection around the preciousness of human life at every stage of development, treating each person with dignity and love.

Moment of Strength: Romans 12:9-21

RESPECT GOD

You must not misuse the name of the Lord your God.
The Lord will not let you go unpunished if you misuse his name.

Exodus 20:7

God's name is a statement of who He is. He is holy, good, true, and beautiful, and His nature, attributes, glory, and works are all included in His wonderful name. In Scripture when a person encountered God, it was often an unsettling experience. Isaiah cried out, "Woe is me!" (Isaiah 6:5, HCSB), Daniel passed out with his face to the ground (Daniel 10:7-8), and John "fell at His feet like a dead man" (Revelation 1:17, HCSB). Scripture makes it clear that God is to be feared—to be regarded with reverential awe.

There is such a thing as being too casual with God. It's not that He is unapproachable or distant; it's that He is great and glorious beyond comprehension. Our worship is diminished when we diminish God. The goal is to see Him as accurately as we can. That will produce true worship.

To misuse God's name means to take Him lightly. It is to shrink His greatness and minimize His glory. It can be an attempt to reduce Him to manageable proportions. It can look like "name it and claim it" theology, where we expect God to give us whatever we want. (To say God is on your side is not to say that God serves your agenda. He does whatever He pleases, whatever is best.) And yet our God is approachable. We can call Him "Abba, Father" (Galatians 4:6). He loves us greatly.

BOTTOM LINE

Respect for who God is, for His name, is a must. And when we see more of how good and great He is, worship and obedience are our natural responses.

Moment of Strength: Exodus 19:16-19

A RESPECTFUL WITNESS

Respect everyone, and love the family of believers.
Fear God, and respect the king.
1 Peter 2:17

WHEN YOU WERE GROWING UP, your parents were there to nurture you. Mom changed your diapers, comforted you when you were sick, and washed your uniform for all your games. Dad cheered you at those ball games, taught you how to drive, and helped you with homework. They both took pictures of you and your prom date, sat through that long convocation when you graduated, and helped you through college.

But in college, you met Christ, and He radically changed your worldview. Slowly but surely, your path began to deviate from that of your parents. Can the wedge between you today be overcome?

As they age, people tend to become more inflexible in their beliefs. If your parents aren't Christians now, they probably won't become believers if you beat them over the head with your Bible. And self-righteousness and judgmentalism will push them away. How can you share God's love with them?

"Respect" is not just the name of an old pop song. It's something we demonstrate with our words and tone of voice. We show it with our sincere responses, not with eye rolling. We give it as we listen attentively and as we serve faithfully. "Everyone" includes our parents, no matter how old we are, no matter if they are Christians or not. In showing respect to your parents, you honor them and are a great witness for God.

BOTTOM LINE

Respecting your parents is a way of loving God. Ask Him to help you love your parents well, despite the differences you may have.

Moment of Strength: 1 Peter 2:11-25

CAREFUL WITH THE COMPLIMENTS

A lying tongue hates those it crushes, and a flattering mouth causes ruin.
Proverbs 26:28, HCSB

WE ALL HAVE CERTAIN EGO NEEDS. Acceptance. Love. Care. Tenderness. And so many voices out there promise to meet those needs or at least convince us that we aren't getting our needs met in the right place. Once we get married, we must meet those needs within the boundaries of our own marriage.

But what if someone else's needs aren't being met? It is quite possible that your female coworker is starved for caring words and tender romance that are long gone from her own marriage. You may mean nothing by your compliments to her, but she may take them the wrong way. She may begin to try to get her needs met through you instead of her husband. When that happens, friend, you are in deep weeds!

Instead of flattering and flirting, show professionalism. Ask yourself: *Would I share this compliment in front of my wife?* Encourage that coworker regarding her work habits, her timeliness, or her character and integrity, as appropriate. And always do it in the company of other people, never alone. Otherwise, you are playing with fire. Proverbs 6:27 says, "Can a man scoop a flame into his lap and not have his clothes catch on fire?"

Save the compliments, the gifts, the flattery, and the flirting for the one whom God has provided for you—your wife. Because some compliments just don't pay.

BOTTOM LINE

Put the needs of your wife before your own. She is your priority.

Moment of Strength: Proverbs 6:20-35

MISSION CRITICAL

If you are faithful in little things, you will be faithful
in large ones. But if you are dishonest in little things,
you won't be honest with greater responsibilities.

Luke 16:10

SO MUCH TIME IN basic training in the military is devoted to disassembling a rifle, cleaning it, and putting it back together. It's a monotonous task that feels like a punishment. It would be easy to skip some steps and do the job halfway. It could also be life-threatening. In a combat zone, you carry your weapon with you constantly, and no one is responsible for its well-being but you. You can't depend on someone else to save you when your weapon jams because you were too lazy to clean it that morning.

Jesus' teaching in Luke 16 highlights that the best proof of a man's fitness for a bigger assignment is the way he fulfills a smaller assignment. On earth, we are in charge of things that are not really ours. We are only stewards of them. But the reward we will receive in heaven depends largely on how we use things on earth. Good stewardship now will be rewarded later.

In other words, if a man can't properly handle worldly wealth, he can't be trusted with the true riches of heaven. Integrity is when we obey in realms that are unenforceable—those areas that no one sees but God. Whom would you rather trust to save your life—the guy who cleaned his rifle thoroughly, or the guy who polished the outside of his rifle but never cleaned the inner parts? Faithfulness in the little things matters a great deal. It's part of living with integrity.

BOTTOM LINE

Ask God to make you a man of clean parts on the inside as well as the outside.

Moment of Strength: Psalm 51:6-13

AN UNDERDOG'S WISDOM

O our God, won't you stop them? We are powerless against
this mighty army that is about to attack us. We do not
know what to do, but we are looking to you for help.
2 Chronicles 20:12

WHEN KING JEHOSHAPHAT FINISHED his prayer, he looked up to see hordes of enemy soldiers amassed and ready to drive God's people into the sea. He faced overwhelming military odds. He felt attacked. He felt powerless. And he felt clueless. He did not know how things would turn out.

Have you ever been in a position where you didn't know what to do? Where you have more questions than answers, and the answers you do have don't work? Maybe, like King Jehoshaphat, you feel powerless. You feel attacked. You feel like an army has come against you . . .

There is a great insight tucked into this verse. Like so many of the Bible's great lessons, it is introduced by the word *but*.

"We do not know what to do," the king prays, "*but* we are looking to God for help and deliverance." To have your eyes on God means to trust Him, to count on Him, and to rely on Him. It means to anchor your peace in who He is rather than in what is happening around you. It is to live by faith and not by sight. In those moments when we step out in faith and trust God, our greatest enemy—unbelief—is defeated.

Faith against the odds is the victory that God wants us to experience most. Yes, there are enemies on the outside that must be defeated, but more than anything, God wants us to trust Him. He never fails to deliver.

BOTTOM LINE

When you face overwhelming odds with overcoming faith, you can't lose. Is
there some area in your life that requires great faith right now?

Moment of Strength: Psalm 27:1-6

WORKING A TEMPORARY JOB

Peter, an apostle of Jesus Christ: To the temporary residents dispersed . . .
chosen according to the foreknowledge of God the Father and set apart by
the Spirit for obedience and for sprinkling with the blood of Jesus Christ.
1 Peter 1:1-2, HCSB

OFTEN WHEN WE READ an epistle from the New Testament, we skip over the introductory verses. But there are golden nuggets of truth to be found there as well. Take the opening sentence that the apostle Peter wrote to Christians dispersed across Asia Minor. He wrote to the "temporary residents" there. Peter fully recognized that our eternal home will be in heaven, not on earth. And he spent the rest of his letter reminding his fellow Christians to plan for their future and not be discouraged by their present suffering.

The Greek word for a temporary resident in a strange land is *paroikos*. This was a sojourner, a man who was in a foreign place but whose thoughts were turned toward his home. A Christian man is one whose eyes are turned toward God and whose loyalty extends beyond the loyalties of this life.

This doesn't mean that we withdraw from this world, but it does mean that we live in light of eternity and see ourselves on a journey toward God. This world is like a bridge. A wise man will walk over it, but he will not build his house on it. This helps us keep the things of this world in proper perspective.

So live in this world. Enjoy it. But you will never own it, so don't waste your time trying to create a permanent home here. You live in the "now and not yet," journeying through this present transitory life as a spiritual pilgrim.

BOTTOM LINE

You won't mind the journey so much when you know the road leads to your ultimate home.

Moment of Strength: Hebrews 11:8-16

BROKENNESS

The sacrifice pleasing to God is a broken spirit. God,
You will not despise a broken and humbled heart.
Psalm 51:17, HCSB

WE STRIVE FOR SUCCESS and prosperity, but when we achieve even the smallest measure of it, we can find ourselves in a spiritual danger zone. When Jesus said, "It is easier for a camel to go through the eye of a needle than for a rich person to enter the Kingdom of God" (Matthew 19:24), He wasn't discriminating against the wealthy. Instead, He was revealing a tendency in man that separates us from God. When things are going well and we feel self-sufficient, we tend to let our spiritual disciplines slide a bit. But when we're poor in spirit, convicted of our sin, or struggling through a hardship, we're forced to admit that things are not perfect. We are not perfect. We need grace and mercy. We need help. And it's this very posture that God desires from us.

Too many people make the mistake of thinking that we must get our lives together before approaching God. But this verse, and many more like it, tells us otherwise (e.g., Isaiah 66:2).

One of the best ways to share your faith with nonbelieving friends or coworkers is to "look for an open nerve." Pay attention for the comment or complaint about something happening in their lives—a relationship, finances, schedule demands, whatever. Then probe into that a little further. Ask what they think the root of the problem is. Then offer the following invitation: "Would you like to hear how I find help in that area?"

BOTTOM LINE

God didn't choose us because we were the strongest and the bravest and the noblest. He chose us because He loves us and we need Him.

Moment of Strength: 1 Corinthians 4:7

STAND FIRM

Be alert, stand firm in the faith, act like a man, be strong.
Your every action must be done with love.
1 Corinthians 16:13-14, HCSB

As FATHERS, we'd be quick to intervene if we saw our kids hanging out with the wrong crowd. We know the power of corrupting influences and peer pressure, and we don't want to see our kids influenced by things that could corrupt their character. We're willing to take big risks, knowing that our kids might become upset with us—at least for a while. We're willing to endure the fallout because we know the cost of ignoring potential danger. We want to do what's right for our children, even if it makes us unpopular in the short term.

But are we as vigilant about monitoring our own work environment for corrupting influences that would undermine our character? We may be more mature than our kids, but we're not immune to negative influences and worldly thinking. When we are aware of lying, cheating, or dishonesty at work, are we expected to look the other way—or worse, to participate? It can be tough to remain faithful.

We're called to take "every thought captive to obey Christ" (2 Corinthians 10:5, HCSB). That means standing firmly by our convictions, even when it's unpopular. We may not have the option to immediately remove ourselves from a job environment we don't like, but we can certainly pray for the courage to be "salt and light" to our coworkers there.

BOTTOM LINE

It's so easy to adopt the ways of the world and drift spiritually. Though we're called to engage the world through our work, our loyalty must be to the Lord.

Moment of Strength: Romans 16:17-19

AN EMOTIONALLY PRESENT FATHER

A voice from heaven said, "You are my dearly loved Son,
and you bring me great joy."
Mark 1:11

LET'S FACE IT. As men, we want to be proficient and successful in the things we undertake. As a result, we often navigate toward situations and circumstances in which we are comfortable and have the greatest chance of success. Because the emotional landscape is often unfamiliar and uncharted territory, we often pull back and avoid it because of our fear of failure or the unknown. No one wants to be exposed as lacking; no one wants to fail.

Being in touch with our emotions is critical, especially as it relates to raising our children. Children need the emotional support of their father when they experience joy, sadness, anger, fear, and frustration. An emotionally engaged father helps his children verbally label all of these emotions and work through them. Our children need to know that they are highly valued because of who they are, not because of what they may or may not be feeling at a particular moment.

In order to teach our children how to verbally label their emotions, we first have to be able to label our own. This skill may not have been modeled for us growing up, so it probably will not come naturally. It will take courage to begin to engage the world around us emotionally and to step into this unfamiliar territory. We might be in the minority, but our children and families are worth it.

BOTTOM LINE

Make sure you understand your own emotions so you can better help your kids deal with theirs.

Moment of Strength: John 10:30

RECONNECTING AFTER CONFLICT

Hatred stirs up quarrels, but love makes up for all offenses.
Proverbs 10:12

JOHN WAS AT A LOSS ABOUT WHAT TO DO. He and his wife, Karen, had experienced a big argument more than two weeks ago, and the emotional climate had been icy in their home ever since. They had settled into a routine of stubbornly giving each other the silent treatment, and neither one wanted to be the first to give in. John found himself longing to reconnect with Karen, but he was afraid that stepping toward her meant he had to take full responsibility for the argument and to admit that he was wrong. He was stuck.

Conflict is part of a healthy marriage, because every marriage brings together two sinners in need of a Savior. Unfortunately, many couples—especially Christian couples—have bought into the idea that good marriages aren't supposed to have conflict. As a result, they spend valuable time trying to avoid or cover up conflict rather than doing the rewarding work of resolving it.

Frankly, it can feel safer to keep our distance and let our wives make the first move toward reconnecting, but playing it safe does not lead to the intimacy that God desires for us. Every fight does not have to have a winner and a loser. The gospel enables us to honestly look at our own failures and recognize that we need grace and forgiveness just as much as our wives do. When a marriage is undergirded by the gospel, conflict isn't something to be feared.

BOTTOM LINE

God calls us to courageously engage in the process of resolving conflict with our spouse.

Moment of Strength: Proverbs 26:20

FINDING JESUS BEAUTIFUL

The Son is the radiance of God's glory and the exact
expression of His nature, sustaining all things by His
powerful word. After making purification for sins,
He sat down at the right hand of the Majesty on high.
Hebrews 1:3, HCSB

EVERY DAY, THE SUN COMES UP AND GOES DOWN. It gives light, energy, and warmth to the earth and makes things grow. The sun is absolutely necessary and incredibly powerful. Without the sun, we wouldn't be able to survive.

Not only is the sun necessary, but it also provides exceptional beauty. Who hasn't seen a kaleidoscope of colors decorate the sky as the sun sets below the horizon or as it greets the day by pushing back the darkness of night? Sunrises and sunsets are some of the most beautiful works of art we will ever witness. And this beauty has the power to captivate and mesmerize us.

The book of Hebrews says the same things about Jesus. Jesus is absolutely necessary. He holds everything together. He sustains life on the earth. He provides atonement for sin. He does for us what we can't do for ourselves. But while many people find Jesus valuable, they fail to see Him as beautiful.

As Hebrews also says, Jesus is the radiance of God's glory. He is matchless. He is magnificent. He has power over us. He has the power to change us and make us more like Him. We "are being transformed into the same image from glory to glory" (2 Corinthians 3:18, HCSB). Our faith revolves around Him.

BOTTOM LINE

May God give you the eyes to not only find Jesus valuable, but also to find Him beautiful. And may God shape you into the beauty that you see in Him.

Moment of Strength: John 1:1-14

BEING WITH JESUS

Jesus went up on a mountain and called out the ones he
wanted to go with him. And they came to him. Then he
appointed twelve of them and called them his apostles.
They were to accompany him, and he would send them out
to preach, giving them authority to cast out demons.

Mark 3:13-15

FIX THE FAUCET. Mow the lawn. Clean the garage. It seems as if there's a growing list of things to do around the house. Our responsibilities as Christians can sometimes feel the same way: Read the Bible. Attend a prayer group. Serve in the community. Give to the poor. When following Jesus is viewed in this way, our closeness with Him can get lost.

Just as owning a home brings big responsibility, so does following Jesus. However, Jesus calls us to a relationship before He gives us responsibility. To say it another way, Jesus calls us to *be* before He calls us to *do*.

When Jesus called the twelve disciples, He had a specific job for them to do. He called them to do the same things He had been doing up to that point—preach the gospel and heal people. But before Jesus sent them out, He first called them to be with Him in order to learn from Him. Jesus called them to be His apprentices.

When you spend time with Jesus, is it merely to check off something from your daily to-do list? Or do you submit yourself to Jesus in order to be taught by Him so that you can live like Him? He desires a personal relationship with you—that's not just popular Christian vernacular. You were made to know Him and love Him, and that comes from spending time with Him.

BOTTOM LINE

Following Jesus is about being with Jesus, in order to learn from Jesus, so that we can live like Jesus.

Moment of Strength: John 1:35-39

STOP FIGHTING

Be still, and know that I am God!
Psalm 46:10

As Eric drives home from work, the only word he can think to describe his life is *chaos*. Today was unexpectedly his last day at work—he was just laid off. His oldest son is on the verge of dropping out of college; there is no peace between his two daughters still at home; and Eric fears that his wife may have cancer. While sitting at a traffic light waiting for the light to turn green, Eric feels the pressure of life squeezing in on him.

Throughout Psalm 46, the psalmist paints a picture of the world in a state of chaos. When life feels out of control, the natural reaction can be to try to fight the chaos by working harder or doing more. But in this psalm we have a counterintuitive invitation from God to stop fighting our circumstances and just be still. However, being still in difficult situations can seem like we are doing nothing and wasting time.

In situations where you feel as if the water is rising over your head, being still before the Lord is often the best thing to do. Elsewhere, the psalmist declares that God is our refuge, our ever-present help in times of trouble, and that He is with us. When we are still before the Lord, we are able to remind ourselves that He is God and we are not. And we receive the peace that only He can give us. So next time you're feeling overwhelmed, slow down and look to the Lord.

BOTTOM LINE

When life feels out of control, instead of trying to fight the chaos, start by just being still.

Moment of Strength: Psalm 46

NO OTHER GOSPEL

*I am amazed that you are so quickly turning away from Him
who called you by the grace of Christ and are turning to a
different gospel—not that there is another gospel.*
Galatians 1:6-7, HCSB

THERE IS SOMETHING IN us that seeks new things all the time. We crave novelty. We get tired of the same old truths we think we know all too well. We want something fresh and different. In some areas of life this may not be a bad thing, but when it comes to the gospel, we must be careful.

The church in Galatia had started to drift away from the simplicity of the gospel, and the apostle Paul felt the need to write a correction. He knew and taught that the only true gospel was the one he preached—a gospel of grace, not works. Moreover, he was amazed that the Galatians would turn from this gospel so quickly. Why the amazement? Because deviations from the gospel are always harmful. The gospel produces life and freedom; any departure from it puts people right back into the bondage of performance-based living rather than faith in God.

To say that the gospel doesn't change is not to say that it is dry and boring—it is anything but that. Moralism—trying to do good things to appease God—is dreadfully dry and boring (not to mention exhausting). The gospel, on the other hand, is the most exciting news ever revealed to man, and it is news that affects how we live. In fact, the gospel produces far greater life change than moralism ever could. We must keep exposing ourselves to its truth. And we should ask God to help us remember it.

BOTTOM LINE

There is only one gospel, and we should thank God for that. Cling to the gospel. Believe the Good News—and share it with others!

Moment of Strength: Galatians 1:6-10

LIVING FOR GOD

When I tried to keep the law, it condemned me.
So I died to the law—I stopped trying to meet all
its requirements—so that I might live for God.
Galatians 2:19

MARTIN LUTHER FAMOUSLY WROTE: "Virtually the whole of the Scriptures and the understanding of the whole of theology depends upon the true understanding of the law and gospel." If Luther is correct, it's obviously important that we get this "true understanding," and it starts with understanding that God's law is good and perfect but that we are unable to keep it perfectly. This led Luther to conclude: "We do not abolish the law; but we show its true function and use, namely, that it is a most useful servant impelling us to Christ." Or as the apostle Paul writes in Galatians 3:24: "The law was our guardian until Christ came; it protected us until we could be made right with God through faith."

The primary purpose of the law in the Bible is to drive us to Christ. And not just for salvation, but to sustain us as we go about living the Christian life. That's what Paul was talking about when he wrote, "I died to the law . . . so that I might live for God" (Galatians 2:19). The law shows us our sin and our desperate need for a Savior. When we see the law rightly, recognizing it as the perfect expression of God's holy will, we don't imagine that we can somehow live up to it. Instead, we turn to Christ, the one who has lived up to it for us. And as we do that, our obedience grows. It's in trusting God that good fruit is produced.

BOTTOM LINE

The law is designed to lead you to the gospel. Progress in the Christian life occurs as we look to Christ, not to ourselves.

Moment of Strength: Galatians 2:19-21

FAITH AND THE HOLY SPIRIT

*Did you receive the Spirit by the works of the law or by hearing
with faith? Are you so foolish? After beginning with the Spirit,
are you now going to be made complete by the flesh?*
Galatians 3:2-3, HCSB

LIKE MANY GOOD TEACHERS, the apostle Paul often uses rhetorical questions to help his readers see obvious truths that seemingly aren't so obvious anymore. A good example of this occurs in Galatians 3:2-3, where Paul asks the Galatians if they had received the Spirit because of their obedience to God's law, or because they had heard the gospel and believed it. The answer, of course, is because they had heard the gospel and believed it.

Christianity is fundamentally about believing in the person and work of Jesus Christ. The Holy Spirit develops this faith in us, and it's our faith in Jesus that fuels our obedience. Additionally, faith in Jesus is opposed to our efforts in "the flesh" to please God. Paul also says that "the law is not based on faith" (Galatians 3:12, HCSB). So the Holy Spirit enables us to believe in Jesus, rather than rely on our own efforts to please God through our obedience—something we can never quite do.

Distinctions between faith and works, between the law and the gospel, and between the flesh and the Spirit may seem like theological nitpicking, but such distinctions are crucial. That's why Paul spent so much time writing about them. The Christian life is a faith-driven, Spirit-inspired glorying in who Jesus is and what He has done. It is not about our trying to be good.

BOTTOM LINE

We began the Christian life by faith, and we continue to live the Christian life by faith.

Moment of Strength: Galatians 5:1

SHARE EACH OTHER'S BURDENS

Share each other's burdens, and in this way obey the law of Christ.
Galatians 6:2

HAVE YOU EVER GONE THROUGH such a difficult trial that, if not for the help and encouragement of your friends, you're not quite sure how you would have made it through? The truth is, we need each other. God designed the church to function as a family, and members of a healthy family are there for each other during the tough times.

Hebrews 3:13 tells us we "must warn each other every day, while it is still 'today,' so that none of you will be deceived by sin and hardened against God." There is a sense in which we *are* our brother's keepers. We are called to love and encourage one another daily. No man is an island, especially in the church. So when we see a brother in need, we're called to step up and help. And when we're hurting, we need to be humble enough to ask others for help and receive it.

In "sharing each other's burdens," we're told, we "fulfill the law of Christ." Jesus is our example here. He is the ultimate burden carrier, as He has removed from us the burden of our sins and the burden of perfect obedience to God's law. He has set us free. But the freedom we have is meant to be used in the service of God and others. That's actually what true freedom is: the ability to love others as God loves us. And God has given us His Spirit to enable us to be burden carriers for others. By God's grace, live a life of love.

BOTTOM LINE

We're called to carry each other's burdens. That's not always easy, but following Christ means being willing to make sacrifices for the good of others.

Moment of Strength: Galatians 6:1-10

CHANGING YOUR FOCUS

*And now, dear brothers and sisters, one final thing. Fix your thoughts on
what is true, and honorable, and right, and pure, and lovely, and admirable.
Think about things that are excellent and worthy of praise.*

Philippians 4:8

THE ARGUMENT WASN'T GOING ANYWHERE. If anything, emotions seemed to be getting hotter, instead of simmering down. *Why can't she see how hard I'm trying to make this work?* Michael thought. *Is she trying to be difficult?*

In order to avoid saying things that couldn't be taken back, Michael asked for a cooling-off period with his wife. He went into his office, turned on his computer, and opened a document. Then he started reading: "She laughs at my jokes. She loves our kids. She's a beautiful singer. She loves God." He kept reading and reading. As Michael pored over this list of truths that he'd written about his wife, the argument seemed less important and more easily resolved.

What changed for Michael? He and his wife were still fighting. But instead of thinking negative thoughts about her, Michael chose to dwell on her good traits. In Philippians 4:8, Paul tells us to focus our thoughts on whatever is true, honorable, right, pure, lovely, and admirable.

In the midst of an argument, it's easy to do the exact opposite. Instead of thinking the best about our wives, we think the worst. If you haven't made a list of the things you love about your wife, take the time in the next few days to start one. In difficult times, it can help remind you of the truth.

BOTTOM LINE

Even during an argument, look for the positives in your wife. Dwell on the fact that she's God's gift to you.

Moment of Strength: Ephesians 4:31-32

FAITH TO MOVE MOUNTAINS

*"What do you mean, 'If I can'?" Jesus asked. "Anything is
possible if a person believes." The father instantly cried out,
"I do believe, but help me overcome my unbelief!"*
Mark 9:23-24

DO YOU HAVE THE FAITH TO move mountains? Mountains are pretty big. Our faith can rise and fall. Sometimes we feel strong in our faith; other times we wonder what happened to it.

Here's the good news: It's not up to our faith to move mountains, because we have nothing to do with it. God does. He's in the mountain-moving business. At times, we may feel that it's up to us to muster up the faith to make something happen. But it's not about muster; it's about mustard. Jesus said nothing is impossible for the person who has faith the size of a tiny mustard seed.

Instead of concentrating on the *strength* of our faith, we should focus on the *object* of our faith—Jesus. In the Gospel of Mark, a father brings his son to Jesus for healing from an evil spirit that the disciples couldn't cast out. When Jesus says that anything is possible to the one who believes, the boy's father shouts, "I do believe, but help me overcome my unbelief!" Then Jesus heals the man's son.

Was the boy healed because of the quantity of the father's faith? No. The father had little faith. In fact, he admitted to his unbelief. But what little belief he had he placed in the right person—Jesus. God's power can help our little bit of faith accomplish big things. He just wants our trust. As we learn to trust Him, He will grow our faith.

BOTTOM LINE

*Don't worry about how much faith you have. Just put your faith in the
right person—Jesus. Put your focus on Him and His grace, not yourself and
your faith.*

Moment of Strength: Matthew 14:28-31

FAME DOESN'T LAST FOREVER

There are many whose conduct shows they are really enemies
of the cross of Christ. They are headed for destruction.
Their god is their appetite, they brag about shameful things,
and they think only about this life here on earth.
Philippians 3:18-19

THESE DAYS A LOT OF people are famous for being famous. In reality TV shows and YouTube videos, people will behave outrageously for a chance at fifteen minutes of fame.

The desire to be seen as special is nothing new. In Acts 8:4-23, Philip travels to Samaria and leads a group of people to the Lord, including a sorcerer named Simon. Soon, Peter and John arrive and pray for the new believers to receive the Holy Spirit. When Simon sees the Spirit's power, he offers Peter and John money to give him the ability to touch people and have them receive the Spirit. Peter's response lets Simon know that's not going to happen.

Simon was used to being famous. He had amazed people for a long time with his abilities. If we're honest, we can easily get caught up in an earthly mind-set of desiring fame. The Bible warns in Philippians 3:18-19 that there are "many whose conduct shows they are really enemies of the cross of Christ. . . . Their god is their appetite . . . and they only think about this life here on earth."

Instead of focusing on making our mark on earth, our hearts should be set on heavenly success. As C. S. Lewis says in *Mere Christianity*: "Aim at Heaven and you will get earth 'thrown in': aim at earth and you will get neither." When we seek God, He rewards us with blessings that last forever, not just for fifteen minutes.

BOTTOM LINE

Our minds should be focused on God—not earthly fame or wealth. Heaven is eternal; all other pursuits are temporary.

Moment of Strength: 1 Peter 1:24-25

MIRROR IMAGE

But the LORD said to Samuel, "Don't judge by his appearance or height,
for I have rejected him. The LORD doesn't see things the way you see them.
People judge by outward appearance, but the LORD looks at the heart."
1 Samuel 16:7

THE WORLD IS OBSESSED WITH IMAGE. Magazines, TV, movies, and the Internet depict a nearly unattainable standard. Several years ago, an eighth-grade girl started a petition that asked a popular teen magazine to print just one unaltered image in its pages every issue. Because the magazine photo-edited all their pictures to make the models look more perfect, many young readers felt an even greater sense of inferiority.

A generation ago, cosmetic surgery was only for the aging or the rich and famous. Today, more and more young people choose to go under the knife for the image they desire. Some researchers call today's kids the most narcissistic group ever. To help avoid that trend, we need to point our children to God and help them see themselves as God sees them.

Who our kids are—and whose they are—is far more important than what they look like. Take time to let your children know how wonderful they are. Then go further to point out a character trait of theirs that you appreciate. As a father, your words powerfully affect how your kids view themselves. Make sure they know that you love them as God does: unconditionally and as His precious children.

BOTTOM LINE

As fathers, we need to help our children reflect Christ—not some earthly standard. What are some ways you can do that this month?

Moment of Strength: Psalm 139:13-14

STAND STRONG WITH BROTHERS

As iron sharpens iron, so a friend sharpens a friend.
Proverbs 27:17

IN THE 1940s, Edward Flanagan, founder of Boys Town, came across a drawing of an older youth carrying a younger boy on his back. The caption read, "He ain't heavy, he's my brother." Flanagan thought that it so perfectly illustrated what his ministry did that he commissioned a sculpture of the drawing that still stands on the Boys Town campus in Omaha.

In 1969, songwriters Bobby Scott and Bob Russell turned the phrase into a popular ballad, and the Hollies turned "He Ain't Heavy, He's My Brother" into a big hit.

As brothers in Christ, it is important that we encourage one another, challenge one another, and help one another stand strong when the ways of the world counter our faith. How do we do that? One way is to make ourselves accountable to a friend or a small group and to have appointed times—weekly is a good plan—when we ask each other hard questions. Some examples: *How much time have you spent studying the Bible this week? In prayer? How have you treated your wife this week? (Would she answer this question the same way?) What have you said or done this week for which you need to apologize? What are you believing about God right now? What are you believing about yourself?* It may not be easy to answer these kinds of questions, but it's worth the effort.

BOTTOM LINE

Find a brother or two who will meet with you weekly—and agree never to shy away from the hard questions. Sharpen each other as followers of Jesus.

Moment of Strength: 1 Thessalonians 3:6-13

STAND STRONG WITH FAMILY

Fathers, do not provoke your children to anger by the way you treat them. Rather, bring them up with the discipline and instruction that comes from the Lord.
Ephesians 6:4

MOST MEN THINK THEY'VE GOT a handle on what it means to be a leader in their families: set the rules, enforce the rules, and discipline the rule breakers. But deep down, we all know it's not always that simple. The same rules don't work with all children. Some children challenge us beyond anything we can figure out, and that often causes us to lapse into "because I said so" mode or the stern-faced, macho man with no feelings.

But leading a family—encouraging and nurturing your wife, challenging and teaching your children—takes a lot more than being a macho man.

When we're backed into a corner, it's a good place to humble ourselves and look at what we may be doing wrong, or at least at what we might do better. For example, author Randy Alcorn, founder of Eternal Perspective Ministries, often shares with audiences a humbling experience he had with one of his daughters at a father/daughter banquet.

Someone at the table asked my youngest daughter, Angela, what I'd done that made the biggest impression on her. I had no idea what she would say, but of course I hoped for something spectacular!

I'll never forget what she shared because it was so powerful to me. She said, "I remember one time when dad was harsh with me. Then a few minutes later he came back into my room, and he cried and asked my forgiveness. I've never forgotten that."

Alcorn concludes, "Being a good example isn't limited to doing great and magnificent things. Sometimes it's when we admit we did wrong." When we're wrong, we have to be ready to apologize and ask our children for forgiveness.

BOTTOM LINE
Start looking for ways to demonstrate your strength by showing your humility.

Moment of Strength: 1 Corinthians 13

DON'T CURSE THE GUARDRAIL

We know that God causes everything to work together for the good of those
who love God and are called according to his purpose for them.
Romans 8:28

LIFE SERVES UP A LOT OF unexpected challenges. Maybe you've been the victim of a lost job, a failed marriage, a chronic disease, bankruptcy, unfulfilled dreams, an accidental death in the family, or deep disappointment.

In those circumstances, it's easy to blame God. But even when it seems your world is falling apart, it is helpful to try to look at the big picture. Don't curse your circumstances. Take comfort in the knowledge that God loves you and that—even though it's painful—He will see you through the hard times.

What are some of the ways God uses our trials and tragedies? First Peter 5:10 tells us He will strengthen and support us after we've suffered. Psalm 119:71 says, "My suffering was good for me, for it taught me to pay attention to your decrees." Sometimes, suffering is the best teacher.

The story of Job is one of history's best-known examples of a good man suffering loss and tragedy. Yet in the middle of his trials, Job was confident that God would eventually purify him, making him "as pure as gold" (Job 23:10). No, testing is never easy, but we must remind ourselves of God's sovereignty. Whatever trial you're going through, let it propel you to search for strength and reassurance in God's Word.

BOTTOM LINE
Use a Bible concordance to find Scriptures and promises that address the issue of suffering. Cling to these during the hard times.

Moment of Strength: 1 Peter 4:1-2

DON'T FLY OFF THE HANDLE

A truly wise person uses few words;
a person with understanding is even-tempered.
Proverbs 17:27

EVER SEE A FATHER GO OVERBOARD in disciplining his child in public? You know, the kind of discipline that tears down and doesn't build up. Feeling embarrassed for the child and hot under the collar about the dad, you vow this will never be a part of your parenting style. Then your son lets a candy bar melt all over the backseat of the van and your daughter spills a drink over all your work on the kitchen table, and you find yourself needing to take a repentance bath after you chew them out.

You know that a man of understanding is supposed to keep a cool head during those times, and you've often considered yourself to be that kind of man, so you figure you should be able to restrain yourself from launching into an angry tirade. But you still may find yourself heading in that direction.

Remember that you were once a child too, and you required a lot of patience. Maybe you didn't receive it from your dad, but you needed it anyway. Imagine that you are the child who is making you mad. How do you look now?

Walk outside and take a deep breath. It's not the end of the world. Tell yourself, "I need to make good decisions right now so I don't add to the problem." A wise man is judicious with his words when disciplining his children. And a wise man seeks help from a pastor or counselor when he needs it.

BOTTOM LINE

Pray daily that God will mold you into the kind of man who doesn't reflexively fly off the handle at his kids.

Moment of Strength: Colossians 3:8

BY MY OWN STRENGTH

The Lord . . . will turn against the king of Assyria
and punish him—for he is proud and arrogant.
He boasts, "By my own powerful arm I have done this.
With my own shrewd wisdom I planned it."

Isaiah 10:12-13

QUICK, WRITE DOWN THE top five accomplishments of your life. Now, how many of those did you accomplish totally on your own, without the help of a coach, teacher, parent, or pastor? Whose shoulders have you stood upon that you might see farther into the distance of your life? Who propped up the ladder against the wall that you've been climbing? What teams have you been on that have accomplished more than the sum of their members?

Pride starts in the heart, but it doesn't stop there. It works its way into our bodies and affects the way we carry ourselves and relate to others. It changes our countenances and then begins to affect our speech. Nowhere is this more evident than in how many times we use the singular pronoun *I* each day. A self-centered, prideful attitude wreaks havoc in our relationships. It also sets us up for a big fall.

Wall Street likes to salute the "self-made man," but truthfully, no such man exists. No matter how great your accomplishments or education, the world doesn't revolve around you. Life is meant to be Christ-centered, not you-centered. After all, who created you and gave you air to breathe and food to eat? Who gifted you and equipped you for life? Who took your sins upon Himself at the cross? A fresh vision of Jesus today will cure your *I* disease and set you free to love others.

BOTTOM LINE

Ask a friend to be a spiritual optometrist for you and point out any I *disease you have in your life.*

Moment of Strength: James 4:6-10

FAITH AND LOVE

When we place our faith in Christ Jesus, there is no
benefit in being circumcised or being uncircumcised.
What is important is faith expressing itself in love.
Galatians 5:6

EVERY DAY IS A NEW OPPORTUNITY TO believe that what God says about us is true—that we're loved beyond measure—and to share with others this amazing love we've received from God. That's our mission as Christians. Galatians 5:6 simply says that "what is important is faith expressing itself in love."

In Matthew 22:37-40, Jesus says: "'Love the LORD your God with all your heart, all your soul, and all your mind.' This is the first and greatest commandment. A second is equally important: 'Love your neighbor as yourself.' The entire law and all the demands of the prophets are based on these two commandments." The Christian life is a life of love that flows from faith.

The Holy Spirit lives inside of us, comforting us, teaching us, and above all, pointing us to Christ (John 14:16-17; 16:13; 1 Corinthians 2:10-13; 3:16). He empowers us to live obedient, God-honoring lives. This unselfish life of love is impossible apart from Him.

In Galatians 5:16, the apostle Paul says, "Let the Holy Spirit guide your lives. Then you won't be doing what your sinful nature craves." Our fruit-bearing for God flows out of our relationship with Him through the Holy Spirit. Because there is an ongoing battle inside us between the flesh (our sinful desires) and the Spirit, we must "let God transform [us] . . . by changing the way [we] think" (Romans 12:2).

BOTTOM LINE

It's easy to get distracted and focus on lesser things. What matters most, though, is faith working through love. That should be our goal.

Moment of Strength: Galatians 5:16-18

JESUS THE WAY

Jesus told him, "I am the way, the truth, and the life.
No one can come to the Father except through me."

John 14:6

ONE BIG PROBLEM MANY people have with Christianity is its exclusivity. "How can there be just one true faith?" is a question that is particularly prevalent in our relativistic age. This question implies that doctrinal differences are unimportant. Well-meaning but uninformed Christians can fall into the trap of saying things such as "Well, I just love God; I don't get into all that doctrine stuff. You know, if we got rid of all doctrine, we would all get along just fine. Don't get hung up on differences—we are all basically the same." But that's not true, is it?

If you have older children or grown children, you may recall the first time you let them walk home from school alone. Did you tell them, "I don't want to be arrogant or narrow-minded, so feel free to take any street you want, or feel free to ride along with anyone, because they will all bring you safely home"? Of course not! Real love dictates that you show your children the right way, that you tell them, "Stay on this road, and don't go anywhere else." That's not arrogance—that's love!

Jesus wasn't being arrogant when He called Himself "the Way." Everyone has a set of exclusive beliefs—even an atheist. Maybe the best question is "Which set of exclusive beliefs can reconcile me to God and deal with the problem of my sin?" The answer is Jesus.

BOTTOM LINE

True love for your children does not allow them to wander on their own. True love trains them in the way they should go (see Proverbs 22:6).

Moment of Strength: 1 John 5:9-13

WHEN DOES WORSHIP START?

I will praise the LORD at all times. I will constantly speak his praises.

Psalm 34:1

WHEN DOES WORSHIP START? At 11 a.m. on Sunday morning? Or maybe it's 10:45? Or does worship start on Saturday nights at 6:00? The truth is, worship encompasses all of life. It's as much a Monday thing as a Sunday thing. We may gather to worship corporately as a church at 11:00 a.m. on Sundays, but we have been worshiping all week. It's just that we may not always be giving our worship to the Lord.

Worship is God's top priority. He is passionate about His glory. The first of the Ten Commandments reminds us that God is to be glorified above all other gods (Exodus 20:3). For King David, worship was a well-established routine. Not only was God's praise continually on his lips, but in Psalm 145:2, he writes, "I will praise you every day."

As men, how can we make worship a constant in our lives? One way is to bring a daily sacrifice of praise to the Lord. As you read Scripture, look for a name or characteristic of God that you can praise Him for. For example, in John 8:12, Jesus says, "I am the light of the world. If you follow me, you won't have to walk in darkness, because you will have the light that leads to life." That single verse has enough in it to ponder for weeks. If you read Scripture carefully and expectantly, you'll be surprised by how rich and full your personal worship will become and how it will influence your thoughts throughout your day.

BOTTOM LINE

May your worship of God never come to an end. It's meant to be a moment-by-moment experience.

Moment of Strength: 1 Corinthians 10:31

LEARNING TO LISTEN

In the same way, you husbands must give honor to your wives.
Treat your wife with understanding as you live together.
She may be weaker than you are, but she is your equal
partner in God's gift of new life. Treat her as you should
so your prayers will not be hindered.
1 Peter 3:7

IN LAW ENFORCEMENT, when officers are teamed together, it is critical that they back each other up. They must be able to trust their partner implicitly as another set of faithful eyes and ears on the scene. And when an 11-99 call goes out over the radio, it brings a swift response because 11-99 means, "Officer needs help immediately."

Your wife is your partner, another set of eyes and ears in the wild and woolly world of parenting, housekeeping, social engagements, and finances. But she needs much more from you than taking care of the car or picking up your socks, as important as those things are. She needs you to listen and be available to her. You may feel as if your wife speaks in code at times. It's up to you to learn her codes, her modes of communication, and respond accordingly. Is your wife struggling with something and could use your help? How do you know when she is sending out an 11-99?

You learn to listen with the ears of your heart. That's a form of listening that is constantly curious about your wife's dreams, hopes, ambitions, and feelings. It gives her room to grow and change, and it affirms the unique person she is and all that God is doing in her life. It is consistently asking questions and talking with her and listening to her. When you do that, she will feel loved and valued.

BOTTOM LINE

This week, ask your wife questions about herself. Don't try to fix her or solve all her problems—just listen and affirm her.

Moment of Strength: Proverbs 1:5

THE PRIVILEGE OF SERVING

God has given each of you a gift from his great variety of spiritual gifts.
Use them well to serve one another.

1 Peter 4:10

WHEN BILLY GRAHAM HELD a crusade in Seoul, South Korea, in 1973, he preached to a live audience of approximately 1.1 million people. Wow! Most folks get nervous talking to small groups of less than ten people! Over the years, Billy Graham's ministry reached untold millions of people around the world.

Countless other Christian servants will never be known outside their own small circles of influence. They serve others selflessly, simply doing what they feel God has called them to do.

There is one very important common denominator between a famous Christian icon such as Billy Graham and Christians who are unknown to others outside their own community. That common denominator is Jesus. No Christian servant is perfect. There's no such thing as a "super Christian." If someone is working effectively for God, it simply shows that God is at work in his or her life.

The grace and peace that God brings to our lives is truly amazing. Jesus says in John 15:5, "I am the vine; you are the branches. Those who remain in me, and I in them, will produce much fruit. For apart from me you can do nothing." The next time you're tempted to admire the service of other Christians, first give thanks that God is at work through them!

BOTTOM LINE

Christian service not only blesses others but also glorifies our heavenly Father.

Moment of Strength: 1 Peter 4:7-11

EVIL WON'T WIN THE DAY

Don't fret because of evildoers; don't envy the wicked.
Proverbs 24:19

YOU'RE DOING WHAT you know to be the right thing at work, but you don't ever seem to get ahead. You do your job without trying to draw attention to yourself and the hard work you put in. You know God put you in this position, and you don't want to disappoint Him by not doing your best.

And then there are some employees at work who don't mind cutting corners and clawing their way to the top. Seemingly, they'll stop at nothing to get ahead and be noticed. They may even go so far as to take credit for somebody else's hard work.

It may seem as if their method is working. They're gaining recognition and even getting promoted, and it's hard not to get discouraged seeing all that. Here's the thing, though. The Bible tells us not to be envious of the wicked. That means we should do our best not to worry about it when other people seem to be getting ahead by doing the wrong thing. That's primarily God's concern. We need to be concerned with our own integrity, knowing that God sees that, too.

The Lord knows the lengths to which others will go to achieve success. Not only does He know how they act, He is also able to put them in their place if they don't turn from their evil ways. Sooner or later, people's actions have consequences. So just keep doing your work as unto the Lord (Colossians 3:23) and let God take care of the rest.

BOTTOM LINE

Injustice may seem to go unchecked for a while, but while striving to reflect God's love at work, you can trust God to make things come out right in the end.

Moment of Strength: Psalm 37

OF LIKE MIND

Make me truly happy by agreeing wholeheartedly with each other,
loving one another, and working together with one mind and purpose.
Philippians 2:2

LARRY COULDN'T WAIT TO get to Sunday school every week. His classmates were all about the same age; most were married and some had kids, just like Larry did. When they were together, everyone laughed and cut up, just like friends do. When it came time for the lesson, everyone had something to share in one way or another. This was Larry's haven from the storms of life.

But as soon as class was over each week, a change came over Larry. He'd had a few disagreements over the years with others in the church, some more serious than others. He trudged into the sanctuary, not looking forward to the service. He felt guilty for feeling the way he did, but he just couldn't help himself.

In the end, the reasons for Larry's discouragement didn't really matter. It was his heart that had become jaded, regardless of how many disagreements he'd had with other church members and how serious those disagreements had been. Try as he might, he just couldn't get past all the hurts, the frustrations, the ill-spoken words, and . . . well . . . yes, the injured pride.

Only God can break down the sorts of walls that had built up over the years in Larry's heart. If you've ever been through something like this in the past, or even if you're going through it now, there is hope. What a joy it would be if Christians could get past their differences and focus on the same goal.

BOTTOM LINE

We know God to be all-powerful, so why not allow Him to break down any walls you may have built up against fellow Christians?

Moment of Strength: Romans 12:14-21

LOOK AROUND

As I looked and thought about it, I learned this lesson.
Proverbs 24:32

MANY COACHES LIKE TO use the phrase "teachable moment" for those times when players can learn from their stumbles. Maybe they went one way on the field of play when they should've gone the other. When that happens, there's an opportunity to learn and improve the next time around—to check out the playbook. It's all there in black and white.

The same thing goes for our lives as Christians. Every day, there are countless teachable moments all around us. Maybe it's the tone of voice you use with your wife and kids. Maybe it's the curse word that slips out when you're frustrated. Maybe it's making the same mistakes that so many others have made.

The context for today's verse is a walk past the field of a lazy person, which is "overgrown with nettles" and "covered with weeds" and has walls that "were broken down" (Proverbs 24:30-31). But the lesson to be learned can also apply to many other situations.

See, and take it to heart. Look, and receive instruction!

We have an infinite number of ways to appreciate God and learn from Him. Some lessons are harder to understand and apply to our lives than others. Some might require us to do our homework again until we get it just right. But don't worry. God's patience is infinite. He is the ultimate teacher.

BOTTOM LINE

Pray for God's strength to take teachable moments and apply them to your daily walk with Him.

Moment of Strength: Proverbs 3:13

MEETING GOD

For where two or three gather together as my followers, I am there among them.
Matthew 18:20

A YOUNG GIRL SAT BESIDE her mother in church. Like most children (and, sadly, many adults), her attention was neither easily captured nor easily held. So much of what happened during church seemed uninteresting. Quite frankly, she was bored.

Then she noticed a bronze plaque prominently placed on the wall, depicting stars, letters, and the American flag. Pointing to the plaque, she whispered to her mother, "What's that?" Graciously, the young mother replied, "Oh, those are the names of the people from our church who died in the service."

There was a long pause. Suddenly, the little girl demanded her mother's attention again. With a sense of concern—almost panic—she asked, "Mom, was that in the first or the second service?"

Though humorous, this story illustrates a common Sunday morning experience for many. It's safe to say that truly life-changing encounters with the living God are all too often missing from our worship services. Sometimes we don't come expectantly, as we should. One of the greatest needs among believers today is an encounter with God. We desperately need a life-changing glimpse of the wonder, power, and mercy of the God we serve.

Worship occurs when people who have fallen in love with the God of the universe engage with Him. It's a meeting between God and His people. Worship does not *lead* to an encounter with God—it *is* an encounter with God.

BOTTOM LINE

The next time you go to worship, seek to encounter the living God. He is ready and willing to meet with you.

Moment of Strength: Psalm 95:6

A PASSIONATE HEART

Love the LORD your God with all your heart, all your soul,
all your mind, and all your strength.
Mark 12:30

AMERICANS ARE A PASSIONATE PEOPLE—passionate about sports, politics, fashion, restaurants, and musical groups. We scream our heads off at football games and concerts. We hurt when our team or candidate loses. We are elated when victory comes. But sometimes we aren't very emotional about our faith. Why is that? If we are passionate about things we love—teams, bands, restaurants—why aren't we also passionate about the God we profess to love—the God who loves us "with an everlasting love" (Jeremiah 31:3)?

Because it's easier to be a fan than a follower. Being a follower takes commitment. It takes listening to and obeying God. It means spending time with Him, learning about Him. It means allowing Him to change us into His likeness. The more we follow Him, the more passionate our hearts become for Him.

In the Bible, the word *heart* refers to the hidden springs of one's personal life, that from which everything flows. When we are passionate about Jesus, that passion will flow from our hearts into every area of our lives, including our emotions.

As men, we may find it hard to talk about or even express certain emotions, but God created emotions as part of our humanity. He commanded us to love Him with all of our hearts, from the very center of our lives.

BOTTOM LINE

As author Mark Batterson observes, "Your reactions reveal what is really in your heart. and if you love God with all your heart, you won't just act like it. You'll react like it."

Moment of Strength: Deuteronomy 4:29

IN THE BAG

"O death, where is your victory? O death, where is your sting?"
For sin is the sting that results in death, and the law gives
sin its power. But thank God! He gives us victory over sin and
death through our Lord Jesus Christ.

1 Corinthians 15:55-57

THE FINAL WORDS OF JESUS AT the cross were "It is finished!" (John 19:30). Jesus had accomplished what was necessary for our salvation. Sin, death, and Satan were defeated. (Jesus' resurrection three days later completed the victory.) Sure, we will continue to have skirmishes because we still have an enemy who wants to wreak havoc on God's people. And though our salvation is secure and "finished," we are still in the midst of a spiritual battle.

But if Jesus' earthly life and ministry are finished, you don't have to run out and find another hero, another savior—all you need you can find in Jesus. If the road to salvation is complete, you don't need to try to earn or keep your salvation through good works. And if Satan is defeated, then you need not fear him or his attacks. Continue to stand firm, and let nothing move you from your commitment to Christ.

Have you had a victory celebration in your life lately? Think back to the last team to win the World Series. How did they celebrate on the field after the final out? If they can celebrate a world championship with such emotion and exuberance, how much more should we as Christians be able to celebrate the victory of Christ at the cross? Despite how difficult life in this world can be, Jesus has overcome the world (John 16:33), and that's reason enough to celebrate.

BOTTOM LINE

Thank God today that your spiritual victory is in the bag! That doesn't mean there isn't a battle still going on, but it's a battle that you're going to win.

Moment of Strength: 1 Corinthians 15:50-58

A WONDER-FILLED SOUL

Let all that I am praise the LORD. O LORD my God,
how great you are! You are robed with honor and majesty.

Psalm 104:1

HAVE YOU EVER BEEN TO a majestic place that takes your breath away? Like the mountains flowing into the ocean along the Oregon coast. Like the crystal-blue waters surrounding the Isle of Capri. Like the Grand Canyon's vastness and beauty. Like cradling your child for the first time. Such wonderful experiences can't be explained; they can only be experienced.

So it is with God. We need to experience Him. When we experience Him, we are filled with the wonder of His presence and love.

This was the essence of what Jesus was getting at when He encouraged His hearers to love God with all their souls (Mark 12:30). The Greek word for *soul* is *psyche*, from which we get the word *psychology*. The soul is the animating principle of life: that which gives life to the body. When we talk about people putting their "heart and soul" into something, we mean they're giving everything they have.

Wonder seems to be a rare commodity these days. A "been there, done that" attitude is common. That cliché suggests spiritual and emotional dullness. We are a people saturated with analysis, explanations, and facts but devoid of wonder. Maybe it's time we rediscovered the wonder of God. All it takes is a renewed awareness of His presence.

BOTTOM LINE

May we become less self-conscious and more God-conscious. That will produce a sense of wonder and joy and worship. Ask God to wake up your soul.

Moment of Strength: 1 Chronicles 16:29

DRASTIC MEASURES

If your hand or foot causes you to sin, cut it off and throw
it away. It's better to enter eternal life with only one hand
or one foot than to be thrown into eternal fire with both
of your hands and feet.

Matthew 18:8

THERE'S A MISLEADING INTERPRETATION OF the gospel that is sometimes preached today. It's really not "good news" because it's not quite true. It's the message that God loves you just as you are and that His main concern is your happiness. The problem with this message is subtle but dangerous. If your happiness isn't completely linked to what brings God glory, then it's not really that important. In fact, you can't be truly happy and fulfilled apart from loving and obeying God. So yes, God does love us as we are, but He loves us too much to let us stay that way. His love is purifying, transformative, and relentless.

Some people give up on holiness before even starting. "I'll never be perfect," they say. True. But holiness doesn't require perfection. Being holy is first a matter of *identity*. It's the mark of a true son with a powerful and loving Father who has given us a clean record. This new identity, then, should change how and why we live. Though we can't pay God back for His gift of grace, we can and should show our gratitude by how we live. If we have habits, influences, or patterns that are sinful, God will help us take measures to break them. It's for our good! God helps us live apart from sin because He wants us to have a deeper, more meaningful, purpose-filled experience with Himself. He created us for relationship.

BOTTOM LINE

God wants us to live holy lives so we can experience Him to the fullest. Is there a habit, influence, or personal pursuit separating you from God?

Moment of Strength: John 14:21

SEEKING APPROVAL

No wonder you can't believe! For you gladly honor each other,
but you don't care about the honor that comes
from the one who alone is God.
John 5:44

YOU GO OUT OF YOUR WAY FOR A STRANGER. You volunteer for your church and other causes. You go the extra mile for a coworker who needs help. You work hard for that promotion. You display diligence, dependability, and excellence, all of which are great character traits. But how do you feel when you don't get so much as a *thank you*? When you don't get recognized for all your unpaid hours? When you don't get the promotion? Or worse, when your slacker coworker does? Do you feel slighted? Offended? Angry? For most of us, the answer is *yes* in varying degrees.

There's nothing wrong with being appalled at injustice. Even standing up against it can be noble. But before we respond, we should consider Jesus' words in today's verse and examine where our motivations lie.

When Jesus said, "No wonder you can't believe," He was making a statement. In effect, He said that our craving for approval from others is an obstacle to true belief in Him. If He's asking anything, it's this: *Where is your priority? Is it some recognition or reputation among your peer group, or are you willing to abandon that pursuit for a more meaningful walk with Me?* It's time to recalibrate our measure of success. At the end of our time on earth, the accolades and praises from others won't matter at all. Only what Jesus says about us matters.

BOTTOM LINE

Pursuing the fleeting, conditional recognition of others is like running in the wrong direction. It takes us further away from God, never closer.

Moment of Strength: 1 Thessalonians 2:4-7

LEARN TO DUCK

Sensible people control their temper;
they earn respect by overlooking wrongs.
Proverbs 19:11

WHEN PRESIDENT RONALD REAGAN WAS shot by a would-be assassin in the spring of 1981, he somehow maintained his charm and sense of humor throughout, even though his life was in greater danger than he or anyone knew. When his frightened wife, Nancy, saw him for the first time in the hospital after the shooting, he joked, "Honey, I forgot to duck."

Though your wife may not be firing bullets at you (we certainly hope not!), learning how to duck a real or perceived insult is a trait that will pour concrete into the foundation of your marriage. Let's face it, we all make slips of the tongue at times and say things we later regret. When you're the guilty party, don't you long for some grace on the other end that is willing to overlook your offense?

You can develop compassion by gaining insight into your wife. If she has offended you with something, ask God to help you understand what your wife is going through. What has her day been like? Whom has she been with? Are there financial or relational pressures involved? Wives often carry the brunt of running the household, which may lead to stressful and snippy conversations at times.

Choose not to be easily offended. You might need to talk with your wife to work out any underlying issues, but endeavor to keep no record of wrongs and thus live out your calling to patiently love her.

BOTTOM LINE

Be the man. Give your wife some grace by overlooking some offenses that aren't a big deal and don't require a conversation.

Moment of Strength: 1 Corinthians 13

THE GRACE AND LAW REMIX

*Don't misunderstand why I have come. I did not come to
abolish the law of Moses or the writings of the prophets.
No, I came to accomplish their purpose.*
Matthew 5:17

THE SCRIPTURES OFTEN speak of God's law as good: "The instructions of the LORD are perfect, reviving the soul" (Psalm 19:7). In fact, God's giving of the law to a sinful people is, in and of itself, an act of grace. Like a father who seeks the welfare of his children, our heavenly Father gave us the law that we might avoid danger and find true life.

Sinful people have no hope of fulfilling the law. And so the law stands against us, accusing us—not because it is bad but because we are incapable of keeping it perfectly. This is one of the reasons Jesus came—to fulfill the entirety of God's law in a way that we cannot.

In your home, you must establish "law" that lines up with the goodness of God's law. In other words, rules designed to protect and bless. The absence of this structure communicates to your children that you do not love them. And yet, you must also balance your law with grace.

Grace doesn't say, "Sin is no big deal." Grace says, "Sin is a massive offense against a holy God remedied only by a massive sacrifice by a loving Savior." In the home, let's teach our children that God's law is good and God's grace is sufficient for us. Let's explain that the Bible is God's standard for life and that Jesus is God's provision to meet that standard.

BOTTOM LINE

*Diluting the force of God's law or the magnitude of His grace leads to an
imbalanced theology, in the home and everywhere else.*

Moment of Strength: Matthew 5:17-48

EASTER AND YOUR MARRIAGE

Be kind and compassionate to one another, forgiving one another,
just as God also forgave you in Christ.
Ephesians 4:32, HCSB

EVERY YEAR AROUND THIS TIME, many in the Western world gather to celebrate the resurrection of Jesus Christ. It's a practice that draws even the most minimally spiritual people. But what most seasoned church attenders don't realize is the power of the Easter story for their own personal lives, particularly the area of life that sometimes produces the most tension and stress: *marriage*.

On the surface, your marriage and what happened on a lonely hill two thousand years ago may not seem to be that closely related. But they are. The gospel is relevant to all of life, especially in areas where we struggle— areas where our selfishness and sin can wreak havoc if we're not relying on God's grace.

Easter intersects with marriage in one simple way: It introduces the idea that both spouses are sinners. Both routinely violate God's standard of perfection. Both need supernatural, extraordinary forgiveness. This simple truth profoundly changes marriage because it profoundly changes the way you relate to your wife. The gospel empowers you to forgive her offenses because you've been forgiven of far worse offenses by Christ. And it allows you to seek forgiveness from her because you don't have to pretend that you're perfect. Easter is about new life, and many marriages are in need of new life that only the grace of the gospel can provide.

BOTTOM LINE

Easter can be the beginning of a radical grace invasion into your marriage. God wants to bring new life and hope to your marriage this Easter.

Moment of Strength: Romans 12:12

EASTER DADS

*The LORD is like a father to his children, tender and
compassionate to those who fear him.*
Psalm 103:13

IF YOU COULD secretly poll Christian dads, you'd probably discover that most of them would acknowledge feelings of inadequacy. They just don't feel as if they are doing a good job as fathers. Some of this is fueled by the knowledge of their own weakness. Or it could be because of an exalted and misguided standard of perfection. As hard as dads try, they continually fall short.

At the heart of this parenting model is the mistaken idea that moral example and moral teaching alone can change the hearts of our children.

It is the Easter story of Christ overcoming sin that breathes out the message kids most need from their dads. It is the message that moral perfection is impossible and that every human soul—from dad to child—is in desperate need of saving grace. The gospel can revolutionize your parenting, empowering your leadership with transforming grace. You'll be a dad who easily forgives, quickly apologizes, sacrificially serves, and humbly teaches. You'll no longer fear your inadequacies. You'll let them drive you to your knees in dependence on your heavenly Father.

The Easter message of a risen Savior who empowers His people gives dads the liberating hope that they can obey the call to spiritually lead their families in a way that honors God.

BOTTOM LINE

Christian dads can't be perfect, but they are being perfected by Christ. Easter shows us that God's grace and power overcomes all our enemies.

Moment of Strength: Colossians 3:21

BRINGING THE GOSPEL HOME

In the same way, you husbands must give honor to
your wives. Treat your wife with understanding as
you live together. She may be weaker than you are,
but she is your equal partner in God's gift of new life.
Treat her as you should so your prayers will not be hindered.

1 Peter 3:7

ONE OF THE BIGGEST MISTAKES a newly married husband can make is to attempt to understand his wife through the lens of his own masculine experience. He can assume the things that bother him also bother her. Or that the things that don't bother him much shouldn't bother his wife, either. These (often wrong) assumptions can lead to arguments and lonely nights on the couch.

The apostle Peter calls men to live with and treat their wives with an understanding of their weaker nature. By "weaker," Peter doesn't imply inferiority; he is simply referring to the natural difference in physical strength between men and women. God intentionally created women to be different from men. And God calls a husband to work hard to understand what makes his wife tick—to understand her dreams, her desires, her emotions, her fears. When a husband shrugs these off, he is not only an obstacle to marital harmony, he is disobeying the Scriptures.

To many men, this kind of relational work seems optional or even irrelevant. But if a husband takes his relationship with God seriously, he'll increase his efforts to understand, sympathize with, and cherish his wife. What's more, a man is encouraged to cherish his wife so that his prayers "will not be hindered." In other words, a husband's relationship with his wife directly affects his relationship with God.

BOTTOM LINE

God calls a husband to learn about his wife's unique emotional, spiritual, and physical makeup. It's a duty and delight to seek to know your wife better.

Moment of Strength: Ephesians 5:25-32

WHAT ARE YOU CULTIVATING?

*As he scattered it across his field, some of the seed fell on a footpath, and
the birds came and ate it. Other seed fell on shallow soil with underlying rock.
The seed sprouted quickly because the soil was shallow.*

Mark 4:4-5

WE LIVE IN A GENERATION THAT, for the most part, knows little about farming and agriculture, though we are heavily dependent on those who work the land. But since we know so little of the process, it is not unusual that we may sometimes misuse common terms that relate to farming.

We may hear people talk about cultivating crops. But the soil itself is what is cultivated, both in preparation for planting crops and in tending the crops as they grow. In a sermon at the Francis Asbury Society's 2011 fall conference, seminary professor Dr. Victor Hamilton made the point that we cultivate the soil, not the crop. Dr. Hamilton then drew a spiritual parallel—we cultivate our hearts, preparing them to receive the seed of God's Word. We then continue to cultivate the heart, allowing the Word to grow and thrive.

To keep our hearts prepared for God's Word to grow requires a few basic things. The first is *desire*. If we don't want the Word of God in our hearts, it won't be there. Everything starts with desire. Second, we prepare our hearts by *studying the Bible*. And third, we prepare by communicating regularly with God through *prayer* and in *worship*. Only as these elements come together in our hearts will we have hearts where His truth can grow.

BOTTOM LINE

Cultivating the soil of your heart to make it more fertile for God's Word is an ongoing challenge and a great blessing.

Moment of Strength: Psalm 51:10-13

SETTING DIFFERENCES ASIDE

Therefore, accept each other just as Christ has
accepted you so that God will be given glory.

Romans 15:7

IT'S PRETTY EASY TO be accepting on a social networking site. Wanna be friends? No big deal. Click the button. No muss, no fuss. Of course, many of those friends are probably not close friends at all but are merely acquaintances and well-wishers. You don't really have to *accept* them, warts and all.

But the clarion call of Scripture is to accept other Christians as they are, not as we might wish they were. And the idea behind the word *accept* is really more active than passive—it is the idea of "take by faith." Just as we accept salvation by faith, we are to accept other Christians by faith. Among other things, this means we don't see them just for who they are now but also for who they will become as God continues to work in their lives.

Sure, some Christians are quite different from you. They come from different backgrounds and see life differently. But at one time, you were on the outside looking in too. And yet you were accepted into God's family by faith. Offer to others the same kind of grace you've received.

Occasionally, you still see this sign outside a business: "No shirt, no shoes, no service." Wouldn't it be great if the sign hanging on your heart said to all around you, "Come Just As You Are"? That kind of grace attracts people. It also pleases your heavenly Father, who offers the same grace to you.

BOTTOM LINE

Be a grace giver. Ask God to help you see and accept others the way He does.

Moment of Strength: James 2:1-4

THE VOICE OF GOD

*The voice of the LORD echoes above the sea. The God of glory
thunders. The LORD thunders over the mighty sea. The voice of
the LORD is powerful; the voice of the LORD is majestic.*

Psalm 29:3-4

IT'S THE MIDDLE OF THE DAY, and the sky overhead is black with storm clouds. The windows are soaked, and it feels as if the house has been submerged in the ocean. The trees are bending to the point of breaking. The lightning is so close you can almost feel it. Being in severe storms can be very unsettling. Just because we are indoors doesn't always mean we are safe. In those moments, we are reminded of the power that nature holds.

In Psalm 29, the voice of the Lord is likened to a severe storm. Christians often use the analogy of a storm to describe trials in life, but in Psalm 29 the psalmist uses it to describe God. It's easy to forget that God is so powerful He can create a world or destroy a kingdom with a word.

Though being in the midst of a severe storm can evoke a fearful response, in this psalm the response is worship. At the end of Psalm 29, the people of God are in the Temple crying "Glory!" Why? Because God is both glorious and good. He may not be "safe"—that is, predictable or manageable—but He is always good. In the aftermath of the storm, God brings peace and strength to those who trust in Him. We see Him come through for us, and we ascribe to Him the glory due His name. So while His glory can be a bit unsettling to us at times—just consider the vastness of the night sky on a clear night—it also leads us to worship.

BOTTOM LINE

The voice of God may not be "safe," but it is good. The more you see how great God is, the more you will worship Him and trust Him.

Moment of Strength: Psalm 29

A CONVERSATION, NOT A "TALK"

Direct your children onto the right path, and
when they are older, they will not leave it.
Proverbs 22:6

As PARENTS, we rarely hold back when it comes to offering instructions to our children. We're more than willing to offer our experiences, thoughts, and opinions on topics ranging from driving responsibly to their taste in music to their choice of friends, but we often overlook or avoid one important topic: *sex*. In most households, if sex is discussed at all, it surfaces as a onetime "talk" and then conveniently goes away, never to be mentioned again. But why do we avoid this important topic with our children?

Many parents shy away from this topic because they don't know what to say or how to say it without feeling uncomfortable. Other parents reason that they can't compete with their children's friends or the media. Many feel that kids will be more curious about sex and want to do it if they talk about it, and some parents are in denial that their children are even thinking about sex.

When it comes to the issue of sex, we should not think in terms of "the Talk" but rather an ongoing conversation. Our children are inundated daily with hundreds of sexually explicit messages from our culture, and as parents we must be diligent to help them hear and understand God's perspective on sex and sexuality. If we are silent, the only message our children will hear is our culture's corrupted view of sex. Remaining silent on the subject is not an option.

BOTTOM LINE

Research shows that parents have the greatest impact on their kids' decisions about sex—more than friends and the media. Take a proactive approach.

Moment of Strength: Ephesians 6:4

HOT PURSUIT

Rise up, my darling! Come away with me, my fair one!
Song of Songs 2:13

EVER SINCE THEIR youngest daughter left home for college six months ago, John and Heather have been strangers living in the same house. Last night, the fighting started when John announced that he was planning an out-of-town golf trip with his buddies. In the heat of the argument, Heather blurted out, "You don't need a wife! You just need a maid and a cook! Do you realize how long it has been since we have taken a trip together?"

The next morning, reflecting on Heather's penetrating words, John knew she was right. He longed to recapture the long-lost passion in their relationship, but he was ashamed to admit he didn't know how. Why couldn't his relationship with Heather be as easy as his relationships with his buddies? Why did marriage require so much work?

It's easy to approach our wives as just another project or task on our to-do list. We once worked hard to win their hearts, and now we have moved on to the next task. But to adequately pursue them, our own hearts must be engaged in the process. This requires effort and intentionality and being willing to step into the often scary realm of the emotions. Rather than shying away, we must courageously pursue in spite of the risks. Our wives and our marriages are certainly worth it.

BOTTOM LINE

Pursuing your wife's heart requires courage. Ask God to give you the courage you need today.

Moment of Strength: Ephesians 5:25

TAKING TIME TO REST

*This is what the Sovereign LORD, the Holy One of Israel,
says: "Only in returning to me and resting in me will you
be saved. In quietness and confidence is your strength.
But you would have none of it."*
Isaiah 30:15

WITH A MYRIAD OF ACTIVITIES and responsibilities fighting for our time and attention, it's often difficult to get everything done. There always seems to be more to do and less time to do it. Without enough time to complete everything, it becomes even more of a challenge to find the time for the rest we desperately need in order to function at peak performance.

According to the prophet Isaiah, our strength is closely tied to rest. In our busy culture, it's easy to think that rest is synonymous with laziness, but it's not. Rest is a disposition of the soul that flows out of a deep trust that God is in control and taking care of us. If we're honest with ourselves, we recognize that much of our busyness may be a result of insecurity about our standing with God. We try to silence our noisy consciences with activity.

You've no doubt heard it said that we are human *beings*, not human *doings*. Still, as men, it's easy for us to define ourselves by what we do and to quickly lose sight of who we are (apart from what we do). Rather than resorting to more activity as a means of dealing with the noise inside us, we should understand that God desires for us to *stop* and *rest* instead. In this stillness, God exposes our desire for self-sufficiency and reminds us that His love for us is based on who we are and not what we do. Don't you long for that? Don't you long for the "green pastures" and "quiet waters" of Psalm 23 (HCSB)? They are available for us.

BOTTOM LINE

If we think we need to earn anything in our relationship with God, we will live restless lives. What will you do today to intentionally rest?

Moment of Strength: Luke 10:38-42

TRUE HAPPINESS

Oh, the joys of those who do not follow the advice of
the wicked, or stand around with sinners, or join in
with mockers. But they delight in the law of the LORD,
meditating on it day and night. They are like trees
planted along the riverbank, bearing fruit each season.
Their leaves never wither, and they prosper in all they do.

Psalm 1:1-3

SOMETIMES YOU HEAR Christians talk about their Bible reading as if it were the equivalent of eating their brussels sprouts so they can have dessert later. What a shame. And how very far from the truth it is! The Scriptures are the gracious revelation of who God is, what His plan is for us and for the world, and, not least, just how much He loves us in Christ. What could possibly be more relevant and exciting than hearing from the God of the universe?

But the goal here is not to guilt you into reading the Scriptures more or to chastise you for the ho-hum attitude you may sometimes bring to your Bible reading. It's to suggest that you may not be thinking about Bible reading the way the Bible itself says we should: with great delight!

Setting aside the distinction that is sometimes made between happiness and joy, Psalm 1 describes a happy man—not a guy who's just a little happy but a man filled with delight. And all because this man loved reading the Scriptures. We can safely assume he read them not in a detached, impersonal way but in a highly personal and enthusiastic way—as if the God of the universe were speaking to him (which, of course, He was). We're told this man meditated on the Scriptures "day and night," and the result was that he prospered. God's Word is a great gift, and reading it is a delight.

BOTTOM LINE

Reading the Bible should be a joyful experience. And it will certainly bear good
fruit in your life. Ask God today to give you a passion for His Word.

Moment of Strength: Psalm 1

GOD'S GLORY, MAN'S DIGNITY

What are mere mortals that you should think about
them, human beings that you should care for them?
Yet you made them only a little lower than God and
crowned them with glory and honor.

Psalm 8:4-5

VERSE 1 OF PSALM 8 BEGINS WITH an almost breathless description of God's glory: "O LORD, our Lord, your majestic name fills the earth! Your glory is higher than the heavens." As much as humanly possible, we should aim to think thoughts of God that are worthy of Him. He is truly magnificent and majestic—utterly matchless.

One way to catch a glimpse of God's glory (and gain a little perspective) is to look around you—and especially *upward*. That's what the psalmist David did. He looked up and was absolutely blown away by God's greatness and his own relative smallness.

"When I look at the night sky and see the work of your fingers—the moon and the stars you set in place—what are mere mortals that you should think about them, human beings that you should care for them?" (Psalm 8:3-4). This is true worship—seeing God's greatness and understanding our lesser place in the grand scheme of things.

And yet Psalm 8:5 says that man is created "with glory and honor." We are made in God's image, and we are of great value to Him. Furthermore, verse 6 says that God gives humanity great responsibility: "You gave them charge of everything you made, putting all things under their authority." We are called to exercise dominion (control) over creation, under God's loving care and rule. And in this His magnificent name is glorified, and we are truly blessed.

BOTTOM LINE

By being created in God's image (and then being recreated to become like His Son), we have been given great dignity, responsibility, and purpose.

Moment of Strength: Psalm 8

A RENEWED LIFE

He lets me rest in green meadows; he leads me beside
peaceful streams. He renews my strength. He guides me
along right paths, bringing honor to his name.

Psalm 23:2-3

EXHAUSTION IS BECOMING the new normal in our culture. It's almost a badge of honor these days to talk about how busy you are, how much you have to do, and how tired you are from trying to stay on top of it all. Our busyness is killing us.

It's not that we necessarily enjoy being ridiculously overscheduled; it's that we don't see a way out of the madness. We drift into unhealthy ways of thinking and living. We aren't intentional enough about how we use our time. We aim for that elusive thing called *balance*, forgetting that there are biblical rhythms of work and rest that, if adhered to, can keep us going without burning out. Perhaps worst of all, we forget that God invites us to find rest in Him whenever and wherever we need it. We are not on our own. He is with us to guide us, strengthen us, and give us rest.

Any progress we make in learning to slow down and live in a sane and sustainable way will ultimately occur as we look to our Shepherd to guide us. In order for that to happen, though, we must be intentional about setting aside some time without distractions to focus on Him. We can't afford to believe the lie that we don't have time to meet with the Lord in quiet, unrushed Bible reading and prayer. When we take time for God, we experience His peace, and it can set the tone for the entire day.

BOTTOM LINE

We can experience peace and renewal as we learn to slow down, spend time
with the Lord, and let Him guide us. Ask Him to help you learn to rest.

Moment of Strength: Psalm 23

NO FEAR

The LORD is my light and my salvation—so why should I be afraid? The LORD is my fortress, protecting me from danger, so why should I tremble?

Psalm 27:1

SOMETIMES WE NEED TO talk to ourselves rather than listen to ourselves. This is especially true when we're tempted to fear. And let's face it, we're tempted on a regular basis. There are just so many things that we could be afraid of—failure, disease, death, relational breakdowns, a bad economy, and on and on it goes.

Living with fear is crippling. It shrinks our world down to what we think we can control, which is actually not that much. It eats away at our confidence—in God and in ourselves. It renders our faith less effective as we slip into survival mode rather than maintain an optimistic expectation of what God can do through us and for us. In summary, fear is a great enemy, and often comes from the enemy, the devil. But we don't have to listen to it. We can prayerfully respond with faith. We can talk back to ourselves in faith-building ways as David does in Psalm 27.

David starts by simply reminding himself that because the Lord is his "light and salvation," his "fortress," he has no need to fear. No matter how bad things were looking on the outside—and they were looking pretty bad for David—he remained confident in God's help and deliverance. In fact, he looked forward to offering sacrifices to God with shouts of joy (Psalm 27:6). That doesn't sound like a guy paralyzed by fear. Instead, it sounds like a guy who is confident in God—and therefore free from fear.

BOTTOM LINE

You may sometimes feel afraid, but you don't have to live in continual fear. You can remind yourself of God's faithfulness. You can worship your way out.

Moment of Strength: Psalm 27

THE JOY OF FORGIVENESS

What joy for those whose disobedience is forgiven, whose sin is put out of sight! Yes, what joy for those whose record the LORD has cleared of guilt, whose lives are lived in complete honesty!

Psalm 32:1-2

GOD IS NOT SHOCKED BY OUR SIN. Nor does it disqualify us from His love. We may feel that way sometimes, but it's not true. Oh, the feelings of guilt when we've done wrong and not confessed it are real enough. In fact, our guilty feelings can be the gracious work of the Holy Spirit convicting us of our sin. When we're convicted, the best thing to do is confess our sin immediately and repentantly and then, by faith, receive God's forgiveness. Otherwise, we may find ourselves feeling a little like David: "When I refused to confess my sin, my body wasted away, and I groaned all day long. Day and night your hand of discipline was heavy on me. My strength evaporated like water in the summer heat" (Psalm 32:3-4).

Sounds pretty miserable, right?

Thankfully, David didn't stay miserable, and we don't have to either. "Finally, I confessed all my sins to you and stopped trying to hide my guilt. I said to myself, 'I will confess my rebellion to the LORD.' And you forgave me! All my guilt is gone" (Psalm 32:5). For some reason, there are times when we would rather conceal our sin, rationalize it, or suppress it instead of simply coming clean and confessing it. We may even attempt to give ourselves a probationary period before returning to God. That never works, though. Confession is the surest path to freedom and joy. Honesty with God is always the best policy. We can't hide anything from Him anyway, and forgiveness is freely available to us.

BOTTOM LINE

Learn to make the connection between confession and joy. God forgives our sin on account of Christ. It's not too good to be true. Confess your sins daily.

Moment of Strength: Psalm 32

HAVE YOU HEARD THE NEWS?

Faith comes from hearing, that is, hearing the Good News about Christ.
Romans 10:17

WHY DO YOU GO TO CHURCH? It's good to gather with the body of Christ and dig into the Bible together. Worshiping the Lord with other believers is an awesome experience. But hearing the Word of God is very powerful. A big part of going to church is hearing the pastor speak the truth.

But apart from your pastor, how often do you hear people talking about God? If you listen to Christian radio, you might get an earful every now and then. But most of us probably don't hear much being said about God during our workweek.

Just as an audiobook proclaims the Good News about Christ through words, we should do the same. The apostle Paul writes, "Faith comes from hearing, that is, hearing the Good News about Christ." The first step in believing the gospel is hearing it. Many people will never set foot in a church building, so it's up to us to reach them with God's life-changing message.

Look for ways to talk about what God is accomplishing in your life. Memorize Scripture and share God's wisdom with the people around you. Let your friends know you're praying for them during difficult times. Don't hide your relationship with Christ. Boldly and prayerfully speak about the difference He's made in your life so others will be encouraged to believe too.

BOTTOM LINE

People need to hear the Good News about Jesus. Boldly, graciously, and prayerfully witness for Him through your words.

Moment of Strength: Romans 10:14

LOVE YOUR JOB

I came to hate life because everything done here under the sun is so troubling.
Everything is meaningless—like chasing the wind.
Ecclesiastes 2:17

JEFF BEGAN TO DREAD going to work every day. The job wasn't so bad; he actually enjoyed working in advertising. But his boss often changed things just to throw his weight around a little bit. And if a client liked an idea, Jeff's boss took all the credit. Not that Jeff was a glory hound; he just would've appreciated a little positive recognition. The only time he did get recognized was if he made a mistake or missed a deadline. Then his boss would come down on him like a sledgehammer, sometimes even threatening his job.

The actual work environment rubbed Jeff the wrong way too. He had never pictured himself working in a cubicle, yet here he was.

Do you ever not want to go to work? Despising your job can make your whole life seem difficult. According to research, dwelling on these feelings drives up your blood pressure, lowers your immune system, and increases headaches. On the other hand, leaning on Jesus and making the best of a bad situation can result in joy and—eventually, perhaps—new opportunities.

If you can't change your job, at least try to change your outlook. Every job has its positives and negatives, so ask God to help you find the positives where you are. Maybe it's your coworkers or the satisfaction of a job well done. You can't always control your circumstances, but you can always control your attitude.

BOTTOM LINE

Ask God to help you find ways to honor Him in your job each day.

Moment of Strength: Ecclesiastes 2:18-26

SWEET REWARD

Taste and see that the LORD is good. Oh, the joys of those who take refuge in him!
Psalm 34:8

SOMETIMES, CHOCOLATE CAN BE GOOD FOR YOU. A study at San Diego State University discovered that people who ate a moderate amount of dark chocolate over a fifteen-day period were able to lower their blood sugar levels and improve both their good cholesterol (HDL) and bad cholesterol (LDL) levels compared to others who ate white chocolate (which contains no cocoa solids).

It should be noted that the people in the study didn't gorge themselves on chocolate or eat huge amounts of chocolate cake and ice cream. But an ounce or two a day can be a great treat. Dark chocolate is a good choice because of its heart-healthy antioxidants.

Chocolate isn't the only sweet thing that can be good for you. In Psalm 34:8, David writes: "Taste and see that the LORD is good. Oh, the joys of those who take refuge in him!" In the book of Proverbs, wisdom is compared to sweet honey. When you savor your relationship with Christ by consuming His Word and building your wisdom in Him, you'll reap a sweet, satisfying reward.

If we're honest with ourselves, we probably don't eagerly anticipate our devotional time the same way we look forward to taking a bite of our favorite chocolate bar. But we should. Think of ways to make your time with God sweeter. Unlike chocolate—where too much can be a bad thing—we can never consume too much of God's Word. We can never have too much Jesus in our lives.

BOTTOM LINE
Look for ways to taste the sweetness of God and His Word daily.

Moment of Strength: Psalm 119:103

NEW CREATION

Anyone who belongs to Christ has become a new person.
The old life is gone; a new life has begun!
2 Corinthians 5:17

IT'S EASY AND NATURAL TO hang on to the past. After all, God has given us the gift of memory, and there are a lot of things worth remembering. (God's faithfulness being foremost among them.) Certainly, the past informs our present and to some degree shapes it. And without the past, we don't have much context for understanding the present or wisdom for how to proceed in the future.

If you're a Christian, your past sins have been forgiven. And they should be forgotten, too. (Of course, we still need to confess and repent of our sins and accept God's forgiveness.) Whether you feel like it or not, you are a new creation with a new life. Colossians 1:13 describes the change that has taken place: "He has rescued us from the kingdom of darkness and transferred us into the Kingdom of his dear Son."

We experience the "new life" that God promises when we believe what He says in His Word. For instance, the apostle Paul tells us to "consider yourselves dead to sin but alive to God in Christ Jesus" (Romans 6:11, HCSB). Because of your new identity in Christ, you are dead to sin and alive to God. You don't have to give in to temptation. You are not a helpless victim of uncontrollable desires. You have been set free, but you need to believe that and consider it true. Remember, the enemy will be telling you a different story.

BOTTOM LINE

Declare your freedom in Christ. God has made you a new creation. By faith, choose to believe your new identity, and live it out.

Moment of Strength: Romans 6:12-14

UNWORTHY

Moses again pleaded, "Lord, please! Send anyone else."

Exodus 4:13

THE TWO INSTRUCTORS HAD a favor to ask of Rick. Recently, he had taken part in a class at the local YMCA to prepare to train for a 5K race. It was hard, but he achieved his goal of finishing in less than thirty minutes. Afterward, he knew the trainers were putting together another course—this one to prepare for a 10K.

What he wasn't expecting was that they would ask him to help out as an instructor. Immediately, a thousand thoughts began racing through his mind, none of them very positive.

I've never done anything like this. I'm not an athlete. I've never done a 10K before. You couldn't get anybody else to do it, right?

When it came down to it, Rick felt a little bit like Moses at the burning bush. No, he wasn't being asked to lead the Israelites out of Egypt, but becoming a running coach was definitely outside his comfort zone. Like Moses, Rick felt uncertain of his own ability, and he thought the trainers were surely making a big mistake. There had to be someone else better suited for this assignment—right?

God knew exactly what Moses' weaknesses were (as well as his strengths), and He called Moses anyway. Many times, accomplishing something for God takes a simple leap of faith. Forget about the reasons why you shouldn't be able to do it, and concentrate on why you can.

(For the record, Rick helped lead the class, and it was a great experience.)

BOTTOM LINE

When you're feeling unworthy of a particular assignment, look to God for guidance, courage, and help. He uses people who aren't perfectly qualified and gives them the strength and direction they need.

Moment of Strength: Exodus 3:1–4:17

DISTRACTIONS

Therefore, since we also have such a large cloud of witnesses surrounding us,
let us lay aside every weight and the sin that so easily ensnares us.
Let us run with endurance the race that lies before us.
Hebrews 12:1, HCSB

HAVE YOU EVER SEEN a group of people sitting at the same table in a restaurant, and everyone is busily typing away on their smartphones? What's so important that they're all practically ignoring each other? Is it possible they're tweeting or updating their statuses about how they're out with their friends? Come on. Put the phones down!

Attention spans aren't what they used to be. Before cable and satellite television, we were stuck with basically three channels. Now, there are hundreds of channels. Don't like what you see when you land on one? Change the channel. Change it again. And again. Let's not even begin to talk about the Internet and how it can . . . oops, wait a second, there's an e-mail coming in!

Life is crazy enough without all these other distractions. You've got plenty of family obligations, and your job keeps you busy enough. You're thankful for your wife, your kids, your job, and everything else, but those relationships and your job require time and care.

As easy as it is to get sidetracked these days, the one constant has to be Jesus. Consider how much time you spend on social media, the Internet, TV, and whatever else you have going, and then think about how much time you spend with Jesus. No matter what else you've got on your mind, stay focused on Him.

BOTTOM LINE

Distractions are all around us. Keep them in their rightful place, and focus on your relationship with Jesus.

Moment of Strength: 1 Corinthians 9:24-27

YOUR CHILDREN'S CHILDREN

Grandchildren are the crown of the elderly.
Proverbs 17:6, HCSB

YEARS AGO, a father arrived to pick up his children at the grandparents' house. Neither of the young boys was very happy about it, and they proceeded to kick up a fuss as their dad struggled to fasten them into their car seats. Frustrated, the dad asked, "Would you rather just stay here and live with Nanny and Papaw?"

Turns out that was a mistake. (Note to self: Don't ask a question that you might not want to hear the answer to.)

Up they came out of their car seats once more. Turns out there was nothing in the world like Nanny and Papaw, who loved them, fed them, and spoiled them just a little bit. The boys hadn't considered that living with their grandparents might be an option. Years later, their dad still couldn't help but laugh at the memory.

There's nothing quite like the relationship between grandparents and grandchildren, is there? Grandparents who have reached retirement age have more time to devote to their grandchildren, and that's obviously a huge plus. And maybe they're more lenient than they were with their own kids.

Whatever the case may be, grandchildren can be some of God's greatest gifts. First, it means that the grandparents have lived long enough to see their grandchildren. Even more important is the blessing that grandchildren and grandparents are to each other. What better gift could there be than to build a legacy of faith with future generations?

BOTTOM LINE

Grandkids are awesome! Love them and have fun with them, all the while giving them a foundation of faith in Christ.

Moment of Strength: Psalm 128

HOW BUSY ARE YOU?

You are worried and upset over all these details!
Luke 10:41

YOU KNOW ALL TOO WELL what it feels like to be up-to-your-eyeballs busy. You're going a thousand miles an hour, but it all seems to be for the right reasons. You're loaded up with responsibilities at work, with your family, and at church. It's a lot to handle, so it's easy to get frazzled. And how much of it truly matters in the long run?

Here's a revolutionary thought: Your children may not need to play on three different sports teams at the same time! That's not necessarily a bad thing, of course, but it may not be a good thing either. It's okay to not be booked all the time. It's wise to move at a more leisurely pace.

Jesus sat and talked while Martha scurried around her home, trying to make sure things were just right. Her sister, Mary, sat at the feet of Jesus and listened intently to what He had to say. When Martha complained that Mary wasn't helping in the kitchen, Jesus responded that Mary had made the right choice. She was focused solely on Him, and Martha was not.

There are several accounts in the Gospels of times when Jesus slipped away from the crowds for some much-deserved peace and quiet. It's okay to slow down once in a while so you can focus on the important things in life. With that in mind, what are some areas where you could possibly cut back? What would you have to do to carve out some healthy margin in your life?

BOTTOM LINE

Do you really have to be as busy as you are?

Moment of Strength: Luke 10:38-42

ALWAYS

Are any of you suffering hardships? You should pray.
Are any of you happy? You should sing praises.

James 5:13

BOBBY WAS ALONE, much more so than he'd ever been in his life. After leaving work on Friday afternoon, he often wouldn't talk to another human being until he arrived back at the office on Monday morning. His meager paycheck was spent before he even received it. Times were tough, and there were many, many nights when all Bobby could do was pray.

Slowly, Bobby's lot in life began to improve. He got an awesome job, one that he truly loved. He met the woman of his dreams. They married and had two happy, healthy children. Every day on the way to school, the kids commandeered the car's CD player so they could listen to a catchy Christian song called "Good Morning." Life was good!

Today's verse is short and to the point, but that's what we need sometimes. When your world has been shaken down to its foundation, this passage doesn't say to mope about it or lash out in anger. It says to pray. That may not always seem like much, but nothing could be more important. Prayer has the power to change our perspective and give us hope.

The same goes for times of plenty. Instead of giving God a quick thumbs-up and going on about your business, praise Him with everything you have. He is the Creator of the universe, and He sent us His Son—the greatest gift possible. Thank Him for that, and don't do it half-heartedly.

BOTTOM LINE

No matter what's being thrown at you, you can pray. And in the good times, you can praise. The important thing is to engage with God from your heart.

Moment of Strength: Colossians 3:15-17

THOSE KIDS ARE NOT YOURS

Children born to a young man are like arrows in a warrior's hands.

Psalm 127:4

FROM THE MOMENT they enter the world, our children are slowly walking away from our care. Those tiny, vulnerable, dependent babies will one day walk down the graduation aisle and into a life of their own. Parents know this, yet there is an innate desire to hang on to our kids, to wrap our arms so tightly around them that, if we're not careful, we can inadvertently end up choking their spiritual lives.

The Bible tells us that our children are not really our own. Sure, they are our flesh and blood, but they are God's children before they are our children. Parenting is not possession but stewardship. For a time, a long season, children are in our care, and we are tasked with the job of providing for them, teaching them, and then releasing them into the world as children of God and ambassadors for Christ and His Kingdom.

The psalmist describes children as "arrows in a warrior's hands." They are meant to be released with power toward a target. This means parents should raise their children with an eye toward God's purpose for them in Christ. Our duty is not to press them into the molds we design, and it's certainly not to help them achieve worldly success; it is to allow the Holy Spirit to shape them for their unique mission in the world. In parenting, as in all things, we must seek first the Kingdom of God and His righteousness.

BOTTOM LINE

Our children are not our possessions to hoard, but God's good gifts to steward.

Moment of Strength: Psalm 127:3-5

HOLD YOUR PREFERENCES LOOSELY

Don't get involved in foolish, ignorant arguments that only start fights.
A servant of the Lord must not quarrel but must be kind to everyone,
be able to teach, and be patient with difficult people.
2 Timothy 2:23-24

THERE ARE CERTAIN truths of our faith that we as Christians should be unyielding about. These are the essential tenets of Christianity. Then there are secondary and tertiary issues that are important but not ultimate. Unfortunately, Christians can sometimes be tempted to go to the mat for things that are more a matter of preference than essential, and in so doing, we can cause strife in the church and distract from the focus of Christ's mission in the world.

Jesus encountered this with the Pharisees, who adhered not only to the Old Testament law but also to several hundred rabbinic additions to the law, which they considered equally important. In fact, as is too often the case with people focused on religious performance, they were more fired up about the nonessentials than the essentials. As a result, they missed Jesus and His gospel.

As leaders in our homes, in our churches, and in the community, we must pray for the wisdom to know when we should show courage and stand up for what is worth defending, and when we should stay out of things, keeping the big picture in mind. It's good to have certain convictions and preferences, but we should not hold them as tightly as we hold to the essential truths of the gospel. In other words, let's keep the main thing the main thing.

BOTTOM LINE

Hold essentials deeply, hold your convictions firmly, hold your preferences loosely. And pray for God to give you the wisdom to know the difference.

Moment of Strength: Matthew 15:9

FRIEND OF GOD

This is eternal life: that they may know You, the only true God,
and the One You have sent—Jesus Christ.
John 17:3, HCSB

EARN MORE MONEY. Get that promotion. Exercise and eat right. Give more. On and on it goes. We live in a society on the move—constantly striving to do more, produce more, and do everything better. We may even be tempted to make our relationship with God all about our performance. We can become approval seekers—employees rather than sons—striving to show ourselves worthy of eternal life. That's exhausting. It's also futile.

We don't need to perform our way to God; in fact, we can't. Eternal life is ours the moment we come to know Him. It's a gift, His gift, that we cannot earn and do not deserve. And it's a "now and later" gift. Eternal, abundant life is found right now—in knowing God and His Son—and later, when we are fully in His presence.

In Luke 10, we have the examples of Mary and Martha. Martha was a striver, a doer. She was taking care of business. Her work ethic would be right at home in our modern world. Mary, on the other hand, was content to simply sit at Jesus' feet and listen. She was experiencing eternal life. Just as young children delight in time spent with their father, Mary found joy in spending time with Jesus. And so can we. There's no need to perform, no heavenly rat race to join—just friendship with the God of the universe.

BOTTOM LINE

Eternal life cannot be earned, nor is it bound up in heaven. It is a gift that is ours right here and now when we become friends with the King.

Moment of Strength: Psalm 16:11

HEALER OF THE HUMBLED

David was furious. "As surely as the LORD lives," he vowed,
"any man who would do such a thing deserves to die!"
2 Samuel 12:5

JESUS ONCE DESCRIBED His ministry like this: "Healthy people don't need a doctor—sick people do. I have come to call not those who think they are righteous, but those who know they are sinners" (Mark 2:17). Every one of us is sick—we're all sinners. And just as a physically sick person needs a doctor, we all stand in great need of a Savior. The people "who think they are righteous" are just as diseased as the rest of us, but they've fooled themselves into believing they're as healthy as can be. They walk through life in a precarious condition, having a fatal but easily treatable disease, but not knowing it.

In order to receive healing, we must first recognize and admit that we are indeed sick.

David was a man after God's own heart, but he was still a man terminally sick with the disease of sin. When the prophet Nathan confronted David with a parable about his sin (2 Samuel 12), David didn't immediately recognize himself as the villain in the story. Though he knew that adultery and murder are wrong—deserving of death, even—he didn't see himself as a sinner. When Nathan finally explained the analogy, David cried out to God. He confessed and repented. And though his actions came with severe consequences, he found forgiveness and renewed joy.

We may not have committed sins like David's, but without coming to terms with our own sinful hearts, we will miss out on the healing that God promises.

BOTTOM LINE

Admitting we're sick and in need of the Great Physician is a tremendous blessing. In fact, it's the first step toward being made whole.

Moment of Strength: Mark 2:13-17

STRONG ON MY OWN

Peter said to him, "Even if everyone else deserts you, I never will." Jesus replied, "I tell you the truth, Peter—this very night, before the rooster crows twice, you will deny three times that you even know me."

Mark 14:29-30

WHEN JESUS TOLD His disciples that one of them would betray Him, they couldn't believe He was serious. They didn't understand what Jesus was telling them about His coming death. Whatever danger was ahead, they declared they would stay right by His side. They were dependable (they thought), and insisted that they would stick with Jesus through thick and thin. Remember Peter's declaration? And his utter failure to keep his word?

As men, we often are far too confident in our own strength. It's a confidence that's frequently rooted in pride. But we are not superheroes. Not even close.

On the other hand, the Bible encourages men to be strong and tells us how. One principle is expressed in Proverbs 27:17: "As iron sharpens iron, so a friend sharpens a friend." It is God's plan for men to encourage and challenge each other to grow in the Lord and fulfill our responsibilities.

An even more critical principle to strengthen our faith is found in 2 Corinthians 12:9, where the apostle Paul writes, "[Jesus] said, 'My grace is all you need. My power works best in weakness.' So now I am glad to boast about my weaknesses, so that the power of Christ can work through me." Staying humble allows God to show His strength in our lives. Our strength comes from dependence on Him.

BOTTOM LINE

Set a goal to begin searching out biblical principles that will help you grow stronger in your faith, yet more humble in your heart.

Moment of Strength: 1 Corinthians 10:1-12

THE TIME FOR ACTION

Do not withhold good from those who deserve it when it's in
your power to help them. If you can help your neighbor now,
don't say, "Come back tomorrow, and then I'll help you."
Proverbs 3:27-28

IT WAS JUST AFTER 3:00 A.M. when the young woman pulled her red sports car into a parking space near her apartment. She got out of the car, locked it, and began the 100-foot walk to her front door. She never made it. A man grabbed her and stabbed her. Her frantic screams for help pierced the night. Lights began to go on as neighbors heard her cry out.

Eventually, someone called the police, who arrived to find the body of twenty-eight-year-old Kitty Genovese. Detectives investigating the crime discovered that thirty-eight people had witnessed the crime from nearby apartments; yet no one had come to Kitty's aid, and no one had called the police until after she was dead. Why? They didn't want to get involved.

That brutal murder, committed in 1964, became symbolic of the dark side of our national character. Psychologists and social scientists even coined a term—*Genovese syndrome*—to describe the group psychology that leads eyewitnesses to a tragedy to choose not to offer aid. "I didn't want to get involved" seems to speak a truth no one wants to face head-on—that we're often so concerned with ourselves and our own well-being that we ignore the needs of others around us whom we could help. Think of it this way: Jesus didn't ignore your desperate need for help. He came all the way down from heaven to save you. That kind of love should move us to love others.

BOTTOM LINE

Because we have been loved so extravagantly by God, we can and should love others out of the overflow. Are you living a life of love?

Moment of Strength: James 1:22

JUSTICE AND MERCY

Judge fairly, and show mercy and kindness to one another.
Zechariah 7:9

LAWS ARE NECESSARY TO maintain order in any society. They keep us safe from burglars and murderers and from those who would take away our rights. They keep our highways and our homes safe. Whether enforced by a law enforcement officer, a judge in the courtroom, or men and women in the jury box, a law that is broken is likely to bring consequences to the lawbreaker.

Laws require justice. Laws require that someone who breaks the law suffers fines, imprisonment, community service, or a revoked license. And we all want justice for the lawbreaker—right? Unless it's us. Then we want mercy.

How do you balance justice and mercy in your life? When a friend betrays you, do you mete out "justice" by severing the friendship? When a client fails to pay his bill, do you immediately take him to court? When your wife lets you down in some way, do you immediately give up on your marriage?

When it comes to mercy, Jesus was the master teacher. He often taught by telling stories about people like the father in the parable of the Prodigal Son. Jesus also told His disciples they should forgive others "seventy times seven" (Matthew 18:22)—in other words, as many times as necessary. Prayerfully ask God to help you extend compassion and mercy wherever and to whomever it is needed.

BOTTOM LINE

Look back over recent months and see whether you can find a broken or wounded relationship in which you can reverse your path and demonstrate mercy.

Moment of Strength: 1 Timothy 1:12-17

THE POWER WITHIN

By his divine power, God has given us everything we need for living a godly life. We have received all of this by coming to know him, the one who called us to himself by means of his marvelous glory and excellence.

2 Peter 1:3

LIVING THE CHRISTIAN LIFE isn't difficult—it's impossible! We learn what God desires, we strive to align our priorities with His will, we meet with other men to keep us on track, and still we stumble. Even Paul, as mature and sold-out in his faith as he was, lamented the pull of sin in his life (Romans 7:15-24). Yet we have this promise from the apostle Peter that "God has given us everything we need for living a godly life." But what does that entail? Read more, memorize more, serve more, pray more? Is that what it takes?

The answer isn't found in our effort; it's found in our relationship with God, who has "called us to himself." When we accept Christ's gift of salvation, we receive the Holy Spirit into our hearts. This is the divine power we now have (Acts 1:8). How we nurture this new relationship will affect our growth in the Christian life. If we go back to our old ways, we'll get nowhere. If we try our best without God, we'll fail. But when we invest the effort to know God through study, prayer, and obedience, He does a transforming work in our minds that we can't do for ourselves. Our desires align with His (Romans 8:5), we make sound judgments (2 Timothy 1:7), and we better recognize His escape hatches when temptation strikes (1 Corinthians 10:13). Best of all, we experience real life. Not just survival—*life!* Growing, fruit-bearing, accomplishing-our-God-given-purpose kind of life!

BOTTOM LINE

God doesn't call us to be holy and then leave us to flop and flail. He gives us His Spirit to transform us into sin-resistant, fruit-bearing men of purpose.

Moment of Strength: Zechariah 4:6

GENETIC DISPOSITION

Because of his glory and excellence, he has given us
great and precious promises. These are the promises
that enable you to share his divine nature and escape
the world's corruption caused by human desires.

2 Peter 1:4

WHEN WE RECEIVE Jesus into our hearts, we are made new from the inside out (2 Corinthians 5:17). The immediate change is to our nature—our spiritual genetics, if you will. Just as a newborn baby has the genetic nature of his or her parents, we receive the divine nature of God. We don't make it happen any more than a baby initiates his or her own conception. "You are saved by grace through faith, and this is not from yourselves; it is God's gift" (Ephesians 2:8, HCSB). As we saw in yesterday's devotion, God's gift is complete—we don't lack anything we need for life and godliness. Now we just need to grow. Our spiritual rebirth is just the beginning.

In addition to giving us His divine nature and divine power, God gives us His very precious promises—His Word—to help us grow healthy and strong in our new nature. We feed our bodies with bread, but we feed our spirits with His Word (Matthew 4:4). As we do this consistently, our appetite for "junk food" (the corruption that is in the world) decreases, and we mature into healthy and strong sons of God who are growing in godliness and service.

Have you received God's divine nature by believing in His Son and accepting His offer of salvation? Are you nourishing that new nature by feeding on His Word?

BOTTOM LINE

God's Word holds the key to knowing what is right, getting back on track when we slip up, and maturing in righteousness.

Moment of Strength: Psalm 119:33-40

AGAIN

*Then the L*ORD *said to me, "Go again; show love to a woman*
who is loved by another man and is an adulteress."
Hosea 3:1, HCSB

AGAIN. It can be such a great word when about it applies to favorable events. When your team wins again, it's a great word. But when your team loses again, someone must pay! The career path of a successful coach is often replete with hirings and firings, because teams have hot streaks and cold streaks.

Marriage is a "team sport" full of ups and downs, but it isn't meant to be a contract based on performance. Marriage is a covenant based not on mistrust but on unconditional love. Hosea's love for his wife, Gomer, certainly wasn't based on her outstanding record of faithfulness. Far from it. She was unfaithful to him time and time again, yet he chose to love her despite her unfaithfulness.

The path of a wandering spouse leads to a morass of pain that is difficult to trace or predict. Yet God said to Hosea, "Go again." Renew your commitment to Gomer—again. Demonstrate your love and affection—again. Risk your heart—again. And Hosea obeyed. Through his obedience, the world saw a picture of God's unconditional love.

Is love really love before it costs us something? The next time your wife dents a fender, makes a poor decision, or blows it once more, forgive her. Again. Because when you consider your own shortcomings and failings, you'll realize that you need plenty of grace and forgiveness too. And if you need to, seek marriage counseling.

BOTTOM LINE

Forgive your wife, not based on whether she deserves it, but based on your
obedience to God.

Moment of Strength: Hosea 6:1-3

SHARED SERVICE

You know his proven character, because he has served with me
in the gospel ministry like a son with a father.
Philippians 2:22, HCSB

WHETHER IT'S IN MINISTRY or the corporate world, athletics or academics, it brings joy to a father's heart to see his children answer God's call on their lives.

The apostle Paul had a unique relationship with Timothy. Though they were not related by blood, Paul was a mentor and teacher to Timothy, and they served together in helping to plant some of the first churches. In writing to the church at Philippi, Paul said he knew no one else who could do the job as well as Timothy (Philippians 2:20). Paul even called Timothy "my true son in the faith" (1 Timothy 1:2).

They were very close—like father and son.

That relationship didn't happen overnight, and your relationship with your sons (and daughters) takes time to cultivate. But in addition to playing catch with them, why not do missions together? They will learn a lot as they watch you serve and as they serve too. Volunteer your family to serve in a soup kitchen. Do a backyard Bible club together. Go to a retirement home and sing songs and chat with residents. Prayer-walk your neighborhood together. Get creative; there are plenty of options.

Doing a small mission project as a family will build lasting memories of serving God together while helping to cultivate a serving heart in your kids.

BOTTOM LINE

There is no greater joy for a dad than to see his sons and daughters serving Jesus. Look for opportunities to make an impact with your kids.

Moment of Strength: Philippians 2:19-24

GOD WON'T FORGET YOU

Can a mother forget her nursing child? Can she feel no
love for the child she has borne? But even if that were
possible, I would not forget you! See, I have written your
name on the palms of my hands. Always in my mind is
a picture of Jerusalem's walls in ruins.

Isaiah 49:15-16

TATTOOS HAVE COME A LONG WAY since Ötzi the Iceman, the 5,300-year-old mummy discovered in the Alps in 1991, had his engraved. Traditionally, tats are reserved for names or symbols that people want to be associated with permanently. Unfortunately, many men are not known for their loyalty to one love. In a famous painting by Norman Rockwell, a sailor is getting a tattoo of a woman's name on his arm. Yet above her name, he has the names of six other women—all crossed out!

Fortunately, God's faithfulness is unparalleled. Just as a nursing mother bonds in a unique way with her infant child, so God bonds with His children. He promises He will never forget you, even going so far as to inscribe your name—not on His back but on His hands, where He is constantly reminded of you. And God knows where you live. The walls of the home of your heart are always before Him; in fact, He is the divine architect who has drawn up the blueprints for your life (Psalm 139).

In this day and age when so much seems temporary—there's even "painless" tattoo removal—it is comforting to know that our heavenly Father will never leave us or forsake us. His love is a permanent inscription on our lives. His faithfulness provides stability in an ever-changing, unstable world. He will never lose sight of us, never stop thinking of us, never fail to take care of us. We don't have to fear being abandoned or forgotten.

BOTTOM LINE

God loves you with an everlasting love, and He will never give up on you. Pray for that knowledge to sink in deeper.

Moment of Strength: John 10:27-30

FLEXIBLE FAITH

If you had faith even as small as a mustard seed, you could say to this mountain,
"Move from here to there," and it would move. Nothing would be impossible.
Matthew 17:20

HAVE YOU EVER HAD BIG PLANS with a lot of details that had to fall into place with perfect timing? Maybe it was when you built the shop in the backyard. There wasn't much extra space, so everything needed to be delivered in the right order. The concrete truck had to be able to turn around in the backyard without piles of building supplies in the way.

Next, you wanted the lumber to frame up the building, then shingles for the roof. And you really didn't want all the stuff for finishing the inside—drywall, paint, electrical, plumbing—until you were ready to use it.

But the building supply company brought the shingles early and left them right where the concrete truck would need to turn around. Then a huge box of light fixtures, switches, and wiring that you'd ordered online was the second item to arrive. Suddenly, you had to adapt and go to Plan B.

Sometimes, faith is like that—we're praying, working toward a goal, and even trusting God to make things happen the way we think they ought to. But we have to learn to be flexible when God works in unexpected ways and to be grateful for however He responds to our faith. As we live by faith, we move ahead by God's timetable, not ours. And we experience a lot more peace when we don't try to control everything, but instead leave it up to God.

BOTTOM LINE

Learning to be flexible will strengthen your faith and help you cultivate
patience and gratitude. Is there an area in your life right now that needs this
approach?

Moment of Strength: Galatians 2:19-21

WORSHIP WINS THE WAR

The LORD is my light and my salvation—so why should I be afraid?
The LORD is my fortress, protecting me from danger, so why should
I tremble? . . . Though a mighty army surrounds me, my heart will
not be afraid. Even if I am attacked, I will remain confident.
Psalm 27:1, 3

IN THIS PASSAGE OF SCRIPTURE, even though the words are confident and hopeful, the imagery is one of a battle. David writes that evildoers and enemies are attacking, but he is not afraid. Armies are deploying against him, but he is confident. War is breaking out, but he is certain that his enemies will fall. Whether David is using this as a metaphor to describe life or an actual war that is going on around him, he finds himself on the defensive. But he knows the one who will shelter him.

We all go through seasons in which life feels like a battle. Relationships aren't working. Situations at work are tenuous. We receive a bad health report. In these difficult situations and in many others like them, when life feels like a battle, how do we stay confident and hopeful? Where can we go for strength and safety?

With war breaking out all around him, David seeks shelter and refuge in God's presence: "The LORD is my fortress, protecting me from danger." Later, he writes: "I will offer sacrifices with shouts of joy, singing and praising the LORD with music" (Psalm 27:6). In the midst of chaotic circumstances, David gains strength and confidence by worshiping God. Worship gives us perspective—it pulls us up above our circumstances. It reminds us that when God is for us, no one can be against us.

BOTTOM LINE

In seasons when life feels like a battle, win the war by worshiping God.

Moment of Strength: Psalm 27

THE POWER OF APPRECIATION

The tongue can bring death or life;
those who love to talk will reap the consequences.
Proverbs 18:21

AFTER A VIOLIN CONCERT BY young Suzuki students, an instructor spoke briefly on how children as young as two years old are taught to play violin. First, the children learn the proper stance. Second, the children learn how to take a bow—even before they have picked up a violin. "If the children just play the violin and stop, people may forget to show their appreciation," the instructor said. "But when the children bow, the audience invariably applauds. And applause is the best motivator we've found to make children feel good about performing and want to do it well."

Adults love applause too. Being affirmed makes us feel noticed and special. Mark Twain once confessed he could "live on a good compliment two weeks with nothing else to eat." He was simply admitting what most of us feel privately—that we all need a lift from time to time. As the writer of Proverbs observes, "A word spoken at the right time is like gold apples on a silver tray" (Proverbs 25:11, HCSB). Praise is a wonderful thing. Yet we are sometimes reluctant to give the warm sunshine of praise and appreciation to the person most dear to us.

If you want to rekindle or sustain the flames of love in your marriage, express your appreciation for your wife. Be specific with your praise, be truthful, and be generous. Put some applause in your marriage, and watch love grow.

BOTTOM LINE

Remember to appreciate your wife every day, not just for the things she does, but for who she is. It is a great way to improve your relationship.

Moment of Strength: Proverbs 10:11

THE SHEPHERD'S VOICE

The sheep follow him because they recognize his voice.
They will never follow a stranger; instead they will run away
from him, because they don't recognize the voice of strangers.
John 10:4-5, HCSB

IT WAS A TYPICAL crowded weekend at the mall. While leisurely strolling through a children's toy store with his wife and two-year-old daughter, Josh felt a tiny hand grab his. Thinking it was his young daughter, he kept walking. Upon glancing down after a few steps, he discovered that it was the hand of a little girl he'd never seen before. At the same moment he looked down, she looked up. Thinking she had grabbed her own father's hand, the young girl was shocked to realize it wasn't him.

Josh took a quick visual pass across the store, saw a man who looked a bit like him, and instantly knew he had spotted her father, even though he'd never met him before.

Just as a little girl can mistake a familiar-looking stranger for her dad, we can do the same with our heavenly Father. Although it may not be a visual mistake, it can be an auditory mistake. Every day we are bombarded with messages and philosophies that claim to have authority and life, but in the end, they may not be true. The way we are able to discern these counterfeit messages as false is by immersing ourselves in the truth of God's Word. Through daily time with our heavenly Father, we learn to not be easily taken in by words that aren't from Him. We begin to think like He does as we consistently renew our minds in His Word.

BOTTOM LINE

The way to guard yourself from misleading messages is by daily meditating on your Shepherd's voice through His Word.

Moment of Strength: Philippians 4:8

THE SHEPHERD'S LIFE

A thief comes only to steal and to kill and to destroy.
I have come so that they may have life and have it in abundance.
John 10:10, HCSB

DAVID IS LYING ON THE COUCH, feet up, enjoying the game he's been waiting all week to watch. All of a sudden, during the commercial break, he's bombarded with ads for a better car, a better body, and a better social life. For a split second he begins to think that someone is holding out on him. In what had been a peaceful, enjoyable Sunday afternoon, he now feels upset, believing there's a better life out there that he could have had.

This is the way the enemy works. He sows little seeds of doubt, suggesting that God doesn't really have your best interests in mind, that He is holding out on you. This is how the story of Scripture begins. Adam and Eve were deceived into thinking there was something better for them apart from God.

The truth is that God has given us everything we need. Just as a shepherd cares for his sheep by giving them his provision and protection, God does the same for us. He knows what's good for us. He knows exactly what we need. And He protects us from the lies of the enemy.

We can easily be deceived into thinking, *If only I had that* or *If only I looked like him*. But that way of thinking only steals our joy. Jesus came that we might have complete joy in Him, not in what we have or don't have.

BOTTOM LINE

Abundant life is found in having Christ—not our circumstances—define our lives.

Moment of Strength: Psalm 23

THE SHEPHERD'S CARE

I am the good shepherd. The good shepherd lays down
his life for the sheep. The hired man, since he is not the
shepherd and doesn't own the sheep, leaves them and
runs away when he sees a wolf coming.
John 10:11-12, HCSB

IF YOU, AS AN EMPLOYER, had to choose between a man who simply needed a job to make ends meet and a man who had great passion for the work of your company, which one (assuming they were both of good character) would you choose? Would you choose the man who had desire and passion? Why? Because the other guy is more likely to bail when the going gets tough. He also might not put as much effort into the work. In the end, you will get a better result from the man who cares about the work of your company.

Jesus is not like the man who bails when things get difficult. Instead, He cares deeply about His mission, which is to save us and sanctify us and bring us safely home. Jesus provides for us and protects us, just as a shepherd does for his sheep. When a threat from the enemy comes our way, He guides us to paths of life. When we wander away from Him, He seeks us out and nudges us back to safety. When we are needy, He shows up with exactly what we need.

Jesus laid down His life for the sheep (us)—He willingly went to the cross to die in our place. He doesn't run away when He sees the wolf come—He goes before us and behind us, giving us abundant life. You can trust in His care.

BOTTOM LINE

Jesus laid down His life so that we can receive eternal life. Do you believe He
will guide you and protect you? Or are you living in fear?

Moment of Strength: Hebrews 13:20-21

WHY WHAT YOU MAKE MATTERS

Whatever you do, do well. For when you go to the grave,
there will be no work or planning or knowledge or wisdom.
Ecclesiastes 9:10

WHETHER YOUR JOB IS slinging salami or crunching numbers, how you perform and what you produce matters, not simply because it makes the boss happy, moves you toward advancement, or cures Third World hunger. It matters to God because, as His image-bearers, we were created to create. When we do, we reflect God's glory as the original Artist, Designer, and Creator.

Imagine how this worldview might reorient our callings. An author doesn't work simply to be published, but to produce good books. A contractor works not simply to make a living, but to build structures whose quality construction reflects the glory of God. A CEO looks beyond the bottom line to the well-being of the employees, whose lives he can influence for good and even for maximum Kingdom impact as people are freed up to work for the benefit of others.

When we have a biblical worldview, we understand that the gospel doesn't simply get us to heaven but also helps us bring a little bit of heaven to earth by giving us a purpose for everything we do—to glorify God. This mind-set—this *reality*—allows the daily grind of work to become a canvas to display God's glory.

What a difference it makes to begin to see all work as God sees it—valuable, important, and a way for us to model His goodness for the benefit of others.

BOTTOM LINE

The gospel renews our vocation, giving eternal significance to our temporal work.

Moment of Strength: Colossians 3:17

LET'S CELEBRATE

They worshiped together at the Temple each day, met in homes for the Lord's Supper, and shared their meals with great joy and generosity—all the while praising God and enjoying the goodwill of all the people. And each day the Lord added to their fellowship those who were being saved.

Acts 2:46-47

A GROUP OF HIGH SCHOOL STUDENTS WERE watching an outdoor wedding reception unfold from the vantage point of their hotel balcony. Lights were strung, music was playing, couples were dancing, and people were laughing. The teenagers stared longingly at the fun they were observing. They longed to join the celebration.

People were born to celebrate—birthdays, weddings, championships, promotions, and holidays. We throw parties and invite our friends and family over. These are big days. And they should be. God never intended for fun and laughter to be excluded from our lives.

The early church knew how to celebrate. They gathered together, acknowledging God's power and praising His goodness. They met in each other's homes, sharing meals, laughing and talking, enjoying life with one another. They worshiped God, their Redeemer. The church's celebrations were so exuberant that even people who weren't believers wanted to join their company because of what they observed.

Celebrations are like that. The exuberance and excitement cause others to want to share in them and become involved. When God's people begin to rejoice in God and enjoy His presence to the point of exuberant celebration, people will want to come just to watch, and eventually some will want to become a part of it.

BOTTOM LINE

When you joyfully worship God, He receives glory, and others are drawn in.

Moment of Strength: Luke 15:23-24

INTIMACY LEAKS

Guard your heart above all else, for it is the source of life.
Proverbs 4:23, HCSB

JAROD WAS CONCERNED. Since starting work on a project two weeks ago with Amy, an attractive coworker, he found himself opening up more and more about his personal life. The more he shared, the more he found himself comparing Amy to Natalie, his wife of thirteen years. Although technically no boundaries had been crossed and nothing they discussed had been inappropriate, Jarod realized it was becoming easier to withhold information from Natalie that he had already shared with Amy. He knew he was on a slippery slope with these "intimacy leaks," and if he didn't quickly make some changes, major boundaries could be crossed.

Men rarely set out intentionally to have an inappropriate relationship. Like Jarod's relationship with Amy, it often starts innocently with small conversations about benign topics that don't initially seem wrong. But the unfair comparisons between the obvious strengths of the coworker and the wife's known weaknesses are often just around the corner. If we aren't careful, these comparisons can lead to resentment instead of the intimacy we want with our wives.

Marital intimacy requires hard work, even when things are going well. Prayerfully ask the Lord to help you guard your heart and love your wife well.

BOTTOM LINE

If you are married, take a moment to honestly assess the intimacy you are experiencing with your wife. Are there any leaks that need to be plugged?

Moment of Strength: Colossians 3:19

RESPONDING WITH GRACE

The son said to him, "Father, I have sinned against
heaven and in your sight. I'm no longer worthy to
be called your son." But the father told his slaves,
"Quick! Bring out the best robe and put it on him;
put a ring on his finger and sandals on his feet."
Luke 15:21-22, HCSB

GREG COULDN'T BELIEVE what he was hearing on the other end of the phone. His chest tightened as the father of one of his sixteen-year-old daughter's friends recounted what had transpired during the past weekend. The words *alcohol*, *party*, and *cops* came through the phone, and Greg found himself vacillating between embarrassment, anger, deep sorrow, and sympathy. He sat down, but the emotional roller coaster continued as more details of Rachel's wild weekend came out.

It should not shock and surprise us when our kids make mistakes. Paul makes it very clear in Romans 7 that doing the right thing isn't as simple as just knowing better. No matter how well we have done our job of parenting, there will be times when our children blow it. How we respond to their mistakes is instrumental in determining how they understand grace and the gospel. If we allow our embarrassment and anger about their mistakes to guide our responses, we risk sending the message that they are loved and accepted only when they behave well. But if we respond to our children's mistakes and sins with appropriate discipline balanced with grace, we can give them a picture of God's unconditional love and acceptance, helping them understand that their value is not based on their performance.

BOTTOM LINE

Has your response to past mistakes given your children a deeper under-
standing of the gospel? Why or why not?

Moment of Strength: 2 Samuel 18:33

GETTING STRONGER

*Keep the Sabbath day holy. Don't pursue your own
interests on that day, but enjoy the Sabbath and speak of
it with delight as the LORD's holy day. Honor the Sabbath
in everything you do on that day, and don't follow your
own desires or talk idly. Then the LORD will be your
delight. I will give you great honor and satisfy you with
the inheritance I promised to your ancestor Jacob.*
Isaiah 58:13-14

SHANE HAMMAN KNOWS something about bulking up. The Oklahoma native is a two-time Olympian who won nine national weight lifting championships and holds every US record in the 105 kg–plus division. At 5 feet 9 inches and 350 pounds, this strong man of God knows where his power comes from: "I realized early that my strength is a gift from God. I totally dedicated my weight lifting to Him to be used for His glory."

Shane trained at the US Olympic Training Center, working with the top experts on muscle building. By properly training his body through strenuous exercise, good nutrition, and proper rest, Shane became incredibly strong. He could squat more than 1,000 pounds, bench more than 550, clean and jerk more than 520, and snatch 435. "Just due to the type of training, it developed me into a really good athlete," Shane says. Try to picture a 350-pound guy pulling a backflip. Shane can do it. Plus, with a thirty-six-inch vertical leap, he can dunk a basketball.

Shane knew his strength came from God and that God required him to rest. God spoke through the prophet Isaiah to remind His people to keep the Sabbath. The Lord wants us to rest and enjoy Him. Without recovery time, you'll just tear through life and not live the way God intended.

BOTTOM LINE

Life—just like weight training—needs to be done according to a rhythm. Make time to rest and recover with God.

Moment of Strength: Exodus 33:14

TAG ALONG WITH YOUR TEEN

Children are a gift from the LORD; they are a reward from him.

Psalm 127:3

THE PSALMIST IS RIGHT: Children are a gift, a reward, from the Lord. And though sometimes you might want to disagree, they are also a blessing—even during the teen years. Maybe your teenagers are pushing you away right now, being disrespectful, and spending more time with their friends than with you and the rest of the family. Even so, research shows that teens benefit from hanging out with their parents as much—or more—than younger children do. So figure out a way to spend time with your teen.

It isn't as important *what* you do, as long as you're doing it together. If your teens are interested in music, visit a music store or go to a concert together. If your teens are more into sports, go to a game or shop for a piece of equipment they need.

As fathers, we know it may take some work to reap the reward that God intended children to be in our lives. Talk with your teens. Invite them to be honest and open with you. Treat them as the valuable people they are, as people made in God's image. Show them kindness and love. Set healthy boundaries, but forgive them when their emotions get the best of them. Try not to treat every conversation as a chance to lecture. And *pray* with them.

By keeping your relationship with your kids strong during the teen years, you'll help them navigate this turbulent time and become the people God wants them to be. It is well worth the effort.

BOTTOM LINE

Don't let your teens push you away. Push back by giving them your time, a listening ear, and your love.

Moment of Strength: Colossians 3:12-14

THE RIGHT ATTITUDE

Do everything without grumbling and arguing, so that you may be
blameless and pure, children of God who are faultless in a crooked and
perverted generation, among whom you shine like stars in the world.
Philippians 2:14-15, HCSB

IT'S EASY TO FIND THINGS wrong with the world. You don't have to go too far to discover imperfection and inconvenience. Even though you could complain about these things, should you? For example, during a quick drive in the car, there are red lights, traffic slowdowns, fast drivers, slow drivers, and drivers who cut you off, and the list goes on. But because God has different standards for His people than what's "normal" or "reasonable," it is possible for us as believers to "shine like stars in the world." This may seem grandiose at first, but a person who takes things in stride without complaining is a rare breed.

On what basis should a Christian not complain? What makes us different from the world? We know our heavenly Father is in control of all things. We know that some of the inconveniences we experience may actually be divine opportunities to help someone else, or for God to grow us. Either way, complaining doesn't honor God.

Here's the bottom line: As Christians, we can rest in the fact that our Father is in charge. He's got us. We can be blameless, pure, and childlike. We don't have to worry and fret and try to control the outcome of everything, getting upset when things don't go our way. Not only does this kind of relaxed trust in God honor Him, but it makes our lives so much more attractive to others and enjoyable to ourselves.

BOTTOM LINE

Living a complaint-free life is a much happier and holier way to live. Besides, complaining never makes things better.

Moment of Strength: Numbers 11:1

A LIVING BOOK

All Scripture is inspired by God and is profitable for teaching, for rebuking, for correcting, for training in righteousness, so that the man of God may be complete, equipped for every good work.
2 Timothy 3:16-17, HCSB

IN HIS INSPIRING BOOK TITLED *Fresh Air*, Pastor Chris Hodges writes: "The Bible is a divine wind machine, inflating our sails with God's breath, giving us direction and purpose, and propelling us forward." Who among us couldn't use a little wind at their backs? With the Bible, we have all the wind power we need to live a godly life. But we have to read it.

Think of it this way: A sailboat with the sail down is not going to be affected by the wind. The sail is useless, extra weight. However, when the sail is up—as it is designed to be—the power of the wind is captured, propelling the boat forward almost effortlessly. It's the same way with reading the Bible—we have to take advantage of Scripture's power to propel us forward in our walk with God. Without it, we won't get anywhere.

It's great to have good intentions about reading the Bible, but it's best to actually have good habits. We are creatures of habit. Though establishing good habits takes some thought, some planning, and the discipline to follow through, it is well worth the effort. Getting into the habit of daily Bible reading soon becomes a joy. And the more we read the Bible, the more we want to read it. Getting started is the first step. It can be a little like running—the hardest part is often the choice to head out the door. Once we're into it, we enjoy it and benefit from it.

BOTTOM LINE

We desperately need the Word of God. It's not optional if we want to grow. So make it a priority to develop good Bible reading habits.

Moment of Strength: Matthew 4:4

PERSISTENT PRAYER

Keep on asking, and you will receive what you ask for. Keep on seeking, and you will find. Keep on knocking, and the door will be opened to you. For everyone who asks, receives. Everyone who seeks, finds. And to everyone who knocks, the door will be opened.

Matthew 7:7-8

CHILDREN TEND TO PRAY much more openly and honestly than adults. Children say what's on their minds; they ask for what they want. They don't dress up their words or have preconceived notions of what they should want. Their motives aren't always perfect, but our infinitely wise heavenly Father loves that they ask.

We could learn a lot about true prayer simply by watching how our children do it. Unfiltered and unashamed. Not overly formal, not based on perceived performance. They just ask, and so should we. Even though our motives aren't always pure, God has extended to us the great invitation to ask, seek, and knock. He wants to bless us, but we must ask and then look for His answers. When answers don't seem to be coming, He says we should keep on asking!

Prayer is talking to God and listening to Him through His Word. It is an ongoing conversation with our Creator, who wants to meet our needs and convey guidance and love to us. "Never stop praying," we're told in 1 Thessalonians 5:17. Keep in mind that prayer is relational more than it is transactional—it's more about getting to know our heavenly Father than it is about trying to get things from Him. That's not to say that He doesn't want to answer our prayers and bless us—He does—but the greatest blessing of all is to get to know Him better and become more like Jesus.

BOTTOM LINE

How is your prayer life? Do you expect great things from God through prayer? Do you pray with confidence? You can! Keep praying, and don't give up.

Moment of Strength: Matthew 19:13-14

EVERYTHING FOR JESUS

Whatever you do, in word or in deed, do everything in the name of the Lord Jesus, giving thanks to God the Father through Him.
Colossians 3:17, HCSB

COLOSSIANS HAS A LOT TO SAY ABOUT JESUS. In fact, it's hard to imagine a more exalted picture of the Son of God. As you read the following excerpt, pay close attention to the degree of Christ's supremacy (which we have highlighted with italics):

> He is the image of the invisible God, the firstborn over *all* creation. For *everything* was created by Him, in heaven and on earth, the visible and the invisible, whether thrones or dominions or rulers or authorities—*all things* have been created *through* Him and *for* Him. He is *before* all things, and by Him *all things* hold together. He is also the *head* of the body, the church; He is the beginning, the firstborn from the dead, so that He might come to have *first place in everything*.
> COLOSSIANS 1:15-18, HCSB

On and on it goes! Just from this section, we can see that everything was made *by* Jesus and *for* Jesus (and that includes *us*). Not only that, but Jesus continues to sustain *all* of creation. In summary, He has "first place in everything."

When confronted with the majesty of Jesus, the proper response is worship—worship that is meant to spill into *every* area of life. "Whatever you do, in word or in deed, do everything in the name of the Lord Jesus, giving thanks to God the Father through Him." That's our joy and calling.

BOTTOM LINE

When we see how great Jesus is, we will be drawn to worship. And when we worship Him, we will become more like the one we worship.

Moment of Strength: Colossians 1:19-20

HARD WOOD

I will give them singleness of heart and put a new spirit within them.
I will take away their stony, stubborn heart and give them a tender,
responsive heart, so they will obey my decrees and regulations.
Ezekiel 11:19-20

PETRIFIED WOOD IS the fossilized remains of vegetation that was once living. Over time, the organic substance of the wood decomposes, and a stone mold forms in its place, preserved exactly in the shape of the wood. It's literally wood that has become stone over time.

In Ezekiel's day, God's people were a lot like pieces of petrified wood. The parts of their hearts that had been alive to God had slowly ebbed away, and their soft, living hearts had been replaced by hearts of stone—cold, unmoving, unloving, dead. And it was because of their corruption and their idol worship.

With every act of devotion to other gods—whether they are work, status, hobbies, or finances—we replace the organic, living material in our hearts with cold, hard stone. We create the idols, but they end up devouring us.

What makes your heart beat faster? What does your bank account say you are more devoted to than anything else? Where do you spend your time? These things reveal what you worship.

Fortunately, God has a remedy for petrified hearts. As we repent of our sin, He will remove our hearts of stone and once again give us hearts that are fully alive to Him. Take some time to search your heart for any signs of hardness. Ask God to renew your heart for Him.

BOTTOM LINE

Repentance makes your heart soft and usable by God.

Moment of Strength: Ezekiel 36:25-27

SEEING WITH THE EYES OF JESUS

Jesus saw the huge crowd . . . and he had compassion on them because they were like sheep without a shepherd. So he began teaching them many things.

Mark 6:34

AMERICAN LIFE IS characterized by busyness. Ask anyone how they are doing and you're likely to hear, "I'm good. Busy, but good." The hustle and bustle of our daily lives can cause us to become so focused on our own needs, agendas, and to-do lists that we don't have the capacity to see or step into the needs of others. When unexpected interactions come along in our day, it's easy to see them as interruptions.

In Mark 6, when Jesus and His disciples have an unexpected interaction with a large crowd, Jesus sees it not as an interruption but as a Kingdom opportunity. His seeing leads to compassion, and His compassion leads to care.

As you go about your day, you will likely catch glimpses of people in need if you're paying attention. Whether it is someone on the street, at work, or somewhere else, there are needs all around you that can tug at your heart. However, seeing their needs and feeling pity doesn't always lead us to action. In Mark 1:41, we're told that Jesus was "moved with compassion." He reached out and healed the man. That's what compassion is: emotion *and* action. When Jesus saw the plight of helpless people, He was moved by their circumstances to the point that His compassion led to action. Don't stop at merely feeling emotion.

BOTTOM LINE

Seeing people with the eyes of Jesus moves us to compassion and leads us to care for others.

Moment of Strength: Mark 6:30-44

INVITATION AND CHALLENGE

His disciples came to him and said, "This is a remote place,
and it's already getting late. Send the crowds away so they
can . . . buy something to eat." But Jesus said, "You feed them."
Mark 6:35-37

GOD DESIGNED US FOR RELATIONSHIP. At our core, we long to connect with people on more than just a superficial level. When Jesus calls people to follow Him, He's not inviting "bad" people to become "good" people. Rather, He's inviting us into an intimate relationship with Him.

In Mark 6, the disciples were returning from being sent out on a missionary journey by Jesus. We don't know how long they had been away, but they had worked hard and had stories to tell of their travels. When they returned to Jesus, His first response was an invitation to come away with Him in order to rest and be with Him (Mark 6:31).

It didn't take long before Jesus' spiritual retreat with His disciples was interrupted by a large crowd. After watching Jesus tend to and teach the crowd, the disciples noticed that it was getting late. They suggested sending the crowd of thousands away to find dinner for themselves. Were the disciples tired and hungry and eager for Jesus to finish? Probably, but Scripture doesn't say.

Jesus' response to the disciples' suggestion was surprising. He said, "*You give them something to eat.*" Five thousand people! Even though Jesus sought to nurture and care for His disciples, He also gently pushed them outside their comfort zones to a place where they had to trust Him and depend on Him. The same thing happens in our lives, too.

BOTTOM LINE

Where is Jesus inviting you to trust Him more? Where is He challenging you to increase your dependence on Him?

Moment of Strength: John 14:1

IMPOSSIBLE BECOMES POSSIBLE

Jesus took the five loaves and two fish, looked up toward heaven, and blessed them. Then, breaking the loaves into pieces, he kept giving the bread to the disciples so they could distribute it to the people. He also divided the fish for everyone to share. They all ate as much as they wanted.

Mark 6:41-42

FOLLOWING JESUS CAN take us to unexpected and overwhelming places. You can imagine that when the disciples came back from their missionary journey, they were excited to get away for some rest and relaxation. Little did they know that their spiritual retreat would begin with an impossible situation. After Jesus taught the crowd of five thousand people, the disciples were ready to send them away to get something to eat, but Jesus said to the disciples, "You feed them" (Mark 6:37).

Jesus was no stranger to leading people into impossible situations. Throughout His ministry, He defied the laws of nature. He walked on water. He healed people with a word. He raised dead people to life. Jesus constantly confronted what we would see as impossible, and He invited His disciples to enter into those places with Him.

Today, Jesus leads us into situations beyond our control. He does this not to cause anxiety or distress but rather to teach us to trust Him and depend on Him. Jesus leads us into impossible situations to show us that when we completely surrender to Him, He makes the impossible possible.

What seemingly impossible situations is Jesus currently leading you toward? How are you responding to your impossible situation? Are you following Him or resisting Him? He can be trusted.

BOTTOM LINE

Jesus grows our faith when we are faced with seemingly impossible situations. Trust Him and watch to see what He will do.

Moment of Strength: Mark 10:27

YOUR MOUNT EVEREST

God is our refuge and strength, always ready to help in times of trouble.
Psalm 46:1

THE MAN WAS AN ADVENTURER who had been all over the world. Although he attempted to climb Mount Everest on three separate occasions, he had made it to the top only once. By far, it was the most difficult obstacle he had ever faced. During his most recent time on the mountain, he nearly died of high-altitude sickness.

He would later say that we all have a personal Mount Everest to conquer, and he is absolutely right. You certainly don't have to travel halfway around the world to find what would appear to be an almost insurmountable obstacle in your life. Whatever it may be—finances, health, issues with family or friends—life isn't always easy.

The list of equipment needed to climb Mount Everest is long and quite expensive. Appropriate warm clothing is an obvious must, in addition to food, supplemental oxygen, ice picks, ropes, and so forth. Most of the time, there's a Sherpa guide to help lug everything up the mountain and back down again.

When a Mount Everest pops up in your own life, however, you don't need any of that stuff. How you deal with the hardest moments in your life means everything. If you try working it out on your own, chances are that it will only get worse. You need Jesus and the promises of His Word. Faith really does conquer the world (1 John 5:4).

BOTTOM LINE

We all face what seem to be insurmountable obstacles. Praise God right now for seeing you through the trials you face.

Moment of Strength: Psalm 32:6-7

ZEALOUS FOR GOD

Then the man said, "Let me go, for the dawn is breaking!"
But Jacob said, "I will not let you go unless you bless me."
Genesis 32:26

BEFORE HE EVEN LEFT his mother's womb, Jacob grasped for greatness, clutching his brother Esau's heel. For years thereafter, he continued to grasp—purchasing Esau's birthright and tricking his way into his father's blessing. He even matched wits with his father-in-law to make himself wealthy.

Jacob's name means "supplanter," and it seemed there was no line he wouldn't cross to get what he wanted. But God blessed Jacob, choosing him to be the heir of His promises. The fact that God chose to bless Jacob despite his multiple and significant failings is good news for the rest of us. God's grace exceeds our sin. And He uses imperfect people.

So what did God see in this natural-born cheater? Deep within Jacob's heart was a desire for God—to know Him, to walk with Him, to carry His promises, and to be blessed by Him. With a fervor and intensity unparalleled in his generation, Jacob wrestled with God. One night, he did so literally.

God desires for men and women to love Him with their entire being (Mark 12:30). Jacob's ethics were sometimes reprehensible, but we should admire how zealously he chased after God. Pursuing Jesus means seeking to take hold of the one thing that matters most—knowing Jesus personally and intimately. Ask God to give you that desire.

BOTTOM LINE

Pursue God with every ounce of your being, even if it means wrestling with Him long into the night. And know that He is pursuing you, too.

Moment of Strength: Luke 14:25-33

A NEW HEART

Run from anything that stimulates youthful lusts. Instead,
pursue righteous living, faithfulness, love, and peace. Enjoy the
companionship of those who call on the Lord with pure hearts.
2 Timothy 2:22

MANY OF US STAND BEFORE the sin in our lives just as the Israelites trembled before Goliath the Philistine. Before we ever enter into battle, we believe defeat to be a foregone conclusion. We have heard that our hearts are deceitful and prone to wander (Jeremiah 17:9). There's a sense in which that's true, even after we come to faith. As the apostle Paul says in Romans 7:18: "I know that nothing good lives in me, that is, in my sinful nature. I want to do what is right, but I can't."

So we continue to struggle with sin, even as Christians. And yet, in the new covenant, God promised to do something about our hearts: "I will take away their stony, stubborn heart and give them a tender, responsive heart" (Ezekiel 11:19).

This promise of a new heart was fulfilled in Jesus' gift of the Holy Spirit. Every Christian has received a new heart. Sin still remains, but like David facing Goliath, we can have confidence in the battle. We need not enter the fight defeated. We fight from victory—Christ's on our behalf—for victory. And this is from God, not ourselves. So rather than focusing on our sinful desires, which have not been completely removed, we can live in the power of God's Spirit. We can focus on Jesus and His grace instead. We have been given a new heart—one that loves God and desires to please Him.

BOTTOM LINE

As Christians, we have each been given a new heart. Knowing this, believing this, and living out of this is a powerful weapon in our fight against sin.

Moment of Strength: Ezekiel 36:22-36

TOUCH ALL THE BASES

Therefore, brothers, make every effort to confirm your calling and election,
because if you do these things you will never stumble.
2 Peter 1:10, HCSB

MARK MCGWIRE'S SUPERSTAR STATUS was destroyed by his eventual confession to the use of steroids to enhance his performance with the baseball bat. His muddied legacy is a lesson about the importance of being men of honesty and integrity.

But in the summer of 1998, when McGwire broke Roger Maris's single-season home run record (61), he taught us another lesson: It's critical to touch all the bases. On that historic run, McGwire rounded first base without touching the bag and had to be called back by the first-base coach. He had to return and tag the base. Otherwise, the record-breaking home run would not have counted.

Details are important—often critical—to the success of an endeavor. Dr. Bailey Smith uses that McGwire story to challenge Sunday morning congregations to make sure they haven't missed any critical points in their faith journey.

Dr. Smith, former president of the Southern Baptist Convention, emphasizes that we must make certain of our salvation. He has preached that sermon many times, and countless church leaders—even pastors—have been among those coming to a living faith in Christ for the first time. It is of eternal importance that we make certain of our relationship with Christ. Use a stake to mark each spiritual milestone in your life.

BOTTOM LINE

We need to be clear about our salvation. God desires us to have great
confidence and assurance.

Moment of Strength: Matthew 13:24-30

ENTRUSTING YOUR WORK TO GOD

"Master," Simon replied, "we worked hard all last night and didn't catch a thing.
But if you say so, I'll let the nets down again."

Luke 5:5

THE APOSTLE PETER WAS tired from a long night of fishing with no catch, but at Jesus' request, he put his boat out a bit from shore. As the crowds drew near, the staple of Peter's livelihood became a floating pulpit from which Jesus preached the Word of God.

It's not just those in full-time ministry who are called to serve Jesus at work. Believers in every career imaginable who are willing to push out a little bit from shore can have an impact on their world for the Kingdom. All it takes is a surrendered heart, the faith to believe that God is working with you and through you, and the knowledge that what you're doing matters. First Corinthians 15:58 says, "So, my dear brothers and sisters, be strong and immovable. Always work enthusiastically for the Lord, for you know that nothing you do for the Lord is ever useless." This refers to ministry, but all work can be done as unto the Lord (Colossians 3:23).

After speaking to the crowds, Jesus told Peter to go out into deep water one last time for a catch. Peter, an experienced fisherman, had just spent a fruitless night on the lake. On top of that, he had just cleaned his nets.

But to Peter's credit, he trusted Jesus with his work life—every last bit of it. The result was a catch so big that the nets began to tear and the boats began to sink. Trust Jesus with your career, let down the nets, and serve Him even at work. He is good!

BOTTOM LINE

Your job can further God's Kingdom and lead you into a deeper relationship with Jesus. Make sure you bring the right attitude of faith to it.

Moment of Strength: Colossians 3:23-24

MIND THE GAP

So be careful how you live. Don't live like fools, but like those who are wise.
Make the most of every opportunity in these evil days.
Ephesians 5:15-16

THE CONTEXT OF TODAY'S VERSE IS the apostle Paul's admonition for us to live as children of light and abstain from sin and immorality. Instead, we should do what we know is pleasing to God. Paul mentions some examples of behaviors we should avoid, such as sexual immorality, greed, coarse joking, obscenity, and drunkenness, but let's not misunderstand what he's saying. Paul is not giving us a checklist of things to do and not do; instead, he is urging us to be purposeful and wise in our choices. His list of bad behaviors are examples of what unwise choices will lead to. We can find ourselves there when we aren't careful about the choices we make, allowing the culture around us to shape our character.

When you walk across a wooden plank bridge, for example, being careful doesn't just mean looking out for things that might knock you off; it also means being deliberate about where you step. Applied to our daily lives, this means finding out what pleases the Lord through time in His Word and in prayer, and then obeying what He shows us.

It's easy to look back at the end of a week and grade ourselves on Paul's list—didn't get drunk, didn't swear, no pornography, played well with others—but were we deliberate? Did we make the most of every opportunity? Pursuing God is more than just trying to avoid sin.

BOTTOM LINE

Being careful is not just being cautious; it also means being deliberate.

Moment of Strength: Deuteronomy 5:32

CHOOSE YOUR RESPONSE

Bless those who persecute you. Don't curse them; pray that God will bless them.
Romans 12:14

ISAAC WAS LIVING IN PHILISTINE COUNTRY, where he was growing successful and wealthy (Genesis 26). At a certain point, the jealousy of the Philistines reached a boiling point, and they decided to do something about it. They sabotaged Isaac's wells (cutting off his water supply) and ran him out of the country. As he moved from place to place, he continued to face opposition from people who claimed ownership of the wells that belonged to him. Each time, Isaac moved on rather than fight back. Why didn't he stand up for himself? Isn't that the right thing to do?

Later in Genesis 26, we see these former enemies come to Isaac to make peace. Why? Because they had seen clearly that God was with him and that he was blessed by the Lord. The forbearance and restraint Isaac showed while being treated unfairly ended up being a powerful testimony to those who needed it. We don't know whether these former enemies ended up seeking after God, but we do know they understood that Isaac's God—our God—involves Himself personally in the lives of those who love Him. That's not a bad place for faith to start.

The next time you're treated unfairly, consider that your response might be what turns someone's attention to their need for God.

BOTTOM LINE

Sometimes the boldest statement about our confidence in Christ is made when we bless those who persecute us.

Moment of Strength: Matthew 5:38-48

PATIENCE IN PARENTING

People with understanding control their anger;
a hot temper shows great foolishness.
Proverbs 14:29

TIM WAS BEGINNING TO wonder whether he had made a mistake in trying to teach Jonah, his twelve-year-old son, how to mow the lawn and trim the hedges. A job that usually took no more than an hour to complete by himself had somehow expanded to more than two hours with Jonah involved. And to top it all off, Jonah had made a few mistakes along the way, resulting in some uneven bushes and several very noticeable scalped places on the lawn. It took all the willpower Tim could muster not to scold Jonah, send him inside, and finish the job himself. But each time his frustration was about to get the best of him, Tim noticed Jonah's beaming smile—soaking in the fact that Dad was entrusting him with real tools.

God has designed our ever-changing sons and daughters as complex, unique human beings. Often, in an effort to do things as efficiently as possible, we find it is easier to do things ourselves rather than patiently invest the time necessary to instruct our children. If we aren't careful, the hearts of our children can be sacrificed on the altar of efficiency and perfectionism. Our ability to recognize who our children are and who they are becoming will only occur with generous amounts of patience. When was the last time you took time to instruct your son or daughter in how to do something?

BOTTOM LINE

It takes patience with our children, and with ourselves, to be good parents.

Moment of Strength: Proverbs 19:11

I WANT IT . . . LATER!

Make sure that no one is immoral or godless like Esau,
who traded his birthright as the firstborn son for a single meal.
Hebrews 12:16

REMEMBER THE STORY OF Jacob and his twin brother, Esau? Esau wanted some of Jacob's stew so badly that he didn't even hesitate when Jacob asked him to trade his birthright for it. In essence, Esau's reply to his brother was, "What good is my birthright right at this moment? I'm more interested in satisfying my immediate hunger than I am in whatever promise might be in store down the road." So without a second thought, even though he knew what the birthright actually entailed, he made the deal. A spiritual blessing, a double portion of the inheritance, leadership of the family . . . traded for a bowl of stew. Sounds ludicrous, doesn't it?

Unfortunately, the story of Esau is being relived by many people, including us sometimes. When we focus our time, energy, and resources on achieving and acquiring what feels good now, we can miss opportunities to participate in the promises and purposes of God. Think about that: We can miss opportunities to join God's work in the world.

Reread Hebrews 12:16 with the following definitions in mind: *immoral* (giving priority to selfish desires) and *irreverent* (treating God in a way that is not respectful). Now ask yourself this question: Is there an area in your life where you're trading away God's blessings for something else that seems more important right now?

BOTTOM LINE

A life lived for Christ is a life focused on Kingdom significance, and a life of Kingdom significance will always far outweigh a life of indulgence.

Moment of Strength: Colossians 1:9-12

MAN UP

The LORD is like a father to his children,
tender and compassionate to those who fear him.
Psalm 103:13

IN 2010, professors at Boston College headed up a fatherhood study called *The New Dad: Exploring Fatherhood within a Career Context.* Researchers interviewed college-educated, first-time fathers of young children. Based on interview data, they concluded that a father's role is more than putting food on the table. A good dad also works hard to share the childcare and home-care responsibilities with his wife.

If you have children, you know that being a father is a 24/7 job. There's little time off, and just when you think you've got it mastered, something happens that makes you doubt your abilities. God wants us to provide for our families, but He also wants us to be there for our children—supporting them emotionally and physically.

Some dads don't have an earthly father whose example they can follow. But, as Christians, we all have a heavenly Father who's worth emulating.

David writes, "The LORD is like a father to his children, tender and compassionate to those who fear him" (Psalm 103:13). It's natural for us to have compassion on our children. We understand our own children in special ways and want to keep them from pain. Sure, part of our role as dads is to guide and discipline our children. But just as our heavenly Father does for us, we need to unconditionally love, nurture, and be there for our kids.

BOTTOM LINE

Think of one way to connect with your children this week. Then do it!

Moment of Strength: Deuteronomy 1:30-31

WHAT'S PAST IS PAST

Do not remember the rebellious sins of my youth.
Remember me in the light of your unfailing love,
for you are merciful, O LORD.
Psalm 25:7

IT WASN'T EXACTLY a weekly thing, but the Knight family routinely had the trees in their front yard rolled with toilet paper by a family friend. His efforts were works of art, if he did say so himself: roll after roll after roll hanging from the limbs, blowing in the breeze, and getting soggy in the rain. Many times, the culprit would help clean it all up.

Fast-forward twenty-five years or so. Now an adult, the former "yard artist" stayed with the Knight family during a visit to town. When he got to his room, it was completely covered with toilet paper. The bed. The pillows. Hanging from light fixtures. Everywhere! It was sweet revenge for the Knights.

The Knights and their friend were able to laugh about the foolish stuff he had done as a teenager, but many people aren't that fortunate. Some kids get into more serious trouble and then spend much of their lives living it down—legally, emotionally, or both. Worst of all can be the guilt. Some people have a hard time experiencing God's forgiveness for the things they did, even though His forgiveness is available to them.

A life of faith is not about feeling guilty about things in your past. God's grace and forgiveness can give you a fresh start. The Cross is not for perfect people; it's for people who aren't perfect and who desperately need forgiveness. So don't believe the enemy's accusations. You are forgiven in Christ.

BOTTOM LINE

You might have messed up big time as a kid or even as an adult, but God's forgiveness is big enough to handle it. Let His grace set you free from your past.

Moment of Strength: Psalm 103:12

MUZZLE

Take control of what I say, O Lord, and guard my lips.
Psalm 141:3

"Even a fool is considered wise when he keeps silent" (Proverbs 17:28, hcsb). When we say the wrong thing at the wrong time, there can be many consequences. But sometimes we just can't help ourselves.

Sometimes we use our mouth to put others down, reveal confidences (disguised as prayer requests), or build ourselves up in the eyes of others. Sometimes we provide a running commentary on life—the good, the bad, and the ugly. James calls the tongue "a world of unrighteousness" and "a restless evil" (James 3:6, 8, hcsb).

Ephesians 4:29 says, "Don't use foul or abusive language. Let everything you say be good and helpful, so that your words will be an encouragement to those who hear them."

Think about that. Is there any better advice when it comes to our speech? It can take years to build trust with someone and only a few ill-chosen words to tear it all back down. Remember that your mouth is one of the most obvious windows to your relationship with Christ. What we say can encourage people in need and give grace to the hearer. Though the tongue can be used recklessly, causing great damage, it can also be used wisely, bringing great good. Allow God to guide your words. Make your speech a matter of prayer.

BOTTOM LINE

Your mouth can be a useful ministry tool or a weapon. By God's grace, seek to use your words for His glory.

Moment of Strength: Proverbs 16:23

A SHINING LIGHT

*In the same way, let your good deeds shine out for all to see,
so that everyone will praise your heavenly Father.*
Matthew 5:16

WHAT DOES IT MEAN TO let your light shine as a good Christian example? It can mean different things to different people. For some, it may look like a willingness to share their faith openly and without reservation. For others, it may look more like living a life of quiet service. The two aren't mutually exclusive, of course, but we all have different strengths and temperaments.

Both examples share at least a couple of things in common. They are both focused on Jesus. He is the light we are shining; we are the conduit. He is the one on whom we're shining the light, not ourselves. And they both involve loving others—something that can be exemplified in countless ways.

How we go about shining isn't necessarily the most important aspect of being a light for Jesus. Can you sing? Consider signing up for the church choir or praise team. Can you teach? Then prayerfully look for opportunities to use your teaching gifts. Do you know people who are struggling? Be there for them. Listen, counsel, and help however you can.

Today's Moment of Strength is a great reminder of how Jesus viewed those who believed in Him. What are Christians? We're the salt of the earth, the light of the world. Jesus wants to live His life through us, bringing glory to the Father. So rely on Him, and let your light shine!

BOTTOM LINE

Through your words and your deeds, do everything you can to shine a light on Jesus.

Moment of Strength: Matthew 5:13-16

TRUST FACTOR

This I declare about the LORD: He alone is my refuge,
my place of safety; he is my God, and I trust him.
Psalm 91:2

HOW DID I LET HIM TALK ME INTO THIS? Richard wondered as he and his son, Josh, slowly rose into the air. The theme park they had visited the day before had been fun, but now Richard found himself strapped to Josh on the world's tallest skycoaster.

"Are you sure we're just three hundred feet up?" Richard asked. "This feels way higher than a football field."

"Don't be a baby, Dad," Josh said. "It'll be fun."

Richard looked at the steel cable that suspended them above the ground. *Okay*, he thought, *my life depends on the strength of that cable.*

Suddenly, Richard found himself speeding toward the ground at more than 70 mph. He was scared, but his fear couldn't wipe the smile off his face.

"This is awesome!" he shouted as they flew back in the other direction.

As Christians, we're supposed to trust Jesus with our lives. But our actions don't always show it. We may use words like the ones David uses in Psalm 91, but then we don't put our faith into action like David did.

Richard and Josh couldn't soar until they trusted the steel cable. It's much the same way in our Christian lives. We're stuck going nowhere until we trust Jesus to hold us up. Is there something you've wanted to do for God but were too afraid to try? Trust Him. Ask Him to increase your faith. He's way more reliable than any steel cable.

BOTTOM LINE

What's holding you back from stepping out for Jesus? Take a risk and discover the adventure that awaits.

Moment of Strength: Isaiah 12:2

SECRET TO A LONG MARRIAGE

"The two are united into one." Since they are no longer two but one,
let no one split apart what God has joined together.
Mark 10:8-9

FOR YEARS, studies have shown that TV watching is bad for your health. All of that sitting increases your risk of heart disease and type 2 diabetes. But some of the latest research shows that TV watching can also be bad for your marriage.

After studying nearly four hundred couples, Dr. Jeremy Osborn of Albion College in Michigan found that "people who believe the unrealistic [romantic] portrayals on TV are actually less committed to their spouses." Most problems aren't solved in thirty minutes, and couples rarely live "happily ever after" without hard work, patience, and commitment. Instead of letting TV dictate what relationships look like, we should turn off the TV and turn on the real-life romance.

When Jesus was asked about divorce, He said, "Let no one split apart what God has joined together" (Mark 10:9). Yet many marriages fall apart not on biblical grounds but because of unmet expectations. Dr. Osborn said he hopes people will look at their expectations of marriage and ask: "Where did these expectations come from, and are they realistic?"

Marriage isn't exciting all the time. Fights don't always end with passionate kisses. But by committing ourselves to our wives and to God, we can create marriages that Hollywood can only dream about.

BOTTOM LINE

What can you do to turn up the romance in your marriage? Have you had unreasonable expectations about marriage?

Moment of Strength: Proverbs 5:18-19

BORE YOUR KIDS WITH CHORES

For we are each responsible for our own conduct.
Galatians 6:5

NOBODY LIKES DOING CHORES. That's probably why adults are doing less housework today than they did twenty years ago. But experts say that children who help their families around the house not only learn the practical skills of taking care of a house or a yard but also learn responsibility, organizational skills, and self-sufficiency, and they get in the habit of serving others. That not only makes them more productive adults but also could benefit their marriages. A 2006 study found that marriages in the United States tend to be more stable when men take an active role in domestic tasks and the housework is shared.

As parents, we should teach our children that all family members must help out around the house according to their age and ability. Obviously, a five-year-old shouldn't be tasked with washing your fine china. But filling water cups, putting clothes in the hamper, or picking up toys could be helpful options.

In Galatians 6:5, Paul says that everyone should carry his or her own load. That's the case in our families and in the family of God. We all need to work together and do our share. What household responsibilities are your kids ready to help with? Make a list, sit down with them, and create a plan. And if your kids are already doing chores, thank them for helping out.

BOTTOM LINE

Families, including God's family, thrive when all members work together to benefit one another.

Moment of Strength: Hebrews 13:16

FROM PRIDE TO THE PIT

We were out in the field, tying up bundles of grain. Suddenly my bundle stood
up, and your bundles all gathered around and bowed low before mine!
Genesis 37:7

FOR A COUPLE OF DAYS, we're going to look at the familiar story of Joseph, one of the Bible's most memorable men. Jacob had twelve sons, but he loved Joseph more than the others (Genesis 37:3). And as expected, such obvious parental favoritism did not play well with the older brothers. Let's recall some of the story's details.

First, Jacob dressed Joseph better than he clothed the older brothers—Joseph's colorful coat contrasted with the brothers' plain, drab robes (Genesis 37:3). Earlier, Joseph had come home from tending sheep and tattled on two of his brothers. Finally, we're told that his brothers hated him and wouldn't even speak to him decently (Genesis 37:4).

When he was seventeen, Joseph boasted about a dream he had in which his brothers symbolically bowed down to him (Genesis 37:6-7). Did he really think this would endear him to them? Was he trying to prove that God was on his side? Not long after this dream, Joseph's brothers threw him into a pit and debated about killing him, but instead, they sold him into slavery (Genesis 37:26-28).

The evidence suggests that Joseph may have been an overly confident teenager. Fortunately, we have the rest of the story: He grew into a godly man of wisdom, integrity, forgiveness, compassion, and humility. Take time now to consider how these godly characteristics are reflected in your own life.

BOTTOM LINE

One of the keys to growing in godliness is spending more time focusing on God
than on ourselves. Even so, sometimes an honest self-evaluation is helpful.

Moment of Strength: Genesis 37:1-11

FROM THE PIT TO THE PALACE

It was God who sent me here ahead of you to preserve your lives.
Genesis 45:5

IMAGINE JOSEPH'S FEARS and feelings as his brothers dropped him into the pit. Surely they were just playing a sick joke on him. Wouldn't they come pull him out any minute? Did he beg them to stop the abuse? Did he hear them haggling with the merchants who bought him?

Fast-forward to Joseph's life as a slave to Potiphar, one of Pharaoh's top officers. We're told that God was with Joseph and made everything he did successful (Genesis 39:3-4). Potiphar grew to trust him. So what had caused Joseph to grow in godly character?

First of all, humility must have come as the result of becoming a slave, isolated from his family (Genesis 39:1). His reputation for integrity was earned by loyalty and faithful service to his master. Remember, Potiphar's wife tried to seduce Joseph, but he ran away (Genesis 39:12). Then she lied to get him imprisoned (Genesis 39:17). Again, Joseph proved honest and upright, even through his years in prison.

The kind of wisdom that made Joseph trustworthy—for example, interpreting dreams about a great famine—could have come only from God (Genesis 41:15-16). Finally, Joseph showed a lot of compassion and forgiveness when his brothers appeared years later, asking to purchase grain (Genesis 45:4). Joseph was finally reunited with his father and family.

BOTTOM LINE

God rewarded Joseph's faithfulness, but it took a while. If you're in a pit right now, don't give up. Believe that God is able to bring good out of it.

Moment of Strength: Genesis 39:1-19

WHEN THE COWS COME HOME

Know the state of your flocks, and put your heart into
caring for your herds, for riches don't last forever.
Proverbs 27:23-24

MANY CHRISTIAN FINANCIAL COUNSELORS cringe when they consider today's shortsighted definition of stewardship. Yes, money is important, but stewardship is about much more than money. It includes our time, talents, and treasure.

There are many aspects of our lives that demand good stewardship—including our family, work, time, abilities, and resources. Our resources include not only our monthly paychecks but also our property and possessions.

As men, our responsibility is to do our best to provide for our families, while also contributing to the work of God on earth and being generous to those in need. Good stewardship is our duty to God, and we must pursue it with diligence.

Here are some items that should be on your financial stewardship checklist: know your financial picture (checking account balance, credit card debt, retirement fund value, etc.); prayerfully build an annual budget with your wife (and children, as age-appropriate) and stick to it; teach your children that money is earned, not an entitlement; accumulate savings and investments for your family's future; give generously. Add to your checklist according to your family's needs.

BOTTOM LINE

Beginning with the list above and a prayer for wisdom, make a checklist to help you begin getting your financial stewardship fully under control.

Moment of Strength: Luke 19:11-27

REST IS NOT A FOUR-LETTER WORD

Better to have one handful with quietness than two
handfuls with hard work and chasing the wind.
Ecclesiastes 4:6

JOHN HUNG UP THE PHONE and slumped back in his office chair. His wife, Claire, had just updated him on her day at the beach with their two children. She was about to send over a video of the sand castle they had built earlier in the day. Although he would be joining Claire and the kids for the weekend, John began to second-guess his decision to stay at work so that he could get ahead on a few projects. "I'm working around the clock to provide for my family," he mumbled to himself, "but I can't seem to stop long enough to actually enjoy my family."

Many of us can relate to John's frustration. The demands of life and the pressure and stress that go along with those demands can be overwhelming. Constantly striving to get ahead or sometimes just survive, we are faced with a seemingly endless stream of deadlines, meetings, and paperwork. In order to have more time, we get up early and stay up late, and inevitably our rest begins to suffer.

But we were not designed for this frantic pace. If our Creator rested, how much more do we as His creation need to rest? Taking time to rest teaches us an essential truth: God is God, and we are His finite, dependent creation. God never asked us to meet life's pressures and demands on our own or by relying on our own strength. God invites us to enter His rest. Have you neglected your rest lately?

BOTTOM LINE

It is a good thing to be a creature with needs, and one of those needs is rest.
Learning to rest is a matter of faith and faithfulness.

Moment of Strength: Matthew 11:28

JESUS KNOWS

Jesus knew that the Father had given him authority over everything and that he had come from God and would return to God. So he got up from the table, took off his robe, wrapped a towel around his waist, and poured water into a basin. Then he began to wash the disciples' feet, drying them with the towel he had around him.

John 13:3-5

FOR SOME PEOPLE, amnesia is a scary reality. Imagine waking up one day not knowing who you are, where you are, or who the people around you are. In such a scenario, it's impossible to know how to live your life. So much of what you do is based on an understanding of who you are. Even people who don't have amnesia spend much of their lives trying to figure out who they are and why they were created.

In John 13, we see how Jesus' identity was shaped by His relationship with the Father. Everything He did flowed out of His identity as the Son. Though we're not divine, we are sons of God, and we, too, are meant to receive our identity from the Father. Just like Christ, we have come from God and therefore belong to God.

Once we understand our identity, we can know how we are to live. It has been said that knowledge is power. In a sense, the more you know, the more you can control people. However, in Jesus' case, He served more because He knew more. For Jesus, knowledge was about humble service. Jesus knew who He was, where He came from, and where He was going. Jesus also knew that all power had been given to Him. But Jesus didn't exert power over people; rather, He voluntarily put Himself in service to other people. The humility of God is incredible.

BOTTOM LINE

Truly knowing our identity and truly knowing our calling lead to humble service. How can you serve Jesus—and someone else—this week?

Moment of Strength: Philippians 2:1-11

CREATED FOR COMMUNITY

As iron sharpens iron, so a friend sharpens a friend.
Proverbs 27:17

DAN FELT THAT HIS WORLD was coming apart. The results were back from a recent battery of tests for his two-year-old son, and his worst fears were realized. This news completed the trifecta in his life, adding the serious illness of a child to the marital struggles between his wife and him and the financial pressure they were facing because of his recent layoff. Dan had no idea how he was going to pay for the expensive treatments his son would soon need. Scared, alone, and feeling overwhelmed by negative emotion, Dan did something he had never done. He reached out to his friend Steve and told him exactly what he was facing. Dan was shocked to discover how much his perspective changed by simply putting into words what he was feeling and having someone else listen.

It's easy to fall for the lie that says men are supposed to be strong no matter what life throws our way. But Scripture makes it clear that God never intended for us to bear life's burdens alone. He has promised to be with us, but we also need fellowship with other Christian men who can love, support, and counsel us when life is hard. A sure sign of strength is knowing when to reach out to others.

What are you trying to face alone right now? Think about a guy you can call and bring into your struggle. The enemy may tell you that nobody cares, but that's just another lie. Reach out for help.

BOTTOM LINE

We were created to live in community with others by a God who also lives in community. Humble yourself and ask for help when you need it.

Moment of Strength: Proverbs 17:17

LIVES OF GREAT MEN

The king of Aram had great admiration for Naaman, the commander of his army, because through him the LORD had given Aram great victories.

2 Kings 5:1

WHO ARE THE GREAT MEN IN YOUR LIFE? Whose life has had the greatest impact on yours? Try to come up with the names of five to seven men if you can. If you're fortunate, you can list your dad among that group. Or you might be able to include a man who took the place of your absent father. Maybe there's a pastor in there, or a layman who shared the gospel with you. It could be a brother, a coworker, or a fishing buddy. Ask yourself what makes these men great in your life. Is it their compassion or wisdom? Their faithful friendship? Their unique skills and talents? Their example?

Naaman is not a prominent name in the Bible, but he is called a "great man." What other biblical men come to mind as being great? There are plenty of examples. Abraham demonstrates great faith in courageously venturing into the unknown with God. David shows us what loyalty looks like in his relationships with King Saul and Jonathan. He also provides an example of failure (his adulterous affair) followed by humility and repentance. From the apostle Paul we can learn many things, including perseverance, as he committed his life to spreading the gospel despite persecution and imprisonment. And of course, in Jesus we have the epitome of a great man.

The great men in our lives and in the Bible can serve as examples to encourage us to walk faithfully with God, creating a positive faith legacy of our own.

BOTTOM LINE

Create a list of the godly qualities you admire in the great men who have influenced you, and ask God to help you begin cultivating those qualities in your own life.

Moment of Strength: 2 Kings 5:1-15

FATHERS AND SONS

A wise son responds to his father's discipline, but
a mocker doesn't listen to rebuke.
Proverbs 13:1, HCSB

WE LIVE IN A TIME when it's harder than ever for teens to be different from the world. There are plenty of Jesus-following students who love the Lord and are respectful to their parents. But our culture seems to be taking countless teens hostage, changing them into rebellious, unreachable kids. Not only do they not listen to their parents, but they also openly rebel against them. A lot of parents are wondering, *Where did we go wrong?* They are desperate to find help and get their kids back on the right track.

Mark Gregston is director of Heartlight, an east Texas home for thirteen- to seventeen-year-olds in desperate need of an alternative residential setting. Typically, residents stay for nine months to a year at the facility, where they attend high school classes and are challenged by counselors and mentors to take another look at where their lives are headed.

Mark says that when he coaches parents in connecting with their teens, he recommends three things to restore damaged relationships. All three have to do with respect and honest communication: (1) Ask relevant questions (don't fake it). (2) Let them think about the answer (don't supply it). (3) Value their response (don't correct it). Connecting with your teenager doesn't have to be complicated, but it must be intentional and loving. Ask God to give you the wisdom and patience you need to love your teenagers well.

BOTTOM LINE

Look for ways to better communicate with the teenagers in your life—your children, your grandchildren, or the teens in your neighborhood or church.

Moment of Strength: Proverbs 17:1-10

LEADING YOUR FAMILY

You must commit yourselves wholeheartedly to these commands
that I am giving you today. Repeat them again and again to your
children. Talk about them when you are at home and when you are
on the road, when you are going to bed and when you are getting up.
Deuteronomy 6:6-7

DR. MEG MEEKER WRITES IN her book *Strong Fathers, Strong Daughters* about
what daughters think about their dads:

> She gives you authority because she needs you to love and adore her.
> She can't feel good about herself until she knows that you feel good
> about her. So you need to use your authority carefully and wisely.
> Your daughter doesn't want to see you as an equal. She wants you to
> be her hero, someone who is wiser and steadier and stronger than
> she is.
> The only way you will alienate your daughter in the long term is
> by losing her respect, failing to lead, or failing to protect her. If you
> don't provide for her needs, she will find someone else who will—
> and that's when trouble starts. Don't let that happen.

Our children—daughters *and* sons—are looking for leadership. They need
someone to follow. They may not always act like it, but they do. Sadly, many
fathers in our society have run away from their leadership role, and it has left
a huge void in families while negatively affecting society at large.

When we live in relationship with our heavenly Father, He provides the
grace and courage for us to lead our families well. May we prayerfully lean on
Him, learn from Him, and obey Him by stepping up to fulfill our leadership
role. Our children will honor us and appreciate our leadership.

BOTTOM LINE

How could you express your leadership in your family in a positive and
proactive way today?

Moment of Strength: Ephesians 6:4

GIVE THEM GRACE

Fathers, do not aggravate your children, or they will become discouraged.

Colossians 3:21

CURT'S WIFE, MANDY, closed the door quietly as she left his office. Curt wasn't sure how he felt about what she had just shared with him. Mandy believed that he had been too harsh lately with their twin thirteen-year-old boys, and she had taken the opportunity to share her concerns.

But I'm their father, and it is my responsibility to make sure they do things the right way, Curt thought to himself. But he also had to admit that his boys had seemed discouraged lately, as if they didn't feel they could ever meet his standards.

The Greek word for *aggravate* in Colossians 3:21 can also mean to stir up, provoke, or irritate. So another way to phrase the apostle Paul's command is "stop nagging your kids."

As fathers, it is our responsibility (along with our wives) to provide rules and guidelines for our children, but these rules should never become a noose that strangles them. Our rules should provide a safe environment where our kids are free to discover themselves and their unique role in the story God is writing. Our rules should never suffocate our children and cause them to lose heart. When our children feel that nothing they do is good enough, it is natural for them to be discouraged and simply give up. It can happen in our relationship with God, too, if we see Him as impossible to please.

In what ways are your rules exasperating your children? How can you show them grace instead?

BOTTOM LINE

A father's words have a great impact. Make sure your instruction builds up your children instead of causing them to become discouraged and lose heart.

Moment of Strength: Ephesians 6:4

WHY AM I HERE?

*For we are God's masterpiece. He has created us anew in Christ
Jesus, so we can do the good things he planned for us long ago.*
Ephesians 2:10

"If you love what you do, you don't work a day in your life." How many
of us have heard this before? We long for that kind of life congruency and
fulfillment of purpose. And yet why is it that so many men hate their jobs?
Why are so many in careers that seem to be a poor match for their gifting?
Why are so many men who are out of work—and who want to work—unable
to find a job at all?

To be sure, many men work hard to support their families, and we should
(1 Timothy 5:8). And there may be seasons of life in which we are called to
perform jobs we don't enjoy that help grow our character and advance God's
Kingdom purposes in our families and ministries. Even so, every man should
pursue the unique calling for which God has placed him on the earth—the
work he is passionate about. But how?

Author Frederick Buechner writes, "The place God calls you to is the place
where your deep gladness and the world's deep hunger meet." Discovering
our God-given purpose involves asking several questions: *What are my
unique gifts and talents? What activities bring me joy? What need do I feel
called to meet?*

These are questions every man should ask God to reveal. Ephesians 2:10
tells us that the gospel launches us into a life of purpose. Each one of us has
a personal mission designed for us by our heavenly Father. We were created
to joyfully pursue it.

BOTTOM LINE

How are you fulfilling the purpose for which you were created?

Moment of Strength: Psalm 37:5

YOU'RE INVITED

Andrew went to find his brother, Simon, and told him,
"We have found the Messiah."
John 1:41

HALL OF FAMER AND San Francisco 49ers receiver Jerry Rice is considered by many experts to be the best receiver ever to play in the NFL. He was once asked, "Why did you attend a small, obscure university like Mississippi Valley State University in Itta Bena, Mississippi?" Rice responded, "Out of all the big-time schools (such as UCLA) to recruit me, MVSU was the only school to come to my house and give me a personal visit." The big-time schools sent cards, letters, and advertisements, but only one extended Rice a personal invitation.

Personal invitations matter. Andrew invited his brother, Peter, to come see Jesus. And it was Andrew who brought forward the boy with the loaves and fishes so that Jesus could feed the multitude.

Elmer Towns reports that 86 percent of new converts say they came to church for the first time because of an invitation from a friend or relative.

Prayerfully look for opportunities to invite others to church. Don't be discouraged if they decline. Don't take it personally if they say yes to coming to church but don't show up. Most important, don't dump them as friends if they won't respond as you would like. Be patient. It may take months or years. You may need to ask repeatedly. Pray that God will soften their hearts, eventually accepting your invitation. It's really an invitation for them to meet Jesus.

BOTTOM LINE

Personal invitations are a powerful way to introduce people to Jesus. Pray for opportunities, and be bold.

Moment of Strength: Luke 14:13

GRACE AND YOUR FINANCES

God will generously provide all you need. Then you will always have
everything you need and plenty left over to share with others. As the
Scriptures say, "They share freely and give generously to the poor.
Their good deeds will be remembered forever."
2 Corinthians 9:8-9

THE BIBLE HAS A LOT TO SAY ABOUT MONEY. Christian financial counselors have done good work in articulating a biblical way to handle the resources God gives us. As faithful Christians, we should strive to be good stewards.

Yet it's so easy to adopt a sort of legalism when it comes to the way we view others who may be in financial distress, or to feel overwhelming shame when we look at our own messed-up pocketbook. Adding to our financial stress are unforeseen circumstances such as long-term unemployment, lost investment value, and plummeting home prices. Many Christians in churches across the country feel like financial failures. They feel sidelined by their financial woes and sometimes even hopeless about ever getting out of the hole in which they find themselves.

We must understand that grace can apply to our finances as well as to any other area of discipleship. God loves those who face bankruptcy or foreclosure as much as He loves those who have their financial ducks in a row. He'll measure the effectiveness of our lives not by how much is in the bank when we die but by how faithfully we've pursued and lived out His purposes for our lives. So if you're struggling in the area of your finances, don't give in to shame or despair. Seek God's help.

BOTTOM LINE

God's grace is available to help us get our finances in better shape. He is the
God of second chances.

Moment of Strength: James 4:6

LAST WORDS

*Jesus came and told his disciples, "I have been given all authority
in heaven and on earth. Therefore, go and make disciples of all the nations,
baptizing them in the name of the Father and the Son and the Holy Spirit."*
Matthew 28:18-19

LAST WORDS ARE IMPORTANT. Whether it's a parent saying good-bye to a child leaving for college, a husband being shipped overseas to war, or even a coach's pregame speech before taking the field, last words are often crucial. They often represent something important, and sometimes they are even memorable.

Jesus' words in Matthew 28:18-19 explain what His followers are to do in the long period between His first coming and His second coming. What Jesus said to His disciples—known as the great commission—would make a difference for all eternity. Those words, spoken on a Galilean hillside, have become the blueprint for His movement. What Jesus said to His disciples that day was certainly of great importance. He wanted them to focus on the mission, and to know that His power and presence would go with them.

Jesus has given us, His followers, the incredible responsibility to be His representatives in the world, to carry His message of love and peace to broken humanity. As we go about our business, we can do Jesus' business by telling others about Him, pointing people to the Savior, and being salt and light in our world. His message becomes our message.

Amazingly, Jesus allows us to share in spreading His gospel. No higher calling or greater privilege exists.

BOTTOM LINE

Whom could you tell about Jesus today?

Moment of Strength: Mark 16:15-16

MOVE AWAY FROM ANGER

Don't sin by letting anger control you.
Don't let the sun go down while you are still angry.
Ephesians 4:26

A MAN TRIED TO DEFEND his bad temper by saying, "I explode, and then it's over with."

"Yes," replied a friend, "just like a volcano—but look at the damage that it leaves behind."

As Aristotle once wrote, "Any one can get angry . . . but to do this to the right person, to the right extent, at the right time, with the right motive, and in the right way, that is not for every one, nor is it easy."

"Don't sin by letting anger control you," says the apostle Paul in Ephesians 4:26. God permits us to be angry on certain occasions. In other words, anger is not always sinful. But with the same stroke of his pen, Paul warns us not to let our anger lead us to sin. Anger can be so destructive because actions taken and words spoken in anger cannot be taken back, nor is the damage easy to repair.

The Holy Spirit within us lets us know when our anger becomes sinful. And it's usually quite obvious to others. Bursts of temper resulting in rage, lack of control, the desire to hurt another person, and profanity are not righteous anger. Far from it.

So how can we be angry without sinning? In addition to praying for God's help, there are some things we can keep in mind. First, we should attack the problem and not the person. Second, we should reprove without rejecting. And third, we should avoid using exaggerations like *always* and *never*.

BOTTOM LINE

Anger is a normal emotion, but we are responsible for how we handle it. We need the Spirit's gift of self-control to help us deal with our anger.

Moment of Strength: Proverbs 29:11

BEAUTY FROM ASHES

*The Spirit of the Sovereign L*ORD *is upon me,*
*for the L*ORD *has anointed me to bring good news to*
the poor. . . . To all who mourn in Israel, he will give a
crown of beauty for ashes, a joyous blessing instead
of mourning, festive praise instead of despair.
Isaiah 61:1, 3

ON JUNE 26, 2012, a wildfire rolled over the mountains and into the city of Colorado Springs. Spurred on by 65 mph wind gusts and fueled by one of the driest seasons on record, the Waldo Canyon fire crested a ridge and dove into the Mountain Shadows neighborhood. In just a few hours, nearly 350 homes burned to the ground.

Dan, one of 32,000 people evacuated from their homes, watched events unfold on TV in a living room across town. Surrounded by his family and closest friends, he waited to see whether his home survived. It did, but many of his neighbors weren't as fortunate.

When Dan and his family returned home, only a handful of houses still stood on his street. The devastation was shocking. Dan walked his neighborhood, helping those whose homes had been damaged or destroyed. Charred wood and ash coated the area, giving it an ominous black feeling.

But just a few weeks after the tragedy, Dan saw the greenest grass imaginable growing up through the ashes. Vibrant, hopeful new life peeked through the black destruction. Though it may have been just a few blades of grass, it reminded Dan that God brings beauty from ashes. Even in the most difficult times, God can create something beautiful and give us hope. So focus on your Father, and don't ever give up. There is always hope with God.

BOTTOM LINE

Are you going through a particularly dark time? Remember that Jesus
promises something splendid instead of despair. Cling to His promise.

Moment of Strength: Hebrews 10:35-36

COMPASSION QUOTIENT

*The LORD is like a father to his children, tender and
compassionate to those who fear him.*

Psalm 103:13

SO YOU'VE BLOWN IT (AGAIN) AS A DAD. Join the club. God calls us to have compassion on our kids, and sometimes compassion is the last thing on our lips and hearts. But God is still merciful toward us, even when we mess up as dads. The trick is not to wallow in self-condemnation or unhealthy guilt. (And ask your kids for forgiveness too.)

What's your CQ (compassion quotient)? Have you learned how to forgive yourself for your parental shortcomings? Learning how to forgive yourself and accept grace and mercy from your heavenly Father is a trait you want to pass down to your own kids. After all, a good CQ toward yourself opens a door for learning that shuts out shame.

Your children can learn from you, even as you make mistakes. Do you expect perfection from yourself? Your kids will tend to carry the same traits they see you model, so a healthy outlook is important. Self-compassion may sound wrong, but compassion is always a godly response to suffering—why would we think it wouldn't apply to our own pain? When you confess your failures, the Lord forgives you, and you can let it go.

Put out your own CQ today to the Lord (repent). Cry out to Him in your distress. He knows. He remembers you. And in your failures, He will forgive you and lift you up with tender compassion.

BOTTOM LINE

Ask God to show you where you need to give yourself grace.

Moment of Strength: Psalm 103:6-14

GREAT HUMILITY

*Don't be selfish; don't try to impress others. Be humble,
thinking of others as better than yourselves. Don't look out only
for your own interests, but take an interest in others, too.*

Philippians 2:3-4

HUMILITY IS VALUED. Just ask any popular athlete. We highly esteem those who are great and who don't feel as if they have to tell us they're great, but we tend to dislike those who are great and who want to let everyone around them know it. Have you ever rooted against a certain individual because of his arrogance?

But humility has not always been a prized virtue. In Jesus' day, it was a dishonorable trait of a conquered people. No one wanted to be referred to as having *humilitas*. It was not a virtue but the trait of a loser. Then Jesus redefined greatness at the cross as He conquered our sin.

What is it to be conquered by Jesus? It is to realize that your life is not your own, and your will is willingly and joyfully surrendered to your Master's will. It is also to understand that your Master is not obligated to justify or explain what He does. God doesn't owe us an accounting of His dealings in our lives. He is infinitely wise and good, and we are not.

A conquered Christ follower works to enhance his Master's name and reputation above his own. Our position is in the background, and our Master is at the forefront. A humble man is actually great in the ways that matter because he uses his power for the gain of others, not for his own personal gain. Will you answer the call to be conquered by Jesus and live a life of humility?

BOTTOM LINE

Ask Jesus to help you lift His name and reputation above your own.

Moment of Strength: Luke 14:7-14

A RISK-TAKER

We tell others about Christ, warning everyone and teaching everyone with all the wisdom God has given us. We want to present them to God, perfect in their relationship to Christ. That's why I work and struggle so hard, depending on Christ's mighty power that works within me.

Colossians 1:28-29

CHRISTIANITY WAS NEVER INTENDED TO be just a body of beliefs to which we give our assent. When we look at it that way, it can become a turnoff. It can seem unreal and ineffective. Christianity was always intended to be a call to action. God doesn't simply reward our knowledge or our good intentions. He rewards what we *say* and *do*. He wants us to join Him in bringing the good news of the gospel to a lost world, demonstrating its power by how we live.

Jesus commands us to love God with all of our strength (Mark 12:30). The Greek word for *strength* in this verse means "the antithesis of apathy." What comes to mind are taking risks, seizing opportunities, and going all out. Living as Christians involves concentrated and consecrated effort, having our whole being focused on obedience.

Jesus is our ultimate example. He took the risk of coming to earth, to a people whom He created but who did not recognize Him. He seized the opportunity to lay down His life as the perfect sacrifice. He went all the way to the cross. He held nothing back.

Loving God means expending time and energy for Kingdom causes. It means servanthood and sacrifice. It means good old-fashioned hard work, empowered by God's grace.

BOTTOM LINE

How is God leading you to serve others today? Do it joyfully to His glory.

Moment of Strength: Colossians 3:23-24

FAITH TO BELIEVE THE IMPOSSIBLE

I do believe, but help me overcome my unbelief!
Mark 9:24

IN MARK 9:14-29, there's a story about a father who brought his demon-possessed son to Jesus, looking for a miracle. The disciples had already tried (and failed) to cast out the demon from the boy. The man was desperate. His son was so completely controlled by this demon that he would sometimes throw himself into fire or water, apparently trying to kill himself.

After explaining the situation to Jesus, the man said, "Have mercy on us and help us, if you can" (Mark 9:22). To this Jesus replied, "What do you mean, 'If I can'? . . . Anything is possible if a person believes" (Mark 9:23). And then came the man's well-known response: "I do believe, but help me overcome my unbelief!" (Mark 9:24). Most of us can relate to this man, at least some of the time. It's not easy to believe things that seem impossible to us.

Try to imagine Jesus' tone when He said to the man, "*If* I can?" Though we know that Jesus wouldn't mock the man's faith, it's easy to imagine Him challenging the man to think more carefully about the one to whom he was making his request. Yes, the request seemed impossible to the man, and yet Jesus seemed to specialize in making the impossible possible, which was no doubt why the man came to Him in the first place. Remember that what can seem impossible to us isn't impossible to Jesus, and pray accordingly.

BOTTOM LINE

It's a challenge to believe God's promises when things aren't looking good. Thankfully, God patiently works with the amount of faith we have.

Moment of Strength: Mark 9:14-29

GOD'S PROMISES

For all of God's promises have been fulfilled in Christ with a resounding "Yes!"
2 Corinthians 1:20

EVERYONE STRUGGLES. That's the nature of life outside Eden. Job 5:7 describes our dilemma: "People are born for trouble as readily as sparks fly up from a fire."

Let's take a look at two common areas of struggle: work and relationships. First, work. We struggle to make a living. Our jobs are often difficult. Sometimes they don't pay as much as we think we need. And for some of us, it can be hard even to find good work. Truly, we experience many "thorns and thistles" (Genesis 3:18) in our work lives. And as men, our pain is compounded by the fact that so much of our identity tends to be wrapped up in what we do, even if we know it shouldn't be that way.

We also tend to struggle in our relationships. Marriage, while a great blessing, is not always easy. Parenting, though rewarding, is challenging too. And being a good friend sometimes requires us to make great sacrifices.

Nevertheless, God's promises in Jesus are enough to sustain us. The apostle Peter writes, "By his divine power, God has given us everything we need for living a godly life. We have received all of this by coming to know him, the one who called us to himself by means of his marvelous glory and excellence. And because of his glory and excellence, he has given us great and precious promises" (2 Peter 1:3-4). *Everything* required for life has been provided through God's power and promises. His Word really can be trusted. He really is enough.

BOTTOM LINE

You can have confidence that, no matter what life throws at you, God's grace is enough to sustain you. Believe His promises. He is absolutely faithful.

Moment of Strength: John 16:33

BIRD-WATCHING

Look at the birds. They don't plant or harvest or store food in barns,
for your heavenly Father feeds them. And aren't you far more valuable to
him than they are? Can all your worries add a single moment to your life?
Matthew 6:26-27

JESUS WAS (AND IS) THE MASTER TEACHER. Though not always easy to understand—He often spoke in parables—His words are always memorable. They always make us think. They usually challenge us to believe more, to exercise our faith more, and to trust Him more despite what we may see or feel.

His teaching in Matthew 6:25-34 about the cure for anxiety is a brilliant example of this. The whole passage is an antidote to worry, which can be one of our most persistent temptations and struggles. Among the components of Jesus' argument is a beautiful analogy between God's care for the birds and His care for us. He poses the rhetorical question: "Aren't you far more valuable to him than they are?" The answer, of course, is *yes*, we are. The inescapable conclusion is that because God takes care of the birds (the lesser), He certainly will take care of His precious people (the greater). Besides, as Jesus points out, worrying will not do us a bit of good anyway.

Instead of worrying, Jesus says, we should "seek the Kingdom of God above all else, and live righteously, and he will give you everything you need" (Matthew 6:33). Will we believe Him? Are we willing to live a worry-free life, trusting God to take care of us? Sometimes a little bird-watching can be good for your faith.

BOTTOM LINE

Worry seems so reasonable. So human. It may even seem necessary. But it's
not—at least not according to Jesus. Pray for the grace to believe Him.

Moment of Strength: Matthew 6:25-34

ASK BIG

O Jerusalem, I have posted watchmen on your walls; they will
pray day and night, continually. Take no rest, all you who pray
to the LORD. Give the LORD no rest until he completes his work,
until he makes Jerusalem the pride of the earth.

Isaiah 62:6-7

HOW MUCH YOU PRAY and what you ask for reveals a lot about your view of God and your relationship with Him. Generally speaking, the more kind and capable you think He is, the more you will want to pray and the more you will pray honestly, boldly, and expectantly. And here's the thing: God encourages us to keep praying until He answers. He wants us to keep engaging with Him in prayer. As today's verse suggests, we should "give the LORD no rest" until He answers.

Of course, our requests must be in keeping with God's will. James 4:3 says, "Even when you ask, you don't get it because your motives are all wrong—you want only what will give you pleasure." God wisely doesn't answer yes to selfish prayers that would do us and others harm. He loves us too much to give us what will hurt us. Even so, we can and should ask for what we want. He is able to sort out the good requests from the bad and to gently teach us the difference.

Think of how children ask for what they want. They make honest requests. They unashamedly express their desires. And a good father delights to fulfill his children's requests whenever he can. Now consider that God is so much more generous than even the best parent (Matthew 7:11). He is not reluctant to bless His children. Our prayer lives should reflect that. As we learn to pray more, we will discover that spending time with God is the greatest blessing of all.

BOTTOM LINE

Prayer is essential to our relationship with God. He wants His children to come to Him for what they need. And what they need most of all is Him.

Moment of Strength: Matthew 7:7-12

LIVE LIKE A MOVIE TRAILER

We are Christ's ambassadors; God is making his appeal through us.
We speak for Christ when we plead, "Come back to God!"
2 Corinthians 5:20

WHAT'S THE BEST PART OF going to the movies? For many of us, the trailers before the featured attraction create the most excitement. Making intriguing movie trailers is big business. Production companies are paid millions of dollars to choose the right music and pick the right scenes, so that after just a few minutes we think, *Wow, I want to see that!* Our first impression of a movie, based on the trailer, is often the deciding factor for whether we'll go see it.

As Christians, we should live our lives like a movie trailer. When people look at us, they should want to see the "rest of the show" and get to know Jesus personally. Second Corinthians 5:20 reminds us that "we are Christ's ambassadors." God makes His appeal through us. What an amazing thought. And what an awesome responsibility we have to encourage others to be reconciled to God.

Our words and actions should attract people to our Lord, not turn them off. As Christ's ambassadors, we must appeal to people and help draw them into God's theater. And unlike many Hollywood features that turn out to be disappointing, Jesus never does. With God, the real show is far better than the trailer. Though trailers often contain the best scenes and funniest lines, God's movie is compelling from beginning to end as it tells the greatest story ever told: the story of Jesus.

BOTTOM LINE

Does your life draw people to God's main attraction? Do they want to know Jesus because of you?

Moment of Strength: Ephesians 6:20

ULTIMATE PROTECTION

Don't turn your back on wisdom, for she will protect you.
Love her, and she will guard you.
Proverbs 4:6

CRIME DOESN'T TAKE A VACATION. During the summer, when families travel, their homes are vulnerable to break-ins. Home security expert Alan Young says some simple steps can keep your house safer. He recommends not posting photos on Facebook or Twitter while you're still on vacation. Surprisingly, many burglaries are committed by someone you know or by someone connected to someone you know. Also, make sure a friend picks up your mail and newspaper and removes any door hangers. Those two things announce to the neighborhood, "Hey, we're not home."

While it's important to take easy steps to safeguard our homes, it's even more important for us to safeguard our lives. The Bible says one of the best ways we can protect ourselves is to pursue wisdom. "Don't turn your back on wisdom, for she will protect you. Love her, and she will guard you."

By making wise decisions, we guard our hearts. Maybe that means waking up early to attend a men's Bible study. Perhaps it's installing a Web filter on your computer to keep harmful images out of your life. Love wisdom by digging into God's Word and asking God to give you understanding for how best to handle the challenging and confusing situations in your life. When we act wisely and pursue wisdom, we protect ourselves and our families.

BOTTOM LINE

Wisdom comes from knowing God's Word and following Jesus. Protect yourself by being wise.

Moment of Strength: James 1:5

MARRIAGE JUSTICE

When God's people are in need, be ready to help them.
Always be eager to practice hospitality.

Romans 12:13

THE BIBLE SAYS IT CLEARLY: "When God's people are in need, be ready to help them. Always be eager to practice hospitality." In recent years, more and more churches are taking those words to heart and taking action. Instead of just talking about the Word of God, people are living it out by helping the needy, donating clothes, and cleaning up trash in public parks.

But according to research compiled by the Heritage Foundation, one of the ways men can best serve their communities is by serving their wives. The facts show that a healthy marriage benefits not only the individual couple but also the community as a whole. Studies prove that strong families are the most effective way to increase education levels, decrease poverty, and keep people away from violent behaviors. Communities with two-parent households also have lower crime rates and greater wealth.

Who knew that social justice hit so close to home? So close, in fact, that it might be best to call it "marriage justice." A strong marriage takes work, but the personal and societal benefits are great. And if you have friends going through some difficulties in their marriage, show some true social justice by reaching out to them and encouraging them to get the help they need to rebuild their relationship. It's one of the best investments you can make.

BOTTOM LINE

A happy wife doesn't just benefit her husband—she can ultimately benefit her community, as well. Marriage is about more than just you and your spouse.

Moment of Strength: Ecclesiastes 4:9

NEW STRENGTH

Even youths will become weak and tired, and young men will
fall in exhaustion. But those who trust in the LORD will find
new strength. They will soar high on wings like eagles. They
will run and not grow weary. They will walk and not faint.
Isaiah 40:30-31

ISAIAH 40:30-31 IS NOT ONLY a beautiful passage—one that is often framed or stitched—it's also an immensely useful one. When we're young, we can feel invincible at times. Yet even when we're young, we get tired. And then as young men, inexperienced and trying to make our way in the world, we sometimes stumble and fall. We experience failure. We discover that we don't have all of the answers and that we're not smart enough or strong enough to make life work on our own. But that's not a bad thing. The truth is that whatever stage of life we're in, we're not sufficient in ourselves but only in God. As we trust Him, we can soar above life's challenges.

Now consider Isaiah 40:25-29:

"To whom will you compare me? Who is my equal?" asks the Holy
One. Look up into the heavens. Who created all the stars? He brings
them out like an army, one after another, calling each by its name.
Because of his great power and incomparable strength, not a single
one is missing. O Jacob, how can you say the LORD does not see
your troubles? O Israel, how can you say God ignores your rights?
Have you never heard? Have you never understood? The LORD is the
everlasting God, the Creator of all the earth. He never grows weak
or weary. No one can measure the depths of his understanding. He
gives power to the weak and strength to the powerless.

This is the God we're asked to trust. Big, powerful, awesome. Worthy.

BOTTOM LINE
The better we know God, the easier it is to trust Him. Passages such as Isaiah
40 recalibrate our small thinking about God and boost our faith.

Moment of Strength: Isaiah 40

KINGDOM LIVING

Seek the Kingdom of God above all else, and live righteously,
and he will give you everything you need.
Matthew 6:33

DURING A TIME WHEN MOST families are struggling just to meet their monthly obligations, it's sometimes difficult to give a part of our income to the local church. For many, mortgage payments, car payments, utility bills, and food expenditures occupy most, if not all, of the monthly budget. Yet in Matthew 6, Jesus tells us not to worry about what we'll eat or drink or wear, but rather to put God first. Jesus is not speaking to independently wealthy stockbrokers here. He's speaking to impoverished people for whom the next meal was a consistent worry. What does this mean?

It means that God cares about our daily needs. In fact, in the rest of the passage, Jesus outlines just how much concern He gives to the important things that keep us up at night. He cares about where we'll find gas money and how we'll pay for our kids' textbooks. In fact, Jesus uses his concern for us as the basis for deeper levels of giving.

Jesus calls us to give when it hurts—giving when doing so may cause us to wonder how we'll get by. It is this kind of generosity that fuels our faith, that forces us to our knees in dependence on God, the creator and sustainer of life. Sustained, sacrificial giving is an act of worship and an acknowledgement that Christ is a caring, providing King.

BOTTOM LINE

God wants us to trust Him with our money. This can be a great test of faith for many of us. Pray that God will help you obey Him in this area.

Moment of Strength: Matthew 6

LESSONS FROM THE WILDERNESS

For everything there is a season, a time for every activity under heaven.
Ecclesiastes 3:1

ARE YOU TORN BETWEEN what you really want to do with your life and what you have to do to pay the bills? You are not alone. This is a real tension for many Christian men.

God has gifted each of us with unique talents, passions, and opportunities. If our hearts are in step with God's, it's okay to pursue this unique calling. But to get there, we may go through seasons of waiting, of frustration, of slogging through jobs we just don't like very much. Moses spent forty years in the wilderness. Joseph spent many years unjustly imprisoned. David used up almost two decades running from Saul.

Looking back, we know that each of these seasons was necessary for the growth and development of their leadership. And so it is with you. The difficult job you're enduring can teach you patience while providing for your family. So don't take your eye off the ball. Work hard to develop the character God will use when it's your turn to step into your calling.

Embrace each season as an opportunity from God. When the timing is right, He will not fail to move in our lives to put us in a place of maximum influence for His Kingdom. Our job is to listen to His voice, obey what we know to be true from His Word, and live our lives in radical service to those He has placed around us.

BOTTOM LINE

If you're not currently doing the kind of work you'd like to be doing, that doesn't necessarily mean that you've missed God's will. Be patient and prayerful.

Moment of Strength: Ecclesiastes 3

WHY MONDAY MATTERS TO GOD

Work willingly at whatever you do, as though you were
working for the Lord rather than for people.
Colossians 3:23

LET'S FACE IT. The average Christian working man doesn't get a paycheck from a Christian ministry, hasn't been to seminary, and is plying his trade in the secular marketplace. What's also probably true is that he often feels as if what he's doing is somehow less important than what happens on Sunday at church. Sometimes, Christian working men feel as if their Monday–to–Friday work is unimportant to God. But this is simply not true.

The Bible obliterates the false divide between secular and sacred work. Genesis essentially tells us that God was the first boss, giving Adam an assignment and a calling even before the Fall. Therefore, our work is not simply a means to make money and provide for our families. Nor do we go to work simply to be evangelists or to have a means to give money to the church. The work itself matters to God. To quote nineteenth-century Dutch theologian Abraham Kuyper, "There is not a square inch in the whole domain of our human existence over which Christ, who is Sovereign over *all*, does not cry: 'Mine!'"

Because the work itself matters to God, we should give our best to whatever vocation God has called us to. The sanctuary at church is not the only place where He exists. Your workplace is also His domain. And if you're currently looking for work, He is with you in that place, too. You will probably need to remind yourself of this truth over and over again.

BOTTOM LINE

Your work really does matter to God, and it matters to your neighbor, too.
Rejoice in that, and do your best for the glory of God.

Moment of Strength: Ecclesiastes 9:10

GOSPEL REENACTMENT

Submit to one another out of reverence for Christ.
Ephesians 5:21

WESTERN CULTURE HAS shaped our minds to believe that the purpose of the institution of marriage is to make individuals happy. People tend to believe that marriage is about finding the right person: a person whose likes and dislikes, hobbies and interests, match our own. We tend to believe it's about finding a person who completes us and makes us whole. This results in a *me* mind-set in marriage. We can foolishly enter into a marriage relationship focused on what we think we will get out of it.

In Ephesians 5, the apostle Paul tells us that marriage isn't about making ourselves happy; it's about making us holy. Marriage is a picture of how Jesus loves the church and gave Himself as a sacrifice for her (Ephesians 5:23, 25). Marriage isn't about *finding* the right person; it's about *being* the right person. Both husband and wife are called to be the type of people who love unconditionally, forgive continually, and serve sacrificially—just like Jesus.

Paul calls us to enter into marriage with a ministry mind-set. Marriage isn't about what you can get out of the relationship but about what you can give to the relationship for God's glory. When you seek to demonstrate love in your marriage, when you are willing to lay down your life for your spouse and serve her sacrificially, the gospel is rehearsed daily in your household.

BOTTOM LINE
Marriage is about having a ministry mind-set of loving service rather than a selfish mind-set.

Moment of Strength: Ephesians 5:21-33

KIDS OF THE KINGDOM

Jesus called for the children and said to the disciples,
"Let the children come to me. Don't stop them!
For the Kingdom of God belongs to those who are like these children."
Luke 18:16

YOU'RE ON THE CLOCK EVERY DAY, starting when your feet hit the floor in the morning, and you don't clock out until your head hits the pillow at night. Even then, you're constantly "on call." You could be needed at any moment throughout the night. There are no days off, and there's no pay. This is the job of a parent.

Because of the demands children make on their parents, it's sometimes easy to see our children as a distraction to the things that we want or need to accomplish. In Luke 18, parents were bringing their children to Jesus so that He would bless them, but the disciples rebuked them. They saw the children as a distraction from the "real work" that Jesus was doing.

Jesus saw this encounter in a different light. He recognized that children can teach us what it looks like to live in the Kingdom of God. Children live in a state of dependence. To make it from day to day, they have to put their confidence in their parents to provide and care for them. That's why Jesus says, "The Kingdom of God belongs to those who are like these children"—it belongs to dependent people. As children of God, we are called to trust Him to provide what we need. In those moments when your children seem like a distraction, remember that God has put them in your life as a blessing and a reminder that He knows what you need because you are His child.

BOTTOM LINE

Children are a gift from God and a reminder to us to walk by dependent faith.

Moment of Strength: Luke 18:15-17

NOT A BIG DEAL

The person who keeps all of the laws except one is as guilty as a person who has broken all of God's laws.

James 2:10

BIG SINS USUALLY GROW OUT OF SMALL SINS. A movie here, a website there, an inappropriate joke, fudging the numbers—our choices may seem harmless at the time, but they create a pattern, a slippery slope, and sin tends to escalate over time. Too often, we lose the battle against sin from the start because we underestimate its danger and damage. We let little things creep up, and we make excuses such as "It's not that big a deal." Before long, our spiritual vision can become blurred so that we don't recognize sin as sin.

The truth is, every sin—even a small one—is dangerous. Simple math reveals that if, instead of walking a perfectly straight line, you stray a mere one inch for every ten feet of travel and continue on that course for a day's walk, you'll wind up about a quarter mile from your intended destination. And that's just one day's walk. Continue on that path day after day and you'll find yourself in a different state, not just a different zip code.

The point is, excusing or failing to deal with sin can establish patterns that become destructive. Not only does it affect our character and our witness, it creates a barrier between us and God. Right now, prayerfully ask God to show you where you're stepping off His path, and then take the courageous step of committing, with His help, to walk the path of obedience.

BOTTOM LINE

Small compromises can be as dangerous as blatant sins because they can go unnoticed. Don't miss the opportunity to make adjustments while you can.

Moment of Strength: Proverbs 3:6

BOY, THAT'S TEMPTING

Pray that you will not give in to temptation.

Luke 22:40

THE BEST WAY TO OVERCOME the temptations we face every day is to fix our eyes on Jesus, our Master. When we rely on our own resolve to keep from sinning, we can hold out only for so long. Eventually, we cave in to temptation and find ourselves repeating the same sins we've fallen into so many times before. Thankfully, God's grace doesn't depend on our getting it right. Better yet, God doesn't leave us to try to be holy on our own. The strength we need to escape temptation comes from Him.

Perhaps the first step in dealing with a weakness or temptation is to take it seriously. That means not overestimating ourselves. Then we should take the matter to God, read His Word for guidance, pray, and write down what He brings to mind. Don't be too quick to dismiss what comes to mind, even if it seems radical. It can be tempting to talk ourselves out of taking action when the source of temptation (e.g., food, our computers, or money) also serves a beneficial and necessary purpose. But God knows what's best for us, and often that involves a sacrifice or inconvenience.

It takes a humble man of faith to value his relationship with God over the temporary pleasures of sin. Ask God to give you strength and faith to fight temptation and win.

BOTTOM LINE

God wants to help us escape what tempts us. Pray and then take action as He directs.

Moment of Strength: Hebrews 2:18

OBLIGATION TO SPEAK UP

Suppose someone secretly entices you—even your brother,
your son or daughter, your beloved wife, or your closest friend—
and says, "Let us go worship other gods"—gods that neither you
nor your ancestors have known. . . . Do not give in or listen.
Deuteronomy 13:6, 8

IF A STRANGER TEMPTS US TO do something wrong, we're usually not compelled to participate, and there's usually no real fallout if we say no. But it gets messy when it's a good friend or family member who's tempting us. Even if we don't give in, we tend to excuse or overlook the sin in those we love, thinking that we're being loyal and loving to them.

In 2 Chronicles 20:31-32, we have the example of Jehoshaphat, who "did what was pleasing in the LORD's sight" but who didn't deal with the sin in other people (signified by the high places where they worshiped idols and false gods). The result was a nation that continued into deeper sin, ultimately bringing severe punishment from God. Jehoshaphat's role as head of the nation included confessing sin and taking decisive action to deal with it. The same is true for us as husbands and fathers and friends.

When Jesus was told that His mother and brothers had come to see Him, He took that opportunity to redefine what true family is: "Anyone who does the will of my Father in heaven is my brother and sister and mother" (Matthew 12:50). Jesus understands that we might face opposition from those closest to us, but He challenges us to take action anyway. Loving others includes graciously confronting them when necessary in the hope that they will repent and walk according to God's will.

BOTTOM LINE

With humble, prayerful hearts, we should confront the sin we see in others for their own benefit, as God leads us to do so.

Moment of Strength: Luke 12:49-53

OUT-REPENTING YOUR WIFE

Instead, be kind to each other, tenderhearted, forgiving one another,
just as God through Christ has forgiven you.
Ephesians 4:32

CRAIG AND HIS WIFE, MICHELLE, had been at an all-too-familiar impasse for the past three days after a heated verbal exchange erupted over their individual spending habits. While a part of Craig wanted Michelle to admit she was wrong and he was right, deep down he knew that at least part of what she had said about his spending was true. Craig finally decided he was willing to humble himself, go to Michelle, take responsibility for his irresponsible spending, and seek forgiveness for the harsh tone and defensive posture he had taken with her during their argument.

In marriage, it's easy to try to minimize our own sin while we magnify our spouse's shortcomings. This often creates a culture where every action and reaction is quietly scored and used to determine which spouse is "ahead" at any given moment. The cumulative effect of years of living in this culture is that we become more focused on getting ahead at any and all costs than on pursuing our wife's heart. God's desire is that we learn to out-repent her instead of trying to outperform her.

An amazing thing about marriage is that God can actually use our spouse's sin to uncover ours. We don't get a pass with a sinful response to our spouse's shortcomings. A healthy marriage is one in which both spouses are free to own their brokenness, weaknesses, and desperate need for a Savior.

BOTTOM LINE

God changes us in community with other people, and there is no closer
community than husband and wife.

Moment of Strength: John 15:12

THE PRIVILEGE OF PRAYER

Never stop praying.
1 Thessalonians 5:17

PRAYER MAY BE ONE OF the biggest challenges Christian men face. Our world demands that we be constantly busy. We scarcely have time for quiet hours of thinking, meditation, or talking to God. We don't have time to sit on the front porch swing and reflect on life. We may not even have a front porch—much less a swing!

Still, the Bible clearly commands us to pray—and not just to pray, but to pray constantly. So let's resolve to start doing it. First, make a list of people and situations you could pray about: your family, a buddy who lost his job, the family whose home is being repossessed, your pastor and church, your workplace, a family friend with cancer, world and national affairs, your local community, or your child's schoolteacher. The list can get long very quickly.

There are at least a couple of different ways to approach prayer. First, pray as a part of whatever you're doing. Pray while you're driving, working, exercising, doing yard work, etc. It takes only a few seconds to say a quick prayer before and during any activity.

Second, set aside time for focused prayer. Be intentional and consistent with this dedicated prayer time. There's no substitute for spending time with God. Practiced together, these two approaches can greatly improve your prayer life and intimacy with God.

BOTTOM LINE

Make sure that you're intentionally cultivating your prayer life. It's a great privilege!

Moment of Strength: Matthew 6:5-13

COURAGE WHEN IT'S TOUGH

From six disasters he will rescue you; even in the seventh,
he will keep you from evil. He will save you from death in
time of famine, from the power of the sword in time of war.
Job 5:19-20

"MEN TODAY ARE facing incredible adversity," says evangelist Phil Waldrep. "They are losing their jobs, their houses, some are losing their wives to death or infidelity. Some men feel they have lost everything."

Have you ever been in those shoes? Are you there now—or do you have a friend who is? The Old Testament book of Job gives us a sterling example to follow when we think we've lost it all, including any hope for recovery. Job was a man who indeed lost everything, yet he stayed faithful to God.

Even when doubt, fear, or loss challenges our faith, we can count on the reality that God never changes. He cares, He knows our hurts, and He want us to turn to Him. Just reminding ourselves that God loves us should restore a measure of peace and assurance, no matter how bad things get. When you're suffering, think about Job. Even though Job's wife had urged him to curse God and even though his friends turned against him, Job remained faithful. Why? Because he knew that God would be faithful. Be sure to read the end of Job's story, where God restores his family and his wealth.

Even in seasons of great loss, we can remain faithful—by the grace of God. If you're going through a tough time, lean hard on your heavenly Father for strength and hope.

BOTTOM LINE

When your world falls apart, it's okay to ask questions and to feel pain. But it's also the best time to remember that God is always faithful.

Moment of Strength: Job 5:8-24

A MAN OF UNDERSTANDING

Paul also wrote to you with the wisdom God gave him . . .
[but] some of his comments are hard to understand.
2 Peter 3:15-16

HAVE YOU EVER READ something in the Bible that you didn't understand? Maybe it was a passage in the Old Testament about war, or something apocalyptic from the book of Revelation. Whatever the case, you're in good company. In 2 Peter 3:15-16, the apostle Peter acknowledges that many people don't understand everything Paul has written in his letters.

The Bible has always been challenged by those who don't understand it, but it seems that the critiques have increased dramatically in our country lately, chipping away at the faith of some. And some people turn away from their faith and deny the Lord because they come across a passage of Scripture that is difficult to understand or even contrary to what they had previously believed.

But think about it: Do you stop loving people just because you don't fully understand them? You probably wouldn't stay married for very long if that were the case. Peter advises us to take God's patience as our cue and to trust that if He wants us to understand something in His Word, He will make it plain to us in His time.

Because God's ways are higher than our ways (Isaiah 55:8-9), it is certain that we will die without knowing all the answers to our questions about Him. We will leave the earth without understanding everything God has said. But in the meantime, let's pursue a deeper and a fuller love for our Savior and trust Him with the things we don't quite understand.

BOTTOM LINE

Practice your Faith ABCs: Admit that God's ways are greater than yours, Believe His Word, and Commit to loving Him despite what you don't understand.

Moment of Strength: 2 Peter 3:14-18

DRIFTWOOD

We must listen very carefully to the truth we have heard,
or we may drift away from it.
Hebrews 2:1

IT'S DOUBTFUL THAT we'll wake up one morning and decide to abandon our faith or commit an atrocious sin. But little by little, our decisions can lead us to slowly drift away from our faith. And the sin we think we'll never commit may become a real possibility down the road if we continue to drift.

The writer of Hebrews says it becomes increasingly important to pay attention to God's Word. Life really is all about Jesus and following Him. But when we make life all about *us*, we will begin to drift, because Jesus now has competition for our affections. When we decide to make ourselves the central character in our lives, it always leads to drifting.

Neglecting the Bible is often both a cause and a symptom of drifting. You may start to think, *I've read that before, heard that before, and studied that before, and I already know it*. And though you may not feel a violent undercurrent, you've begun to break away from the structure and foundation of your faith.

Prayerfully invite a Christian buddy to ask you the tough questions about your thought life, your financial habits, and your time alone in prayer and in the Word. Ask your friend to help you discover any currents in your life that are leading you to drift away. Then thank your friend for speaking the truth in love, and thank God that He rescues and repurposes driftwood of all kinds.

BOTTOM LINE

It's so easy to drift and so easy to ignore it for a time. But though we can sometimes drift, it is never too late to repent and refocus on God and His will.

Moment of Strength: 1 Corinthians 10:11-13

PARKING LOT PERMANENCE

May the Lord our God show us his approval and make our efforts successful.
Yes, make our efforts successful!
Psalm 90:17

BORN WITH A SILVER SPOON IN HIS MOUTH, Richard, the Duke of Gloucester, had untold wealth and privilege. He was eventually crowned as King Richard III of England, but he later lost his life in a decisive battle in the Wars of the Roses. He was buried without honor, his grave unmarked for more than five centuries. In 2012, his remains were discovered beneath a parking lot, buried among the commoners of his day.

Both pauper and potentate come to the same end. No matter how the world sees you, your power is extremely limited, and your clock is ticking. You may have worked hard to establish your own paradise here on earth. But it is all fleeting, and once you are gone, you will have no control over how people remember you.

The key is to live in light of eternity, because only what is done for Christ will last. King Solomon writes in Ecclesiastes 1:11, "We don't remember what happened in the past, and in future generations, no one will remember what we are doing now." What will be your legacy? What message would you want to shout from beneath the asphalt pavement? Only God can establish permanence in the work of our hands, so put your life in His good and faithful hands. A legacy of faith is the result of living under His lordship.

BOTTOM LINE

Ask God to lead you into work that has eternal significance.

Moment of Strength: Ecclesiastes 11:8-9

JULY 22

PROFIT WITH A PURPOSE

The Scripture says, "You must not muzzle an ox to keep it
from eating as it treads out the grain." And in another place,
"Those who work deserve their pay!"
1 Timothy 5:18

ONE OF THE BIGGEST MISCONCEPTIONS in contemporary culture, even among many Christians, is that there is something inherently evil in turning a profit. The Bible warns against making wealth an idol (1 Timothy 6:10), but it doesn't discourage the responsible accumulation of wealth by God's people.

Scripture may not make a clear case for capitalism, but it is apparent that some capitalist principles are rooted in a biblical worldview. For instance, Scripture encourages us to work hard for honest wages (2 Thessalonians 3:10; 1 Timothy 5:18); to create goods that enrich others (Proverb 11:25); to buy and sell and make a profit (Proverbs 31:16-24; Leviticus 25:14); and to responsibly invest our resources (Luke 19:11-26; Proverbs 11:24). We're also told to support our families (1 Timothy 5:8).

Wealth, like any of God's good gifts, can easily become an idol, hence the many warnings against a full-fledged pursuit of money at the expense of a life focused on knowing God. Materialism and greed can sap our spiritual life (1 Timothy 6:17-18). Indifference to the poor is a denial of the gospel (James 2:14-20). So we should hold our wealth loosely, but we shouldn't feel bad if hard work and thrift result in financial gain. We can prayerfully use that gain to bless our family and give to others.

BOTTOM LINE
It's not a sin to have wealth. It's a sin for wealth to have you.

Moment of Strength: 1 Timothy 6:17-18

NEW LIFE

Go and sin no more.
John 8:11

THE STORY OF HOW Jesus treated an adulterous woman is one of many amazing examples of forgiveness and redemption in the Bible. The woman was guilty; she was actually caught in the act of adultery. But not only did Jesus save her from being stoned to death, but He also declined to condemn her for living the kind of life she had been living.

It's not hard to imagine the woman as she left the area that day, a happy and relieved smile spreading across her tear-streaked face. With that redemption came a responsibility. Jesus didn't give her a free pass to keep acting as she pleased. Her life had been saved, and she was free to live a new life now.

Don't make the mistake of using your faith in Jesus as a get-out-of-jail-free card. Forgiveness is not a license to keep sinning. Although your debt has already been paid by God's grace, don't keep piling up charges.

More than two thousand years later, the lesson of the woman caught in adultery still resonates with us. She was given a new lease on life from the author of life Himself. And rather than see her go right back to living the way she had been, He invited her to live the life of a cleansed, forgiven, free-from-condemnation woman. God's grace not only covers our sin; it also enables us to live a whole new life of joyful obedience.

BOTTOM LINE

As forgiven Christians, we're free from the shackles of sin. It's up to us not to put them right back on again.

Moment of Strength: John 3:16-18

BE ON GUARD

Beware! Guard against every kind of greed.
Life is not measured by how much you own.
Luke 12:15

IN THE GOSPELS, Jesus gives more warnings about the deceitfulness of money than the destruction of adultery. Why? Perhaps it's because the deceitfulness of wealth is more subtle than sexual sin. A man who is having an affair is very aware of his actions and sin, even though he may try to justify his actions. If he's honest, he'll know how he got there. With wealth it's different. Greed has a subtle way of telling us that we always need more, and it has the ability to justify the desire for more. *It's for the family. I've worked hard for this. I deserve it.*

The parable Jesus tells in Luke 12 makes the point that pursuing riches with no regard for God is a bad idea. Wealth isn't necessarily a bad thing—Jesus never said that money in and of itself is bad—but He does warn us to be on our guard because it's so easy to transfer our confidence and security from God to the money in our bank accounts.

We can prevent this from happening by seeing all of our money as God's money to be stewarded for His glory. We must remember that it is God who has given us what we have. Near the end of this section, Jesus says, "Wherever your treasure is, there the desires of your heart will also be" (Luke 12:34). If our wealth is our treasure, we will hoard it for ourselves. But if God's Kingdom is our treasure, we will hold our wealth with open hands.

BOTTOM LINE

Money for money's sake is fruitless and ultimately empty. Money for God's sake is a means to His glory.

Moment of Strength: Luke 12:13-34

ENDURING TRIALS

The temptations in your life are no different from what others experience. And God is faithful. He will not allow the temptation to be more than you can stand. When you are tempted, he will show you a way out so that you can endure.

1 Corinthians 10:13

WHEN YOU GO THROUGH DARK TIMES, it's easy to imagine that no one else can understand and that no one has ever suffered like you. Yet the apostle Paul—a man beaten and imprisoned for his faith—could declare that trials are trials and that somebody has already victoriously gone through whatever you are facing. The exact details may not be the same, but the core experience is: the feeling of loss, the agony of separation, the humiliation of failure, the anger at injustice, the heartbreak of broken relationships, the frustration of loneliness, the emptiness of grief, the pain of illness and disease. In a fallen world, this is our common lot. You're not the first person to walk a path of suffering.

God knows exactly what you can bear. He is faithful. He lives within you to give you strength (Philippians 4:13). He comforts you in your sorrows (2 Corinthians 1:4). His grace is sufficient (2 Corinthians 12:9). If you bear your trials with confidence in God's goodness and power, your heart will find peace. You will be able to step through your heavenly escape hatch, bloodied but not beaten.

Self-pity, bitterness, lashing out, or giving up are signs of a temper tantrum against God. Don't let yourself go there. Fight to take every thought captive to obey Christ (2 Corinthians 10:5). Depend on His grace to sustain you in the tough times. He will come through for you. He is faithful.

BOTTOM LINE

Whatever you're going through, you can handle it with dignity and grace through the power of Christ in you.

Moment of Strength: James 5:10-11

EXCUSES, EXCUSES

But they all began making excuses.

Luke 14:18

REMEMBER THE GIRL IN high school who didn't want to go out with you but was too nice to come out and say it? She had all kinds of excuses. The more reasons she came up with, the more determined you became to overcome them. Then she really lowered the boom. She thought of you like a brother!

All these years later, we're still surrounded by reasons why something can't be done. Some are valid, and some are not. Kids have excuses for not cleaning their rooms. We have excuses not to mow the yard or help with the dishes, and the list goes on.

We also might make excuses when it comes to helping out at church. We're too busy. We're not gifted in that area. The kids are in sports. We've never done that before. We wouldn't be very good at it. It's perfectly acceptable to want to serve in areas where we're gifted, and trying something new won't earn us points with God. But sometimes it's great to get out of our comfort zone a little bit.

The key here is a willingness to serve if you possibly can. What are you good at? If you're the creative sort, prayerfully consider helping out with the church website or newsletter. If you're an organizer, there are bound to be all kinds of committees that would love to have your help. Do you love kids? Help out in the nursery or with the student ministry. Just go for it, wherever opportunity and ability meet.

BOTTOM LINE

Ask God where He wants you to serve in your church and for His Kingdom.

Moment of Strength: Luke 14:16-24

HIDDEN TREASURE

Wherever your treasure is, there the desires of your heart will also be.
Luke 12:34

JESUS TALKED A LOT about treasure. He said if we find hidden treasure in a field—the Kingdom of Heaven (Matthew 13:44)—we should sell everything to buy the field. He said to store our treasure in heaven, because earthly treasure doesn't last (Luke 12:33). Jesus knew that our hearts will follow our treasure. We pursue and are passionate about what we value. When we store up treasures in heaven, our hearts are there (Luke 12:34).

Our hearts should be focused on heaven. Our relationship with God is our first priority. But right after our relationship with God, we should treasure our wives.

By consciously storing up treasure in your wife, your heart will grow closer to hers. But "storing up" takes action. Look for the gems in your relationship. What's most precious to you about your wife? How can you show her what she means to you? Even if you've known your wife for decades, there's still plenty to explore and discover. When you find these relational gems, polish them. Make them brighter and more valuable. Tell her often what you appreciate about her. Be as specific and sincere as possible. Let her know that you treasure her and that she is valuable to you. As you seek to understand, value, and store up treasure in your wife, you'll better appreciate the precious gem you have in her.

BOTTOM LINE

How can you treat your wife more like the treasure she is? Do it, and watch your heart grow closer to hers.

Moment of Strength: Proverbs 31:10-12

BROKEN FOR HIS GLORY

"It was not because of his sins or his parents' sins," Jesus answered.
"This happened so the power of God could be seen in him."
John 9:3

NICK VUJICIC IS a public speaker and author. In the last decade, he has spoken to more than 3 million people in more than twenty-four countries on five continents, challenging audiences to live life to the fullest and embrace the gospel of Jesus Christ. But Nick almost gave up on life at the tender age of ten years old.

You see, Nick was born with Tetra-Amelia Syndrome, and he has no arms or legs. When he was a child, the taunts he received at school so depressed him that he tried to drown himself in the bathtub. But then Nick met Jesus and discovered that God loves him and has a special purpose for his life. Now he travels the world, sharing Jesus' love with everyone he meets.

In the ancient world, people born with disabilities were considered cursed by God because of their sin. In John's Gospel, Jesus confronts this worldview (John 9). Our challenges are not divine accidents, and they're not punishments; instead, they are a means of displaying God's power. As the apostle Paul discovered in his own life, "[Christ's] power is perfected in weakness" (2 Corinthians 12:9, HCSB).

Have you considered that God may be using your unique challenges to make Himself known to the people around you? Like Nick Vujicic, you may discover that an obstacle you've been trying to overcome may be the very thing God uses to accomplish His purpose in your life.

BOTTOM LINE

God's glory shines through weakness, so let your brokenness be bright.

Moment of Strength: 2 Corinthians 12:7-10

DON'T QUIT YOUR DAY JOB!

Each of you, dear brothers and sisters, should remain as
you were when God first called you.
1 Corinthians 7:24

MANY YEARS AGO, a young man was interviewed for a job with an internationally recognized ministry. The interview went well, and as it was wrapping up, the hiring manager asked him if he'd be willing to commit to work for one year. He responded, "I go wherever the Lord calls me, so I can't commit even for one week."

As it turned out, the young man ended up working for that ministry for more than twenty-five years! Though we tend to believe God's calling on our life will be like Abram's or Paul's—to a new place or to a new line of work—God often calls us to stay put, right where He has placed us.

When Paul wrote to the believers in Corinth, many expected that God would call them to something new now that they had come to know Jesus. Instead, Paul says that they "remain as [they] were when God first called [them]." For the moment, they were exactly where God wanted them to be.

You may not think that you're where you should be, but God can provide opportunities to minister to others through your job, your location, and even your daily routine. The entire universe is in God's control—from the migration patterns of birds to the prosperity of nations. At least for the time being, you can prayerfully seek opportunities to make an impact for the Kingdom right where you are.

BOTTOM LINE

Be sensitive to God's calling, but don't forget your calling to follow Him right now, right where you are.

Moment of Strength: Isaiah 46:10

WHAT DO YOU HAVE?

"What can I do to help you?" Elisha asked. "Tell me, what do you have in the house?" "Nothing at all, except a flask of olive oil," she replied.

2 Kings 4:2

HER HUSBAND HAD DIED, leaving her with a massive debt and no means to pay it back. Her husband's creditors were threatening to take away her two sons and make them slaves. So when she came to the prophet Elisha for help, she was looking for a miracle. And through Elisha, God did indeed perform a miracle in this widow's life. He multiplied the leftover oil in the bottom of a jar so that it filled every jar she and her neighbors could spare. The money she would be able to earn from the sale of the oil would pay off the debt, leaving her and her sons with money to live on (2 Kings 4:1-7).

When money is tight, it's easy to focus on what we don't have. But what about what we do have? That's where Elisha started. The poor woman had a few drops of oil and faith in God.

The widow probably didn't think much of her nearly empty oil jar. But in God's hands, it became more than enough. We, too, have been given gifts from God—talents, skills, and even assets that we may not think much of. God can provide for our needs, but it may be that He wants to work through the gifts He has already given us. Often they're a lot more than we think.

Are you offering what you have to God? Are you thankful for what you have? God can take whatever you have and turn it into a lot.

BOTTOM LINE

No doubt you have gifts from God. Offer them up, and see God use them to provide for your needs.

Moment of Strength: Matthew 6:25-34

INVESTING TIME

Husbands, love your wives and never treat them harshly.
Colossians 3:19

WADE WAS SO THANKFUL that he and his wife, Miranda, had scheduled a weekend getaway to the mountains. Three children, two jobs, and volunteer commitments hadn't left much time for them as a couple lately. The retreat helped them to reconnect emotionally and talk about things of substance.

We may have felt as if we married our soul mate, but unfortunately, many couples end up with nothing more than a roommate after a few years of marriage. With the demands of our careers, school, kids' activities, church responsibilities, and so on, pursuing intimacy seldom is an urgent priority like a deadline at work or getting kids to an event on time. Even if our marriage is not in immediate jeopardy, are we simply "getting along" as a couple, or are we experiencing the intimacy we long for?

Most couples work on their marriage during leftover time between events and obligations. Many marriage experts recommend at least a quarterly getaway without the kids: a day trip, a weekend outing, or a long night out. But instead of this time being spent as a regular date, this time could be reserved for asking the tough questions, assessing our roles as husband and wife, as father and mother, as lovers, etc.

When was the last time you and your wife planned a time to discuss the health of your marriage?

BOTTOM LINE

To have the intimacy we desire in marriage, we must be intentional with our time.

Moment of Strength: Proverbs 18:22

TRUSTING GOD WITH YOUR KIDS

*Timothy, my dear son, be strong through the grace
that God gives you in Christ Jesus.*
2 Timothy 2:1

WARREN COULD NOT BELIEVE that his daughter was graduating and would be leaving home next month. It seemed such a short time ago that he and his wife, Marcie, had brought home this beautiful bundle of needs from the hospital. And now, here she was—all grown up. Lately, Warren had found himself worrying about whether he had properly prepared his daughter for the rest of her life. *Who will protect her? Will she have enough money? Will she marry the right guy? Will people take advantage of her?* Once the questions started, they were endless as he realized that he had absolutely no control over her future.

Questions like these, especially at times of transition when we feel as if we are out of time, can cause fathers great anxiety. The responsibilities that come with being a dad—protector, provider, teacher, nurturer—can be overwhelming, especially when we beat ourselves up over past mistakes or how we could have done better. But in these times of worry and anxiety, we must remind ourselves that our children have a perfect Father who is always with them to protect, provide, instruct, and nurture. This knowledge allows us to confidently release our children into their future, trusting that God is good and will never abandon them.

BOTTOM LINE

Your children's future is in God's hands and is not wholly dependent on how well you parented them.

Moment of Strength: Philippians 4:6

COMING AS A CHILD

Let the children come to me. Don't stop them!
For the Kingdom of God belongs to those who are like these children.
Luke 18:16

JACOB WAS TERRIFIED AS he looked at the imposing letter. Things were already tight financially, and now he was being told that he owed more than $7,000 in back taxes. His first thought went to the money he had lost that year in a risky investment. Was this God's punishment for his irresponsibility? Jacob had spent hours beating himself up over that deal, and now all those feelings of self-loathing and inadequacy came rushing back.

"How can I pray and ask God for help when it was my irresponsibility that created the problem?" Jacob muttered.

It is tempting to believe that God expects us to be completely responsible, self-sufficient adults who need Him only when we have exhausted all other options. But nothing could be further from the truth. In today's verse, Jesus doesn't tell the crowd that they enter the Kingdom of God as self-sufficient, responsible adults who have no needs. Rather, He says, we're to come as little children.

Infants are completely dependent on others for their well-being. The basic necessities that sustain life—food, water, and shelter—must be provided by others. Even when infants sleep, they must be monitored. Though it may be hard, especially for men, to admit we are needy, it is what God desires. And it is our reality as dependent, created people made in God's image. We need Him for everything.

BOTTOM LINE

There's no shame in childlike, dependent faith. In fact, that's the kind of faith Jesus is looking for from us.

Moment of Strength: John 15:5

SIMPLE KINDNESS

The generous will prosper;
those who refresh others will themselves be refreshed.
Proverbs 11:25

THERE ARE AS MANY WAYS TO show simple kindnesses as there are stars in the sky. A soldier and his mother are behind you in line for the cashier at the restaurant, and when they get to the cashier, you've already taken care of their bill. In the parking lot of the grocery store, you offer to take an elderly lady's cart back inside. You decide to visit a fellow church member who's been going through a rough spell. You have a basketful of groceries, and you allow someone with a carton of milk to go ahead of you in line. It can be as simple as holding a door open for someone.

Kindness doesn't have to be a major production. More often than not, there's no need for planning, strategy, or committee meetings. Some of the most sincere kindnesses take place at the spur of the moment. You see a chance to do something nice, and you take it! Pray that the Holy Spirit will give you eyes to see, and He will. Kindness and goodness are part of the fruit of the Spirit (Galatians 5:22-23).

The key here is simple. It may be easy to put money in the offering plate on Sunday, but it's the attitude behind the gift that's truly important. A truly generous heart seeks to do for others without any desire for recognition whatsoever, and it's not just a once-in-a-while thing, either. It's 24/7/365.

BOTTOM LINE

Whether the kindness is big or small, it's the heart behind it that truly counts.

Moment of Strength: 2 Corinthians 9:6-8

IT'S SIMPLE, BUT NOT EASY

*One day Jesus told his disciples a story to show that
they should always pray and never give up.*
Luke 18:1

IN LUKE 18:1-8, Jesus tells the parable of the persistent widow. A fitting summary might go something like this: "An unjust judge finally gives in to a lady's annoying requests so that she'll leave him alone and he can get on with his life." It may not be a lovely story, but it's effective. Jesus tells us that if a man like this unjust judge, who doesn't "fear God or care about people" (Luke 18:4), can be worn down by a woman's requests, then God, who is not unjust and who is our loving heavenly Father, will certainly answer our persistent prayers. Jesus adds, "I tell you, he will grant justice to them quickly!" (Luke 18:8).

Great news, right? We keep praying, and God is supposed to answer quickly. That's what you might think Jesus is saying. But that interpretation raises a question: Why should we have to keep praying (and not become discouraged) if God *quickly* grants us justice (or whatever it is we need)? Perhaps our definition of *quickly* and God's are not the same. It's probably best for us to focus on the need for *persistence* rather than on the timing of God's answer. Otherwise, there's a good chance we will become discouraged. So what's the takeaway from the parable? In the words of Winston Churchill, "Never give in, never, never, never." Keep praying and trust God to answer in His perfect way and timing.

BOTTOM LINE

Prayer may be simple, but it isn't easy. It's good, though—not just for receiving what God gives us but also for growing our relationship with Him.

Moment of Strength: Luke 18:1-8

FORGETTING WHAT IS BEHIND

I focus on this one thing: Forgetting the past and looking
forward to what lies ahead, I press on to reach the end
of the race and receive the heavenly prize for which God,
through Christ Jesus, is calling us.
Philippians 3:13-14

LEARNING FROM THE PAST, remembering God's faithfulness—these are good things to do. But dwelling on mistakes we've made and living with constant regrets about the past generally has very little value. We can't change the past, no matter how much we think about it. Regrets tend to diminish our current experience of life and make us afraid of the future.

The apostle Paul had a lot in his past that was regrettable. In 1 Corinthians 15:9-10 he says, "For I am the least of all the apostles. In fact, I'm not even worthy to be called an apostle after the way I persecuted God's church. But whatever I am now, it is all because God poured out his special favor on me—and not without results."

What a great perspective!

Paul had persecuted the church. It doesn't get much worse than that. He could easily have allowed his horrible past to keep him from pursuing God's call on his life. (Satan would have liked that.) Instead, Paul readily admitted that he was "not even worthy to be called an apostle," and he didn't let it bother him. He chose to focus on God's grace, not on his own failings, and the result was that he lived an incredibly fruitful life for God.

Are you punishing yourself for past mistakes? Technically, we can't forgive ourselves, because our offenses are against God, but it certainly doesn't make sense to beat ourselves up for what God has forgiven. By God's grace, let go of your regrets.

BOTTOM LINE

Holding on to regrets can seem humble, but it doesn't do anyone any good. It keeps you focused on yourself instead of on God and others.

Moment of Strength: Psalm 103:12

ADVANCE DECISION-MAKING

Don't lust for her beauty. Don't let her coy glances seduce you.

Proverbs 6:25

FREDERICK BUECHNER DESCRIBES lust as "the ape that gibbers in our loins. Tame him as we will by day—he rages all the wilder in our dreams by night. Just when we think we're safe from him, he raises up his ugly head and smirks." Lust has been called the athlete's foot of the mind—an insatiable itch. Bill Hybels writes,

> Lust is taking a complete, complex human being, made in the image of God, and reducing him or her to just a body dedicated to the gratification of the luster's sexual desires. A person caught up in lust doesn't care about the other person's thoughts, feelings, spiritual condition, worries, anxieties, or aspirations. Lust is fundamentally self-seeking and completely devoid of love.

In Proverbs 6:25, King Solomon advises, "Don't lust." But how? Winning the war with lust involves making a commitment when we are strong as to what we will do before we become weak and vulnerable to the powerful forces of sexual temptation.

Seventeenth-century theologian François Fénelon writes, "We are not masters of our own *feeling*, but we are by God's Grace masters of our *consent*." In other words, we can control what we allow ourselves to be exposed to. We can choose to plan ahead. We can choose a path of wisdom that leads us away from temptation. When it comes to lust, the best time to make that choice is far ahead of time—not in the moment of temptation.

BOTTOM LINE

Decide in advance to live according to God's standards.

Moment of Strength: James 1:5

BEWARE OF SEDUCTIVE WORDS

*For the lips of an immoral woman are as sweet as honey, and
her mouth is smoother than oil.*

Proverbs 5:3

MIKE HAD BEEN STRUGGLING with the question of identity. For all of his bravado on the outside, he was weak and insecure on the inside. He needed someone to pat him on the back; kiss him on the cheek; and tell him how good he was, how good-looking he was, how wonderful, great, strong, and powerful he was. He found that someone seated in the restaurant booth next to his as he was eating alone while his wife was out of town. The conversation got out of hand and eventually led to a rendezvous in a motel room. This meeting led to another and another until it became a full-blown affair.

Benjamin Disraeli was correct: "Talk to a man about himself and he will listen for hours." Mike listened, and it cost him dearly—his self-respect, his happiness, and his marriage. If only he had heeded Solomon's advice.

The immoral woman that Solomon writes about in Proverbs understands men's longings. She uses her speech to flatter, engage, and ambush unknowing victims. Many a man has fallen prey to smooth talk and flattering speech. Beware of deceptive speech, inappropriate conversation, exaggerated compliments, and coarse jokes. When your warning antenna goes up with the soft touch and the flattering words of a woman who is not your wife, pay attention. Those words may lead to destruction.

BOTTOM LINE

Sexual sin often begins with unwise conversation. Always be on your guard.

Moment of Strength: Proverbs 7:21

CONSIDER THE CONSEQUENCES

In the end she's as bitter as wormwood and as sharp as a double-edged sword. Her feet go down to death; her steps head straight for Sheol.

Proverbs 5:4-5, HCSB

AFTER A CHRISTIAN LEADER HAD an affair, he said: "If only I had considered the cost this relationship would have on my family, my career, my witness, and my reputation, I would not have done it."

Perhaps before you venture down that same path, you should stop and weigh the long-term penalties. Adultery tries to cancel tomorrow's consequences by emphasizing today's delights. But it always costs more than you think. Adultery demands a toll, and the price is high.

Adultery will cost you your closest relationships. Consider the hurt and pain it will inflict on your wife and family. It will also hurt your relationship with God. Adultery can cost you your strength. You will end up weak and worn out through your deceit and cover-ups. Adultery may cost you your money. You could end up spending a great deal of money on legal expenses if your marriage ends in divorce. Adultery can negatively affect your health. Long before people heard of chlamydia, syphilis, hepatitis, HIV, or AIDS, Solomon warned that those who commit adultery experience consequences "as bitter as wormwood." Adultery will cost you your reputation and destroy your Christian witness. You will lose respect and trust. In the end your sin will find you out. Minutes of gratification can cause a lifetime of pain.

BOTTOM LINE

Before you cross the line into sin, weigh the cost—and then don't cross the line!

Moment of Strength: Proverbs 6:27-29

GUARD YOUR HEART

Guard your heart above all else, for it determines the course of your life.
Proverbs 4:23

A PROGRESSION IS always evident in an affair: Verbal leads to visual, and emotional leads to physical. Most affairs can be traced back to conversations that became intimate—flirtation, sharing problems, connecting as friends. These conversations led to viewing that person—often a friend, coworker, or neighbor—sexually. Then the emotions got involved—thinking too much about her or spending too much time with her—which eventually led to the physical act of adultery.

Affairs begin in the mind, not the bedroom, because the heart is the doorway to the mind. That's why Solomon advises us to guard our hearts, putting a garrison at the door, stopping unwanted and unwelcome visitors before the line is crossed.

Signs that you may be standing at the brink of an emotional affair include feeling that your wife is not meeting your needs; thinking that you can unwind easier with someone else; talking outside your marriage about your problems; rationalizing a friendship with a female coworker, churchgoer, or neighbor; looking forward to being with this person; and wondering what you would do if you didn't have this relationship.

Beware, back off, and flee from these entanglements. You are teetering on the edge of an affair. When the emotions become engaged, most people are simply looking for an opportune time to take the final and destructive step into sin.

BOTTOM LINE

If you find yourself in an emotional relationship with a woman who is not your wife, you are playing with fire. You need to end this relationship immediately.

Moment of Strength: Proverbs 7:25

CAPTIVITY: THE LIE

"But we are descendants of Abraham," they said. "We have never
been slaves to anyone. What do you mean, 'You will be set free'?"
John 8:33

IN THE VERSES PRECEDING JOHN 8:33, we see Jesus teaching that those who continue in His Word will know the truth and find freedom. "Freedom from what?" the Jews asked. Their defensive response exposed both their pride and their spiritual blindness. For one, the claim that they had "never been slaves to anyone" was clearly wrong, and they knew it. Just a few generations earlier, their forefathers had been living in captivity in Babylon. More important, though, they missed the point of Jesus' life and message: He came to give us freedom from the bondage of sin.

Let's look at two of Satan's most successful tactics for keeping us in bondage:

1. *Convincing us that we're not even in bondage.* If there's any kind of recurring sin in your life—an area in which you've stumbled on multiple occasions—then think twice before accepting this lie.
2. *Convincing us that freedom isn't worth it.* Change is hard, especially when it involves altering your daily routine, the influences you allow into your life (friends, media, etc.), or the way you handle your finances.

If you've sensed unrest in your spirit about how you are spending (or not spending) your time, make this a matter of deliberate prayer. Ask God to remove any spiritual blinders and reveal the truth of where you are and where He wants you to be.

BOTTOM LINE

Spiritual captivity is deceptive. We may think we're not slaves to anything, yet we tend to repeat our mistakes. Ask God for wisdom and clarity.

Moment of Strength: Proverbs 5:22

FREEDOM: THE TRUTH

*I will say to the prisoners, "Come out in freedom," and to those in
darkness, "Come into the light."
They will be my sheep, grazing in green pastures and on hills that
were previously bare.*
Isaiah 49:9

WHAT EXACTLY IS FREEDOM IN CHRIST? We hear about it, read about it, and sing about it, but what does it really mean? Freedom is "the absence of necessity, coercion, or constraint in choice or action." In other words, we're not confined to only one option. Too often we interpret "freedom in Christ" as being a release from the penalty our sins deserve. It includes that, for sure. But it's just as much the option to choose what we do next. We have been given the ability to say no to ungodliness and yes to Christ. That's true freedom.

When we read today's key verse and the context around it, we see three beautiful aspects of freedom in Christ:

1. *We have a choice.* We don't have to keep doing things that separate us from God. This includes any sinful habits as well as our ambitions and goals that are contrary to what God wants for us.
2. *We have a model.* Jesus came to show us what God desires and how to live in the world without conforming to it. He is our light—we don't have to stay in darkness wondering what His will is.
3. *We have God's provision.* If we're on the road to which He's called us, we'll find our sustenance in Him, and we'll find rest in our spirits. We find an unexplainable peace when we're doing what we know God wants us to be doing.

BOTTOM LINE
Enjoy your freedom in Christ! You have everything you need.

Moment of Strength: Galatians 5:1

CAPTIVITY OR FREEDOM?

Get out! Get out and leave your captivity, where everything
you touch is unclean. Get out of there and purify yourselves,
you who carry home the sacred objects of the LORD.
Isaiah 52:11

ARE YOU A CAPTIVE? Try this exercise: Think of the things you've done in the past week that you know displeased God. Now narrow the list down to those things that were a first for you. In other words, consider how many of your sins are areas where you find yourself stumbling over and over. We may fool ourselves into thinking we'll be stronger next time, but that's what we said last time. The truth is that we tend to repeat our sins because we don't take the radical steps needed to prevent a "next time."

Jesus paid a high price for our freedom. Though we've been given the opportunity to enjoy this freedom, we have to take action to actually become free. It seems foolish to sit in a dark dungeon for no reason, yet that's essentially what we do when we don't make the changes needed to break our sinful habits.

In Jeremiah 14:10, God points out that part of our problem is that we don't restrain our feet. "You love to wander far from me." Later, He pronounces judgment on those who haven't changed their ways: "I will winnow you like grain" (Jeremiah 15:7).

Men, this message is for us. Now is the time to remove the things from our lives that present temptations or distractions. Let today's verse be an encouragement to get serious about dealing with the areas that trip us up. Remember, we have a model in Jesus and the promise of His help. Lasting change is possible. There's no reason to become hopeless that we'll never change; there's no reason to remain as captives.

BOTTOM LINE

List the areas that tend to trip you up. Pray through your list, then take the courageous step to make the necessary changes.

Moment of Strength: 1 Samuel 7:3

WITHERING FLOWERS

*The grass withers, the flowers fade, but the word of
our God remains forever.*
Isaiah 40:8, HCSB

WHAT'S MORE IMPORTANT? A bright, shiny sports car that looks better than it runs, or a reliable, but not at all flashy, car that gets you from Point A to Point B, day in and day out, without fail? Would you choose a huge mansion, or a comfortable house where you and your family can relax without a monster mortgage hanging over your heads? A lot of flashy jewelry, or a simple wedding band? The latest and greatest smartphone or electronic gadget, or ones that are functional?

There are all kinds of choices to be made every day, and each one says something about who we are as men. Are we focusing on bringing attention to our socioeconomic status, or are we focusing on providing for our families?

We all are probably guilty of focusing on the wrong things to some extent, but chasing things that really and truly don't matter isn't the pathway to peace and contentment in life. There's always going to be another bauble to catch our attention. There's always going to be a technology upgrade. In the end, however, the most important question to ask is a fairly simple one: Is God impressed?

In the Bible, God assures us again and again that He can take care of us. We can trust Him. That doesn't mean we're all going to be chauffeured around in Bentleys. The key is learning to be content with what He does provide!

BOTTOM LINE

Take a good look at your priorities in life. Are they things that one day will wither away, or are they Kingdom focused?

Moment of Strength: Psalm 119:89-94

NURTURING DEVOTION

Love the LORD your God [and] walk in all his ways.

Joshua 22:5

THE PROGRESSION IN today's verse is first to love the Lord and then to walk in His ways. As you help your children develop their relationship with God, it is vital to guide them in that order. Too many dads stress the importance of walking in the ways of God and miss the critical importance of first cultivating a love for God. Like other human beings, your kids will do far more out of love than they will ever do out of mere duty.

When we cut the process short and emphasize duty before cultivating a relationship, we can unwittingly set our kids up for rebellion. Avoid the temptation to "lay down the law." You can win the battle and lose the war. Invest the time, energy, and creativity needed to paint a picture of God that is gracious, kind, and inviting. Your kids will respond far more easily to grace than to law—they're not so different from you that way.

The human heart longs for deep relationships based on love. When we really see who God is—when we begin to be bowled over by the grace of Jesus Christ—we gain not only a greater capacity to do the right thing but also a far stronger desire to be holy as He is holy. Grace trumps law as a way of relating to God, and that is just as true for your kids as it is for you. Remember, the gospel is meant to be received as good news. And not just once, at salvation, but always. Give your kids grace.

BOTTOM LINE

God is lavishly gracious, kind beyond measure, and deeply loving to His children. A right view of God is the surest way to generate a right response to God.

Moment of Strength: 1 John 3:1-3

CONQUERING FEAR

I prayed to the Lord, and he answered me. He freed me from all my fears.
Psalm 34:4

WE ARE LIVING IN A TIME OF UPHEAVAL. The global economy is still reeling, millions are out of work, governments around the world are toppling, nations threaten war, terrorists still plot to kill on a mass scale, and we wonder what kind of world our kids will inherit.

In the middle of all this chaos, believers are called to trust the Lord with the assurance that He can deliver us from all our fears. *Trust* does not mean "believing that every circumstance will turn out great." It means having confidence in the character and love of God even when hard times deliver crushing blows. Indeed, the Bible is filled with examples of faithful men and women who had great outcomes and terrible outcomes. Peter was miraculously delivered from prison, but John the Baptist was beheaded. Why? That is known only to God. Even though the circumstances may be horrible, a mature Christian recognizes that God is still worthy of our trust.

The Cross of Christ has forever settled the question of whether God is utterly committed to us. But the Cross also demonstrates that God, in His providence, can allow even His own Son to experience extraordinary pain to accomplish His broader purposes. Much of God's plan will not make sense until we are in heaven. In the meantime, He offers us deliverance from our fears if we will seek Him.

BOTTOM LINE

God does not want us to live our lives paralyzed by fear. He is able and willing to give us a peace beyond human understanding if we will trust Him.

Moment of Strength: Hebrews 11

AT HER SERVICE

Even the Son of Man came not to be served but to serve others
and to give his life as a ransom for many.
Matthew 20:28

HUSBANDS ARE CALLED TO love their wives as Christ loved His church. The mark of Jesus' love is service and sacrifice. That's what love does. As God in human form, Jesus had every right to arrive on earth and demand our service. But He didn't do that. Instead, He looked for opportunities to bestow mercy, to speak the truth in love, to weep with those who wept, and to take the death sentence we had coming to us. Service flowed from Him naturally because He had the heart of a lover and giver. And He calls us to be like Him.

Being like Jesus is a tall order—impossible, humanly speaking. But God never issues a call without also making a way for us to rise to it. Lean on Him for the strength to serve. Pointedly and continually ask Him for the ability you do not have on your own. If you are married, service begins with your wife. Look for ways to give to her, especially when it is difficult, because you promised to do so "in sickness and in health." Remember, Jesus did not bail out on us when things became difficult. He wants us to trust Him for strength beyond what is humanly possible.

God will empower us to do His will as we take on the role of a servant. As you commit yourself to serving others, you just might find a new and unexpected exhilaration as you discover that the joy of the Lord really is your strength.

BOTTOM LINE

Service may not be glamorous, and it may well be that only God really
understands how much you sacrifice; but He will enable you to do it joyfully.

Moment of Strength: Galatians 5:13

OUR TRUE IDENTITY

Because we are his children, God has sent the Spirit of his Son into our hearts,
prompting us to call out, "Abba, Father." Now you are no longer a slave but
God's own child. And since you are his child, God has made you his heir.
Galatians 4:6-7

KEVIN COULDN'T BELIEVE what was happening to him. Panic and gut-wrenching fear swept over him as he left his boss's office with the dreaded pink slip in his hand. All he could think about as he staggered back to his cubicle was how he was going to tell his wife that he had been downsized after twenty years of loyal service. So much of his identity was wrapped up in his job that he wasn't sure he knew who he was apart from being an accountant.

What about you? Where do you find your identity? Where do you find your value? You may call yourself an accountant, a doctor, a sales professional, a student, a devoted husband, a retired executive, or a farmer. But just as Dan discovered, any of these titles could be gone in a matter of minutes. Now who are you? What is your value? There is only one identity that is unshakable and everlasting. That is your identity in Christ.

Knowing who you are and *whose* you are brings a confidence into your life that cannot be taken away. Your career may change; you may acquire or lose your skills; your relationships with others might change. But your identity in Christ is permanent.

Have you allowed your identity to be tied too closely to your achievements and occupation? Take some time to reflect on what it means to be an heir to God's Kingdom.

BOTTOM LINE

Our identity is who we are, not what we do.

Moment of Strength: Titus 3:6-8

IN GOD WE TRUST

No one can serve two masters. For you will hate one and love the other; you will be devoted to one and despise the other. You cannot serve God and be enslaved to money.

Matthew 6:24

THE REMINDER IS ON the front of every US coin and on the back of every US bill. Four simple words: *In God We Trust*. It sounds simple enough, yet if we are completely honest, many of us depend more on the piece of paper the phrase is printed on than we do on the God we claim to trust.

More than 15 percent of Jesus' teachings dealt with money and possessions. Jesus taught more about money than He taught about heaven and hell combined. Could it be He knew how hard it was for us to trust that He has given us a new heart and has promised to provide for our needs? Or was it that He knew we would struggle with living as orphans when in fact we are sons of the King?

For orphans, the world can be especially frightening because they lack parents to provide love, protection, and a sense of belonging. We can also be guilty of "orphan thinking" when we live as if we are completely on our own or when it comes to taking care of our needs. When we fail to trust that what God says about us is true—that we are His beloved sons—we will always resort to trusting in our own resources to make life work.

Does your anxiety level rise and fall in direct proportion to the rise and fall of your bank account balance? Take a moment and reflect on the fact that you are a beloved son of a King who promises to provide for you and who doesn't want you constantly worrying about money.

BOTTOM LINE

There is a strong connection between our spiritual lives and how we think about and handle money.

Moment of Strength: 1 Timothy 6:10

CHIPPING AWAY

Thank you for making me so wonderfully complex!
Your workmanship is marvelous—how well I know it.
Psalm 139:14

SOME JOURNALISTS HAVE a love/hate relationship with those who edit their copy for style, punctuation, and grammar errors. They've written a story that to themselves seems perfect. The lede is a good one (and not buried), the research is great, and the quotes are interesting. This piece could very well be an award winner somewhere down the road.

When the story goes to an editor, though, there are quite often big changes. Writers are always having their words chipped away and refined. If a writer is willing to be humble and recognize that there's a purpose to the process, the end product can turn out to be so much better.

When we allow God to hone our imperfections—no matter what they may be—we become better husbands, better fathers, and ultimately, better Christians. The process can often be agonizing for any number of reasons. Pride could be involved, and maybe some shame, too. There might even be a good deal of ignorance of what God has in store for us.

We're not perfect, and we can't pretend to be for long. It might be possible to fool other people for a while, and we might even be able to fool ourselves for a time. Yet no one will ever be able to pull the wool over God's eyes. He sees the things in our lives that need chipping away. Allow Him to do something about it.

BOTTOM LINE

No matter how hard you may try, you're not perfect. Ask God to sand off your rough edges today.

Moment of Strength: Hebrews 12:6

MEASURING UP

Therefore, since we have been made right in God's
sight by faith, we have peace with God because of
what Jesus Christ our Lord has done for us.
Romans 5:1

IN TODAY'S WORLD, men have to "qualify" in so many different areas of life. We have to make the grade for loans to buy a home. If we want a particular job, our skills and experience must measure up. Every sport known to man has a playoff system to determine which team or player is good enough to continue on to the championship.

There's always a temptation to compare ourselves to others, whether they're celebrities we'll never meet or the guy next door. He's got six-pack abs. He drives a better car. His children are so well-behaved (whereas we have to peel our kids off the ceiling when we go out to eat). Whatever the point of comparison, there's always someone who seems to have it more together than we do.

One of the most comforting truths about the Christian faith is that we don't have to measure up when it comes to our salvation. In fact, such a thing is impossible: It is by God's grace, and God's grace alone, that we've been saved. We can't ever do enough, say enough, earn enough, or be enough on our own.

So get over yourself and stop making pointless comparisons.

When you try to stack up your life against someone else's, the end result is that you're living for yourself, your own dreams and desires. But if you trust the fact that God accepts you just as you are (not that He wants you to *stay* that way), you may experience an overwhelming, unquenchable desire to live for Him.

You're worthy, so why worry?

BOTTOM LINE

You'll never be able to measure up against everyone, but that simply doesn't matter to your Savior.

Moment of Strength: Romans 5:1-11

JUST ONE WON'T HURT, WILL IT?

The next day John saw Jesus coming toward him and said,
"Look! The Lamb of God who takes away the sin of the world!"
John 1:29

YOU'VE BEEN TRYING TO get in better shape, so watching what you eat has become a way of life. You work out. You jog. You're doing all the things you're supposed to do, and in the long run, it's paying off. But there are certain little treats that you miss, and they're oh-so-tempting sometimes.

Maybe you love tortilla chips, so you rationalize: One tortilla chip is not going to kill you, right? So you take one—okay, maybe two—and enjoy them. You savor the taste. And then you get on with your day, right?

Right?

Like habits we know are not good for us, and like the ways in which we rationalize our unwillingness to give them up, the temptation to sin can also be very deceptive. A sin can seem insignificant: maybe fudging a bit on a job application or letting a curse word slip out. We may rationalize that "one tiny little sin" won't doom us to eternal damnation, and that God doesn't hold such things over our heads, waiting for us to slip up again.

But just like your favorite snack food, sin has a way of quickly spinning out of control. Before you know it, you've eaten the whole bag of chips. In the same way, one small sin can quickly become a daily habit that spirals into an unhealthy addiction—something you feel that you can't live without. So fight against sin with all your heart, relying on God's strength to give you lasting victory. And ask Him to help you with those bad habits, as well.

BOTTOM LINE

God forgives the biggest and smallest of sins, but always, always, always fight against them.

Moment of Strength: Romans 6:12-14

CLEAN, CLEAR WATER

Anyone who believes in me may come and drink! For the Scriptures declare,
"Rivers of living water will flow from his heart."
John 7:38

THE DEAD SEA IS a popular tourist attraction in Israel, boasting a string of luxury hotels offering mud baths and spa massages. Why is it called the Dead Sea? Because it has no visible outlet to allow water to pass out of the sea, all the salty sediment remains in the basin, hypersalinating the water and making it impossible for fish, plants, and other organisms to survive there. You may have seen photos of tourists leaning back as if sitting in a family room recliner as they read magazines while floating in the Dead Sea. That phenomenon is possible because the heavy concentration of sediment increases the water's density.

Contrast the Dead Sea with the Sea of Galilee in northern Israel. The Sea of Galilee receives water from the Jordan River to the north and releases water back into the Jordan as it continues downstream to the Dead Sea.

The New Testament has many references to Christ as living water. The Sea of Galilee might be considered an example of living water as well. It stays clean and clear because it receives fresh water regularly, and it drains water out. But even a cup of clear water left sitting long enough will stagnate and allow impurities to develop.

In Psalm 23, David declares that his cup is filled to overflowing. As we take in the living water of Christ, we must make sure that He overflows from our lives into the lives of others around us. Otherwise our lives will become stagnant and unhealthy.

BOTTOM LINE

Begin looking for more ways to ensure that the living water of Christ flows not just into your life but through your life to others.

Moment of Strength: Psalm 23

STRAIGHT AS AN ARROW

Children are a gift from the LORD; they are a reward from him.
Children born to a young man are like arrows in a warrior's hands.

Psalm 127:3-4

To SAY THAT A MAN IS "straight as an arrow" means he's a man of honor and integrity. It tells us he is living a life above reproach. His life is honest, trustworthy, and dependable.

Arrows—even handcrafted ones from ages past—require careful attention to detail to ensure optimal performance. The shaft of the best arrow is perfectly straight. If an arrow is to hit its mark, it takes more than simply pulling back on the bowstring. To do its job, an arrow must also have a sharp, hard tip capable of piercing its target to the core.

To maintain a straight path, the arrow depends on fletching, which are feathers that keep it balanced and true in its flight. Finally, while the arrow itself needs these qualities, it also requires a good marksman in order to hit its target.

A good archer needs training and practice if his arrows are going to fulfill their intended purpose. In the same way, a successful dad makes sure to get his training by spending time in the Bible each day, praying regularly, and practicing discipline in his own life. To truly teach his children, a man must not only instruct with words but also model with his life. When he does that, his words will have much more authenticity and power. Your kids need your involvement and direction, or they will fly off in the wrong direction. Ask God for help.

BOTTOM LINE

How well are you training yourself so that you are prepared to teach your children?

Moment of Strength: Ephesians 6:1-4

YOU ARE RICH

*Therefore I, a prisoner for serving the Lord, beg you to lead a
life worthy of your calling, for you have been called by God.*
Ephesians 4:1

YOUR POSITION IN CHRIST IS A GREAT TREASURE. You possess all the privileges of a royal child of God. All that is His is yours. You are an heir of God and a coheir with Jesus (Romans 8:17). You partake of Christ's inheritance. Your name appears on the deed to all His "endless treasures" (Ephesians 3:8).

Not only are you rich in spiritual possessions before the throne of God, but you also are rich in identity. Whatever labels the world has put on you are false. You are who God says you are. He labels you *beloved*, *holy*, *chosen*, and *friend*. He labels you *powerful*, *worthy*, and *good*. God has entrusted you with the great privilege of displaying the riches and identity of Christ in the world. This is the high calling you have received.

Do you walk in a manner worthy of this high calling? Do you seek out your treasures and use them? When the Bible talks about walking, it refers to your daily way of living. Words. Feelings. Thoughts. Actions. Relationships. Choices. Does the daily stuff of your life reflect your riches in Christ?

God has declared you able to do all things, and He has provided all you need to walk worthy of your calling. By faith you can become the person God designed you to be. It's a matter of believing that what God says about you is true and living in full reliance on His promises.

BOTTOM LINE

Live today with the humble faith that you are the richest man you know, and leave no unclaimed treasures in your spiritual portfolio.

Moment of Strength: Romans 8:28-37

FAITH IS THE VICTORY

*For every child of God defeats this evil world, and
we achieve this victory through our faith.*

1 John 5:4

GOD IS THE POTTER, AND HIS PEOPLE ARE THE CLAY. He has the right to shape us as He wills. Sometimes God answers prayers the way you prayed them. The job is offered, the child healed, the money supplied, the marriage saved. In those glorious moments, it's easy to praise God and be thankful.

But what about the other times? What about the people of faith in Scripture whose lives had no happily ever after? That's when you have to steadfastly entrust your life to the Lord of outcomes. Your prayers do not box God into a corner. His plan and ways are immeasurably higher than yours. He can use every circumstance of life, good and bad, to accomplish His Kingdom purposes in the world. Thankfully, His purposes are good, and "God causes everything to work together for the good of those who love God" (Romans 8:28).

God's job is outcomes; your job is faith. Regardless of outcomes, keep faith in God. In the spiritual realm, faith is the victory. Even if the illness returns, the job evaporates, or the child goes astray, it is your determined faith in the darkest hour that amazes angels and wins the applause of heaven. Your faith will be tested again and again. Expect it, and keep trusting and following God when the trials come.

Remember, outcomes are secondary, but faith is primary. Keep your faith in God and let Him take care of the rest. That's the path to victory.

BOTTOM LINE

Faith is the victory, even if the outcome is not what you hoped for.

Moment of Strength: Hebrews 11:32-40

THE SHOW

Always be full of joy in the Lord. I say it again—rejoice!
Philippians 4:4

IT'S THE THICK OF THE BASEBALL SEASON, and the pennant races are beginning to heat up. Soon, players in the minors will be called up to the big leagues, many for the very first time. Can you imagine what that moment must be like, when they get the news that they're going to the Show? They've worked a long time for this, and now it's actually happening.

Not everyone gets to play professional baseball, but joy and satisfaction come in pursuing countless other goals. Maybe you've always wanted to be a writer and you finally get an article published. Or a promotion finally comes through at work. Or you want to get in better shape, and your waistline slowly but surely begins to shrink.

Most people have some sort of lifelong dream, and many may even get to experience theirs. Yet those pursuits pale in comparison to the day we'll achieve our ultimate prize—the day we're called home to heaven. Spending eternity with Jesus is so unimaginably wonderful that it's hard to comprehend it.

Revelation 21:4 promises a day when God "will wipe every tear from their eyes, and there will be no more death or sorrow or crying or pain. All these things are gone forever." What else could anyone ever want? Thank God for the gift of salvation that will allow you to spend eternity with Him.

BOTTOM LINE

Many people get to live out their lifelong dreams, but we all have the opportunity to land the ultimate prize—life with Jesus in heaven. Praise God!

Moment of Strength: Revelation 5:9-13

NOT TOO MUCH, NOT TOO LITTLE

First, help me never to tell a lie. Second, give me neither poverty nor riches!
Give me just enough to satisfy my needs.

Proverbs 30:8

MANY CHRISTIANS TODAY ARE confused about money. On the one hand, there's the prosperity gospel that says that God wants to make us wildly rich based on our faith. On the other hand, some seem to think that money is always evil and that having little of it makes one more spiritual. Neither extreme is true.

The Scriptures offer a more nuanced view of money and possessions. The accumulation of wealth isn't viewed in Scripture as something necessarily immoral but often as the reward for hard work, ingenuity, and risk taking. And yet the prophets, Jesus, and Paul warned the rich against finding ultimate security and happiness in their prosperity.

Proverbs 30:8 strikes the proper balance: "Give me neither poverty nor riches!" Paul echoes this refrain in preaching contentment in every financial season (Philippians 4:12). Wealth acquired through hard work is considered a blessing (Proverbs 13:11) as long as the rich man realizes that the source of his ingenuity and strength is God and not himself (Luke 16:19-31).

Ultimately, it's not our money that God is after, but our hearts. The American Dream of financial security is no substitute for God as the object of our worship. The antidote for some may be radical lifestyle changes. For others, it may mean reordering some priorities to make sure that God is first.

BOTTOM LINE

A biblical view of money rejects both the prosperity gospel and the poverty gospel.

Moment of Strength: Ecclesiastes 5:10

MAGNIFICENT OBSESSION

Those who hunger and thirst for righteousness are blessed, for they will be filled.
Matthew 5:6, HCSB

RICK AND JASON WERE COMPLETELY STUMPED. They had come across a trivia question related to one of their favorite sports, and they couldn't put their finger on the correct answer. They mulled it over, texted and e-mailed back and forth, called friends, checked newspaper accounts, and posted the question on Facebook.

The harder they tried, the longer it seemed to take to nail down a decisive answer. Just when they thought they had the problem licked, yet another theory would pop up to burst their bubble. Still, they kept trying and finally came up with the information they'd been so determined to find.

To what extent will you go to search out God, to find the peace and comfort that only He can provide? In Psalm 42:1, David is as eager to experience God's presence as "the deer longs for streams of water." In the next verse, David says, "I thirst for God, the living God." This is no half-hearted pursuit of the Lord; it's an all-out search.

We're filled with all kinds of different passions, whether it's our jobs, our hobbies, or something else. And we'll often go to great lengths to get what we want. But for what? Some sort of temporary satisfaction? Apply that same kind of passionate drive to your walk with Christ, and the reward will truly be satisfying.

BOTTOM LINE
Allow God to be the focus of your obsession, rather than chasing after some trivial pursuit, possession, or accomplishment that will eventually fade away.

Moment of Strength: Psalm 42:1-8

IS HELL FOR REAL?

The rich man shouted, "Father Abraham, have some pity!
Send Lazarus over here to dip the tip of his finger in water and
cool my tongue. I am in anguish in these flames."
Luke 16:24

SOME BELIEVE IT IS MERELY SYMBOLIC. Others believe *hell* is a word that shouldn't be used because it sounds "intolerant" or "judgmental." After all, would a good God really send people to hell? The really crazy thought, though, is not that some will go to hell but that anyone will go to heaven!

Jesus taught about a literal hell that was originally designed for the devil and his angels, not for us (Matthew 25:41). It is a place of despair and pain. In hell, people will be given over to their sins. Imagine an addiction so severe that even momentary bursts of gratification are gone, and all that's left is slavery to a hunger that can never be satisfied. In the throes of sin here on earth, the alcoholic, the sex addict, and the gossip all feel a momentary buzz. But even temporary pleasure will not be found in hell.

Hell will mean great physical and relational anguish for those who experience it. The rich man in Jesus' parable not only suffered to the point where a drop of water became precious; he also suffered because he didn't want his brothers to experience hell.

As C. S. Lewis observed, "There are only two kinds of people in the end: those who say to God, 'Thy will be done,' and those to whom God says, in the end, 'Thy will be done.' All that are in Hell, choose it." Now is the time to pray for those who don't know Christ, and share your faith whenever you can.

BOTTOM LINE

May the truth of hell motivate us to share God's love with others.

Moment of Strength: Luke 16:19-31

ADJUST YOUR TONE KNOB

Gentle words are a tree of life; a deceitful tongue crushes the spirit.

Proverbs 15:4

EVER HEAR THE PHRASE, "It's not what you say, but how you say it"? It's true to a certain degree. Too often our tongue and our tone are out of sync with each other. We may praise our kids with a disinterested tone or tell our wife "yes" when our volume says "no." How we say what we say matters a lot.

Jesus warns about this when He says in Matthew 5:37, "Just say a simple, 'Yes, I will,' or 'No, I won't.' Anything beyond this is from the evil one." He knows that truthful speech ultimately comes from the heart, not just the lips. And when the heart's motives and the tongue's words don't match up, the result can be speech that harms, maims, even crushes others.

So how can you develop a tongue that heals? It takes ruthless self-examination to adjust your tone. Memorize verses about the tongue. (Proverbs is full of them.) Find stopping points in your day to pause for thirty seconds, asking God to show you how your tongue and heart are incongruent. Confess any ways you've broken another's spirit with your speech.

One man, eager to shed himself of his hurtful speech, was held accountable by a friend. He paid his friend five dollars for every word he used that hurt someone. After writing a couple of checks, his speech cleared up pretty quickly. The point is, do whatever it takes. And start by asking God to help you.

BOTTOM LINE

A *"tree of life" tongue will bear sweet fruit for the future.*

Moment of Strength: James 3:3-12

REVISING HISTORY

*It was God who sent me here, not you! And he is the one
who made me an adviser to Pharaoh—the manager of
his entire palace and the governor of all Egypt.*

Genesis 45:8

AT FIRST GLANCE, you'd think Joseph has an awfully short memory. "Wait a minute, Joe! Remember that day out in the fields with the coat and the cistern and the caravan, and later with the captain's wife and the cell and the cupbearer and the crazy Pharaoh with the dreams? It was your brothers who put you through that!"

But Joseph chose to view his history through God's eyes. Even in his darkest moments—at the bottom of a well (Genesis 37:23-24), falsely accused (Genesis 39:17-18), and forgotten in a foreign prison (Genesis 39:20)—he recognized God's sovereign hand of protection and provision on his life. Near the end of his life, he even told his brothers, "You intended to harm me, but God intended it all for good. He brought me to this position so I could save the lives of many people" (Genesis 50:20).

It's easy to ascribe all the blessings in our lives to God and attribute the tough times to Satan. But look again. There are lessons we can't learn, joys we can't experience, and knowledge of God we can't attain until we go through the valleys of life.

Take a look back over your history, especially some of the recent tough times. The same God who was with Joseph is with you, too. When you see your life through His eyes, you, too, will say, "It was God who brought me to this place."

BOTTOM LINE

Learn to recognize the sovereign hand of God in all your affairs—including the difficult times.

Moment of Strength: Genesis 39

DORM DAD

But when I am afraid, I will put my trust in you.
Psalm 56:3

FROM THE MOMENT they bundled her into your arms at the hospital, you've protected her. You swore that stray dogs, mean kids, and scary shadows would never touch her. You encouraged her before her piano recital, helped her study for numerous tests, and smiled awkwardly when she posed for pictures before the prom. Now you've driven many miles to a college and toted her stuff into a coed dorm, and it's time to say good-bye.

There's a lump in your throat the size of Pikes Peak, and you start to worry. Does she have enough money? Does she know how to change a flat tire? Will she make good friends? And most important, will she continue her walk with Jesus?

Just remember the game plan. It was never drawn up on the blackboard that you would go everywhere with her. You can't move into the dorm. Healthy parenting includes facing down your fears and cutting some of those ties at the right moment.

Rest easy, Dad. God is going places with her that you can't go—behind her, in front of her, and beside her. Read Psalm 139 through the eyes of your child. His plans for her are greater than even you could ever dream. Letting go is a fearful thing—but keeping her chained to you and the past would be an even scarier thought.

BOTTOM LINE

You can trust God with your fears as you release your children to Him.

Moment of Strength: Psalm 139

STRAIGHT A'S IN LOVE

Again I say, each man must love his wife as he loves himself,
and the wife must respect her husband.

Ephesians 5:33

MAYBE YOU HEARD A SERMON ON marriage and got overwhelmed by the message. Perhaps it was a book on relationships, and reading it felt like torture. Does marriage have to be so complicated? Where can a guy go to learn the basics about marriage?

Ephesians 5:33 is one place. Paul adds up all the previous wisdom about marriage, and shares the bottom line: Love your wife as you would want to be loved. No one wants to receive a barely passing grade in love. We all want the best, go-to-the-head-of-the-class, A-plus love!

What's that like? Apply some *A* words to your relationship with your wife.

Attention is one of those words. Every wife needs attention, which means you are fully present in relating to her. An occasional grunt in the middle of watching a ball game on TV does not a conversation make.

Acceptance is another area in which you need to earn an A. Love your wife for who she is, not for who you want her to be.

Appreciation is important too. Your wife performs all manner of little tasks and chores that get overlooked during the week. Shower her with appreciation on a daily basis.

Affection is a final A. Women need affection that doesn't always have to be sexual. Give these A's to your wife, and you will go to the head of the class in Marriage 101!

BOTTOM LINE

Ask God to help you make straight A's in your marriage.

Moment of Strength: Ephesians 5:25-33

THE RIGHT EXPECTATIONS

We are pressed on every side by troubles, but we are not
crushed. We are perplexed, but not driven to despair.
We are hunted down, but never abandoned by God.
We get knocked down, but we are not destroyed.
2 Corinthians 4:8-9

THE APOSTLE PAUL CERTAINLY didn't live a carefree life. Not even close. He describes going through times of being "pressured," "perplexed," "persecuted," and "struck down." Most of us consider Paul to have been a strong Christian, so what gives? Why wasn't Paul enjoying the good life of ease and comfort, secure under God's protective blessing? Because that's not what God promises, and that's not how the Christian life works.

Despite experiencing a great deal of suffering, Paul says that he was "*not* crushed," "*not* driven to despair," "*never* abandoned," and "*not* destroyed." Paul doesn't deny or downplay suffering in the least, but he knows that suffering doesn't have the final word—God does. Without our sufferings, we would never appreciate God's great rescues. We would never really learn to trust Him instead of ourselves. So while suffering hurts, it's not meaningless.

What attitude do you bring to your present sufferings? Do you see them as cruel and random and ultimately meaningless? Or do you see them as opportunities to persevere and overcome by the grace and mercy of God? When you know that God is absolutely wise, faithful, and loving, you know that you will win in the end if you just continue to trust Him. Ask God to give you faith to believe.

BOTTOM LINE

Suffering is normal and to be expected. Overcoming suffering by God's grace is normal, too, and to be expected by every Christian, including you.

Moment of Strength: 2 Corinthians 4:7-18

A CLEAN SLATE

Finally, I confessed all my sins to you and stopped trying to hide my guilt. I said to myself, "I will confess my rebellion to the LORD." And you forgave me! All my guilt is gone.

Psalm 32:5

IF YOU LET GARBAGE PILE UP, it begins to stink. It's the same with unconfessed sin. Pretending it isn't there or hoping it will somehow go away on its own does absolutely nothing to remove the growing stench that results when we don't confess our sins to God and ask for His forgiveness. The truth is that sin must be dealt with, or our relationship with God will feel unnecessarily distant and unsatisfying.

The enemy would have us believe that sinning isn't a big deal. Then, when we do sin, he is quick to heap on the guilt and condemnation. The problem is, we don't recognize that it's the devil. Sometimes, we actually imagine God up in heaven with His arms crossed and a ticked-off look on His face, thinking of ways to teach us a lesson. And instead of immediately doing the one thing that will solve the problem—come clean, confess to God that we've sinned, and ask for His forgiveness—we wallow in our guilt, feeling miserable.

The main reason we don't confess our sins is that we really don't believe that God is as gracious as the Bible says He is. Nothing in this world prepares us for the amazing grace that God offers. It seems too good to be true. So we hide. We duck and dodge rather than face the music. But we're wrong. That's not who God is. He delights in forgiving us. He longs to give us a clean slate and a clear conscience.

BOTTOM LINE

Someone has said that "to admit our sin is positively the most cheerful thing any of us can do." Do you believe that? Are you willing to come clean?

Moment of Strength: Psalm 32

BEAUTIFUL PRAISE

*Let the godly sing for joy to the L*ORD*; it is fitting for the pure to praise him.*
Psalm 33:1

IN GENERAL, it's good for us to rejoice, to be thankful, to praise what we find praiseworthy. Think about it: It's almost impossible to be miserable while you're praising something, just as it's almost impossible to be happy while you're complaining about something. So praise is a good thing, and we ought to be offering it as much as possible.

Yet there are many things that can keep us from feeling joyful, thankful, and full of praise. If our strategy is to wait until all of our circumstances are perfect before finally choosing to give praise—and it often is a *choice*—we'll never praise. Ever. Well, not until heaven, anyway. The good news, though, is that there is *always* a solid reason to give praise *now*, and that's because the object of our praise—the Lord—is *always* worthy of it. That's wonderfully good news that can take us far beyond mere positive thinking and a good attitude.

Our heavenly Father delights in the praises of His children. It absolutely thrills His heart when His children offer their praises to Him out of thankful hearts. Why? Because we were made for that purpose. It's not that God has a huge ego that needs to be continually stroked. It's that we desperately need to understand that God is supremely worthy of our praise and that praising Him is what we were designed to do.

BOTTOM LINE

You don't have to wait for a good reason to praise when God is your heavenly Father. Let it flow freely for your good and His glory.

Moment of Strength: Psalm 33:3

STICKY CHANGE

The Lord is like a father to his children, tender and
compassionate to those who fear him.

Psalm 103:13

RICK COULDN'T BELIEVE WHAT HE WAS SEEING. The drinking cup—the full drinking cup—had somehow been crushed as his son was getting out of the car, and now there was sticky soda everywhere. It not only completely filled its own cup holder, but the one next to it and an adjoining change holder as well. And Rick's jacket was a soggy mess.

Rick was so angry that words escaped him. He couldn't even express in complete sentences to his son what was wrong. "Cup crushed. Soda mess. Car cup holders. Paper towels, now!" The poor kid's eyes were as big as saucers. He was in trouble. Dad had told him not to get in the car with an uncovered cup.

We are God's children, and we mess up all the time. Thankfully for us, though, God's patience and mercy go far beyond what we deserve or expect. When we seek His forgiveness, He willingly grants it. His Son gave His life to assure us that we wouldn't have to pay for our sins. Yes, there can be consequences, but there is no condemnation or punishment from God.

Did Rick's son deserve punishment? Maybe. But in the grand scheme of things, it could have been much worse. There had been plenty of times when Rick himself had done careless things as a kid. Wouldn't it be amazing if we showed everyone—not just our children—something like the same kind of compassion that God has for us?

BOTTOM LINE

God calls fathers to offer their children grace and mercy just as He offers us
grace and mercy. Discipline should always be administered with love.

Moment of Strength: Psalm 130:3-4

GIVE TILL IT HURTS

Remember this—a farmer who plants only a few seeds will get a small crop.
But the one who plants generously will get a generous crop.
2 Corinthians 9:6

WHEN IT COMES TO GIVING financially to God's work, we've all heard the story of the poor widow who dropped two tiny coins into the Temple treasury. Jesus saw this and told His disciples that she had given more than anybody. "They have given a tiny part of their surplus, but she, poor as she is, has given everything she has" (Luke 21:4). That kind of generosity is rare. Were it not for Jesus holding her up as an example, we'd probably call her foolish for not taking care of herself first.

The widow gave until it hurt. That's a high standard to strive to attain. The widow's two coins have proven mighty over the last couple of millennia as an example of sacrificial giving.

Today, studies show that people continue to give sacrificially. Those who can least afford it often give the highest percentage of their income.

No matter how much you've given or haven't given in the past, make it a priority, starting today, to give back to God in a way that honors Him. As God blesses us, we need to remember to bless others. The apostle Paul reminds us in 2 Corinthians 9:6 that "a farmer who plants only a few seeds will get a small crop. But the one who plants generously will get a generous crop." When we give generously to God, He can bring in a huge harvest that benefits us and others far beyond the accumulation of more money.

BOTTOM LINE

Prayerfully look for specific ways to give this year that will have the greatest impact for God's Kingdom.

Moment of Strength: Acts 20:35

BELIEVE THE BEST

Do to others as you would like them to do to you.
Luke 6:31

THE YOUNG COUPLE SAT WITH giddy anticipation across the desk from their pastor as he pulled the test results from a manila envelope and looked at the googly-eyed couple. He scanned the analysis from their premarital assessment.

"You know," the pastor said, "nobody is as good as you each think your future spouse is. You're wearing rose-colored glasses."

More than twenty years later, the couple looked back on that meeting in the pastor's office and laughed. They'd faced difficulties in their marriage, fought on occasion, and disappointed each other numerous times. But those rose-colored glasses had stayed firmly planted on their faces. They'd continued to look at each other in the best possible light, and because of that, they actually helped each other become the person they each were hoping for.

Jesus may not have been talking about marriage in Luke 6:31 when He said, "Do to others as you would like them to do to you," but the principle still applies. How we treat others must be our focus.

Do you want your wife to think the best of you or to harbor resentful feelings? Easy question. Then you need to stay away from negativity as well. Acting positively toward your wife strengthens both your love for her and your marriage relationship. When you choose to believe the best, you're usually right.

BOTTOM LINE

When you think the best about your wife, it'll help you get through the worst times.

Moment of Strength: Philippians 2:3

GET THE MESSAGE

I am not ashamed of this Good News about Christ. It is the
power of God at work, saving everyone who believes.

Romans 1:16

WHENEVER YOU GO TO THE MAILBOX, you can probably count on finding two things: bills and junk mail. Normally, you may toss out the junk mail without looking at it. But sometimes you have to admit that something catches your eye. Maybe it's a great sale. Perhaps it's an offer for a free vacation.

Direct-mail professionals know they'll have more misses than hits. If they get a 3 percent response on a piece, they're pretty happy. Then they'll continually change the packaging, design, and promotions to get an even greater return.

As Christians, we can learn a lot from the direct-mail approach when it comes to telling others about Jesus. God wants us to be His witnesses. Maybe we don't do much to spread the Good News message because we feel that everybody's heard it before or because we've already told the people around us. But we can't give up.

Romans 1:16 says we shouldn't be ashamed of the gospel, because "it is the power of God at work, saving everyone who believes." We need to keep sending out the message and not give up. God promises that the gospel message has power. Most of the time it may be discarded, but eventually (with persistence and creativity) our message will catch somebody's eye and pay eternal dividends. And that's the best return of all.

BOTTOM LINE

Commit to telling two people this month about the life-changing message of Jesus Christ, and pray that God would lead you to the right people.

Moment of Strength: Romans 10:14

A TIME AND A PLACE FOR YOU

*From one man he created all the nations throughout the whole
earth. He decided beforehand when they should rise and fall,
and he determined their boundaries.*

Acts 17:26

DO YOU EVER WONDER HOW you got to where you are? For many of us, where
we are now is nowhere near where we thought we would be geographically,
relationally, professionally, or spiritually. Rarely does life go as planned. The
truth is, we are not ultimately the masters of our own fate—as popular as that
idea may be. ("If you can dream it, you can achieve it" is not always true.)

In light of the winding, unpredictable road you may have traveled thus
far, does your life ever seem random, maybe even purposeless? How do you
respond to that feeling? Do you decide to quit dreaming and planning? Or
dismiss the idea that God created you for a purpose and may have you precisely where He wants you, despite all your sins, mistakes, and bad decisions?
Giving in to doubt and despair is the kind of resignation that destroys hope
and further clouds your purpose.

Part of the problem is that we often forget that our main purpose is to
know God. "This is the way to have eternal life—to know you, the only true
God, and Jesus Christ, the one you sent to earth" (John 17:3). When we're
overly concerned with seeing our own plans come to fruition, we forget that
knowing and loving God is what life is all about. When we get that right,
everything else begins to make more sense. We start to see that every part
of our journey is necessary, and that God can tell a good story with our lives
despite the confusing parts.

BOTTOM LINE

*Your life is not random. God is weaving together a great story with your life.
Your job is to trust Him and embrace the adventure.*

Moment of Strength: Acts 17:27-28

ANXIETY FREE

Give your burdens to the LORD, and he will take care of you.
He will not permit the godly to slip and fall.

Psalm 55:22

CAN YOU IMAGINE HAVING absolutely no worries? Think about how much happier and freer and full of life you'd be. You'd be off the charts! It sounds a lot like heaven. It certainly doesn't sound much like earth.

Sadly, life on this troubled planet is full of things that can tempt us to worry. In fact, it almost seems irresponsible *not* to worry. Unconsciously, perhaps, we figure that if we don't worry, bad things will happen to us. We think that things will spin out of our (illusory) control and that we'll suffer terrible consequences for our lack of concern and attention. But is that really true? Has worrying about something ever really helped? As Thomas Jefferson once wrote in a letter to John Adams, "How much pain have cost us the evils which have never happened?" So true, and yet we fret.

Mr. Barrow, a character in a story by Mark Twain, offers some helpful advice: "Drag your thoughts away from your troubles—by the ears, by the heels, or any other way, so you manage it; it's the healthiest thing a body can do." The solution for Christians, of course, is to drag our worries to the Lord. Psalm 55:22 tells us to "give your burdens to the LORD," and then *leave* them there! Every time you're tempted to pick them back up again, remind yourself that you can't carry them, that they only make you miserable, and that God is willing and able to handle what you can't handle and weren't designed to handle. You *don't* have to worry.

BOTTOM LINE

Worry is useless and unnecessary. Cast your burdens on the Lord and trust in Him. He can handle them much better than you can!

Moment of Strength: 1 Peter 5:7

A PERFECT FATHER

You have not received a spirit that makes you fearful slaves.
Instead, you received God's Spirit when he adopted you as his
own children. Now we call him, "Abba, Father." For his Spirit
joins with our spirit to affirm that we are God's children.

Romans 8:15-16

THE ARAMAIC WORD ABBA—used here and in only two other places in Scripture—is the intimately tender term of endearment that a boy would use for his father, his Daddy. What a scandal that anyone would use such a tender word to refer to God, but that is exactly what Jesus did in the garden of Gethsemane when He was facing the agony of the cross. And because Jesus endured the cross, our adoption has been made possible, and we can now join our Savior in crying out, "Daddy!" in the scary and broken world in which we find ourselves.

It can be difficult for a grown man to admit that he is, at the same time, a scared, needy child. Growing up, when you were angry, maybe you were sent to your room and told not to come out until you had a smile on your face. When you were sad, maybe you were told to cheer up or snap out of it. So maybe now, as an adult, you've come to expect that you're on your own emotionally and that if you were honest about your emotions, you would risk being abandoned or left alone in your pain.

If you experienced emotional distance growing up, you may have come to expect that same feeling of distance and neglect from God. But God is eager to heal us and restore us, and He invites us to crawl into His lap. He is strong and loving, and He wants you to come to Him to find the strength and comfort you need.

BOTTOM LINE

No matter what wounds and insecurities you carry with you from your childhood, God desires to "re-father" you and heal you in those areas.

Moment of Strength: Psalm 68:5

FOOLISHNESS

As a dog returns to its vomit, so a fool repeats his foolishness.
Proverbs 26:11

JEFFREY MOTTS WAS executed by lethal injection for the 2005 murder of a fellow inmate at the Perry Correctional Institute in South Carolina. He also murdered two elderly people in 1995. What was particularly revealing was a comment he made in his final statement, which was read by his attorney: "I was the child everyone wanted their children around until I got on drugs. Drugs will destroy your life."

Jeffrey Motts was a good kid who became addicted to drugs. He is not alone. Many people today struggle with addictions—if not to drugs or alcohol, then to food, exercise, pornography, shopping, work, or the Internet. Habits that were once called compulsions or weaknesses are now described as addictions.

Addictions destroy lives. They undermine confidence and self-respect. They produce painful, destructive patterns. They create a black hole of despair. They make people insensitive to the feelings of those who care for them, because addicts will stop at nothing to feed their addictions. Addictions rob children of loving parents. And they rob people of health and well-being.

Solomon painted a grotesque picture of the addict as one who keeps going back to his "drug" over and over again, thinking that surely this time it will satisfy. But it never does. It will only continue to get worse apart from God's liberating intervention.

BOTTOM LINE

Addictions are not glamorous. The next time you are tempted, flee to God for strength and help.

Moment of Strength: Proverbs 23:29-35

THE POWER OF HABITS

Look straight ahead, and fix your eyes on what lies before you.
Proverbs 4:25

IN A 1984 ARTICLE IN *SPORTS ILLUSTRATED*, Ron Fimrite wrote about former Los Angeles Dodgers manager Tommy Lasorda's battle with bad habits. As Lasorda told him,

> I took a pack of cigarettes from my pocket, stared at it and said, "Who's stronger, you or me?" The answer was me. Then I took a glass of vodka and said to it, "Who's stronger, you or me?" Again the answer was me. Then I took out a plate of linguine with clam sauce, looked it in the eye and said, "Who's stronger, you or me?" And the answer came back, "Linguine with clam sauce." I cannot beat linguine.

Solomon reveals that getting into a routine or a habit is easy but getting out is harder. Think about debt: easy to obtain, but harder to relinquish. Or weight: easy to gain, but harder to lose. Sleeping late, procrastinating, watching too much television, and surfing the Internet are all easy, comfortable ruts we fall into that are hard—but not impossible—to break.

Overcoming bad habits takes time. According to studies, it takes six weeks to break a habit, but sometimes we give up too soon. As with any habit, a simple decision to change is not enough. Proactive, prayerful steps are needed. What step can you take today to break a bad habit? Imagine how much better your life would be with God-honoring habits.

BOTTOM LINE

Replacing a bad habit with a good habit is critical to success. Willpower and wishful thinking are not enough. Ask God to help you take the first step.

Moment of Strength: Proverbs 4:26-27

THE POWER OF REASON

Avoiding a fight is a mark of honor; only fools insist on quarreling.
Proverbs 20:3

A COMPANY WAS CONVERTING TO a group medical plan that required 100 percent participation. Everyone signed up, except for one employee. He refused. His friends and coworkers tried to convince him to sign up, but to no avail. Finally, his boss visited him and told him either to sign up or be fired. He signed up. His friends asked him what made the difference. He replied, "The boss explained it in a way I could understand."

Solomon reminded us that honor exists in doing what is right. Anyone can take the path of least resistance. Anyone can give in to pressure. It takes a strong person to take the difficult choice and make the right decision.

Studies have shown that an immediate health effect will make more people change a habit than some distant threat. In other words, the more real and pressing the consequences, the greater the chance of change. That's why when confronted with the reality of death, people will stop smoking, lose weight, and start exercising.

Our bad habits, though often pleasurable, may be the reason we are not achieving the results we long for. We need a strong reason like health, success, better relationships, and, most important, the glory of God to ditch a bad habit.

Let the hope of a better future motivate you.

BOTTOM LINE

Are the things you're doing leading you to where you want to go? What do you need to change? Where do you need to look for motivation?

Moment of Strength: Proverbs 3:1-2

THE REPLACEMENT PRINCIPLE

Only simpletons believe everything they're told!
The prudent carefully consider their steps.
Proverbs 14:15

PSYCHOLOGIST ROBERT EPSTEIN REVEALS three keys to changing a bad habit into a good one.

First, modify your environment. One student started a new habit of bike riding simply by placing her bicycle in the doorway before she left for school. When she returned home, the bike was the first thing she saw, and that was all she needed to get started.

Second, monitor your behavior. Psychologists don't know why monitoring works, but studies have shown that if we monitor what we do, we'll probably do better. If we keep a record of what we eat, we'll probably start eating better. When we track our spending, we'll probably end up saving money.

Third, make a commitment and tell someone. When we make a commitment to another person, we put pressure on ourselves to follow through. That's why people have exercise partners and pay money to attend seminars. Commitments help us to persevere and accomplish our goals.

Solomon reminds us that the right steps have to be taken to move us in the right direction. It's sensible. Taking the appropriate action steps and moving forward toward our goals yields results in the long run.

Is there an area in your life where you need to apply Epstein's advice? How could you put each step into practice? Breaking a bad habit will not be easy, but it can be done with the right actions, fueled by the right motivation, and sustained by the grace of God.

BOTTOM LINE

Good habits aid our growth in godliness. Ask God to help you make the connection between how you're living and the results you're achieving.

Moment of Strength: Psalm 119:45

SHOW THEM THE MONEY

Even while we were with you, we gave you this command:
"Those unwilling to work will not get to eat."
2 Thessalonians 3:10

HAVE YOU EVER NOTICED IT's easier to spend other people's money than your own? The same is true for your children. Your kids probably have no problem spending lots of your money on clothes and toys. But if they *earn* a dollar, they might spend twenty minutes agonizing over just the right candy bar to purchase.

Many financial experts agree: If you want to teach your children money management, let them earn an allowance. Most parents wait too long to begin. Start the training early. Once your child understands the concept of money and shows material desires, you can introduce an allowance. For some kids, that's as young as age five.

The sooner your kids learn the relationship between work and money, the better. Many children grow up feeling entitled. That kind of thinking needs to be replaced with an attitude of gratitude and a solid work ethic. The beauty of an allowance is that it is earned, not simply given. Your child's allowance can be tied into chores and other duties around the house so that everybody wins.

Make sure to explain to your children that all money is God's, so it's important to honor Him by giving some back for His work. Saving money for bigger purchases can also be a good lesson in delayed gratification. The Bible talks a lot about money, so you should do the same with your children.

BOTTOM LINE

By passing down sound financial strategies, you can help your children grow up with the right attitude toward money.

Moment of Strength: Luke 12:15

IN THE NEWS

"The time promised by God has come at last!" he announced.
"The Kingdom of God is near! Repent of your sins and believe the Good News!"
Mark 1:15

THE INTERNET CAN BE A WONDERFUL TOOL. It places a plethora of news and facts at your fingertips. As fictional office manager Michael Scott (Steve Carell) once said on the popular TV sitcom *The Office*: "Wikipedia is the best thing ever. Anyone in the world can write anything they want about any subject, so you know you are getting the best possible information." As helpful as the Internet can be, we obviously can't trust everything we read there. We have to check our sources to make sure the news is reliable.

God's Word is always reliable. Jesus Christ came to the world saying, "The time promised by God has come at last! . . . The Kingdom of God is near! Repent of your sins and believe the Good News!" (Mark 1:15). We can confidently share Jesus' Good News with others because it's the truth.

When God's Son said He was bringing Good News, it was rock-solid truth—whether people believed it or not. For those first disciples who believed, it changed their lives, and they took the Good News to the world.

God's truth is just as transformational today as it was two thousand years ago. Jesus may not ask you to leave your family or change your career, but He does expect your life to be different. And that's good news. It's so much more than good advice. It's something that happens to us, rather than something we make happen ourselves. Our job is to continually expose ourselves to God's Good News.

BOTTOM LINE

Think of how God's Good News has changed your life. Praise God for His truth and be sensitive to opportunities to share the Good News with others.

Moment of Strength: Luke 9:6

PROBLEM AREA

Wise words bring approval, but fools are destroyed by their own words.
Ecclesiastes 10:12

MEN AND WOMEN ARE DIFFERENT. No shock there. Just looking in the mirror reveals that. But some differences are subtler than others. Studies show that women consistently speak more than twenty thousand words a day. Men, on the other hand, say fewer than ten thousand on average. How we communicate and what we talk about differs greatly between the sexes too.

Many women love to talk things out. The mere act of communicating makes them feel better. Most men don't share that opinion. They tend to speak less and problem-solve more. University of Missouri professor Amanda J. Rose has studied this dynamic and says it can lead to difficulties in romantic relationships.

"Women may really push their partners to share pent-up worries and concerns because they hold expectations that talking makes people feel better," Rose says, "but their partners may just not be interested." You can see why it's important to understand these differences in disposition and expectations.

As you communicate with the women in your life, try to be aware of their needs as well as your own comfort zone. Talking things through with your wife will help her feel more bonded to you. During times when you don't feel like talking, be gentle and considerate as you explain your needs. By being gracious with your speech, you'll avoid conflict and build a better relationship. Wise words are gracious.

BOTTOM LINE

Even when you don't feel like talking, always speak kindly to your wife. Your gracious words will help prevent misunderstanding.

Moment of Strength: Ephesians 4:29

GOOD SPORTS

Share each other's burdens, and in this way obey the law of Christ.
Galatians 6:2

DEPENDING ON WHOSE WEBSITE you're looking at, everything from flag football to canoeing to pickleball (a combination of tennis and Ping-Pong played on a small court) claims to be the fastest-growing sport for adult men. The truth is that a lot of guys still love to compete well past their college days. Jamar Johnson, chief commissioner of the Community Basketball Leagues, observes that people like to play sports for three reasons: *competition, camaraderie,* and *community*. Relationships forged on the playing field often last the longest and grow the deepest.

The anticipation of striving together makes playing sports exciting. Wouldn't it be cool if going to church were like walking into the YMCA for a rec league game?

Church can be like that. In fact, God desires that we get some of the same things out of church that we look for in sports—camaraderie and community (probably not competition, though). When we go to church, we should try to build lasting, deep relationships. As Galatians 6:2 says, "Share each other's burdens, and in this way obey the law of Christ."

Look for opportunities to help others. Though we don't need face paint and team jerseys to go to church, we do need to "get in the game" and connect with our brothers and sisters in Christ.

BOTTOM LINE

Look for a church to help you grow in Christ—and in your personal relationships.

Moment of Strength: Hebrews 10:24-25

SURF'S UP

O LORD of Heaven's Armies, what joy for those who trust in you.
Psalm 84:12

ONE OF THE BASIC SKILLS OF surfing is learning how to catch a wave. As a wave approaches, you must turn toward the beach and paddle as hard as you can. The wave will then lift you and your surfboard. While your natural inclination will be to lean back, it's important to keep your weight forward and your arms paddling. If you do it right, you'll find yourself at the highest point of the wave with a decision to make: commit to riding it or bail out.

It may feel scary, but if you lean in and keep going, you'll start sliding down the face of the wave. Soon the wave will pull you, and then all you have to do is stand up and enjoy the ride! It can actually begin to feel effortless, even natural.

Catching a wave requires taking a risk. But if you don't take the risk, you'll end up sitting on your surfboard going nowhere, bobbing up and down in the water. Living out your faith involves a similar risk. Sometimes God will ask you to lean into a situation when all you want to do is bail out. At those times, you have to trust the Lord.

Psalm 84:12 reminds us that trusting in the Lord results in happiness. Why? Because God is trustworthy! When you give up control and trust God, that's when you begin to experience the abundant life. That's when faith becomes exciting. That's when your understanding of God's power and grace really begins to grow. Don't be afraid to risk.

BOTTOM LINE

To enjoy true happiness, you have to fully commit yourself to God, even if it feels scary. Is there something that God has been nudging you to step out and do?

Moment of Strength: Psalm 37:5-7

DON'T WASTE YOUR TRIAL

When your endurance is fully developed,
you will be perfect and complete, needing nothing.

James 1:4

TRIALS ARE INEVITABLE AND INESCAPABLE. We have no power to determine their size and scope. They often burst upon us with little or no advance warning. But we can choose what we do with our trials.

James, leader of the early church in Jerusalem, cautioned his people against shortcutting God's work of sanctification. He reminded them that trials can be the very tools God uses to shape the character of His children. But there's a catch. We have to trust the process and remain patient.

There are two kinds of people in the world: those who—when blindsided by hardship—complain, resist, and push away from God, seeking temporary relief in substances, distractions, or friendships; and those who cling to God under the same circumstances.

Make no mistake, patient endurance isn't a Pollyanna, head-in-the-sand approach to suffering. It isn't a call to maintain a fake smile when sorrowful. Trials can crush the soul, dredging hidden idols to the surface and provoking soul-piercing questions. But the wise man of God chooses to filter his emotions through the truth that God is sovereign and good, no matter how things look. A wise man of God trusts the process whereby God reveals the false gods that people are tempted to trust in, so that we might learn to put all of our trust in Him, the only one worthy of it.

BOTTOM LINE

Trials can be a source of either sanctifying joy or unending discontentment. Don't waste your trials.

Moment of Strength: James 1:1-13

THE WEIGHT OF YOUR WORDS

*Dear brothers and sisters, not many of you should
become teachers in the church, for we who teach will be
judged more strictly. Indeed, we all make many mistakes.
For if we could control our tongues, we would be perfect
and could also control ourselves in every other way.*

James 3:1-2

THE WORDS OF A LEADER MATTER because words are powerful instruments, especially in the hands of someone in a position to communicate biblical truth. The book of James reminds us of the gravity of the things we say on behalf of God. This is why pastors and Bible teachers should not teach more or less than what the Bible says.

You may be reading this and thinking to yourself, *Whew, glad I'm not a pastor*. But this sober warning in James 3 applies to leaders at all levels. The Scriptures urge us to weigh our words because they can have such a profound impact. They are more powerful than we realize—they're compared to the bridle of a horse, the rudder of a ship, and the spark of a fire. And this is by design. God intended language to be powerfully used for good. But sin has made the tongue a potential force for evil.

The only one who can tame the tongue is Jesus. He gives you the power to harness your tongue for good. So the question for every Christian man is simply this: How are you using your words? For good, or for evil? As a leader, you can move masses of people to positive action with words of truth and grace. Or you can move masses of people to frustration and sorrow with words of evil. The tongue is that powerful. Ask the Lord to help you control your tongue so that it will be an instrument of blessing to others.

BOTTOM LINE

Leaders at all levels must consider the gravity of their words.

Moment of Strength: James 3:1-12

WHAT MOVES GOD'S HEART?

When the Lord saw her, his heart overflowed with compassion.
"Don't cry!" he said.

Luke 7:13

JESUS WAS ON HIS WAY TO the town of Nain when He came upon a funeral procession. A woman, who was already a widow, had just lost her only son. Moved with compassion, Jesus did what only God can do: "He walked over to the coffin and touched it. . . . 'Young man,' he said, 'I tell you, get up.' Then the dead boy sat up and began to talk! And Jesus gave him back to his mother" (Luke 7:14-15).

Jesus could have raised every dead person and healed every pain for every single person that crossed His path. But He didn't. We can feel bewildered or even slighted by God when we read about these momentous miracles that never seem to happen for us. Are we second-class saints? No, not at all. Jesus did not come to create paradise on earth. He came to save us from our sin and even from some (but not all) of the pain of living in a fallen world. He came to restore our relationship with the Father now and for all eternity. The best is yet to come.

The miracle Jesus performed for the widow of Nain is not a promise to do a miracle for us. But it does testify to the power of God to one day raise us from the dead, and it shows that there is something deep within God's nature that is "moved with compassion" when He sees our pain. We may not see a healing miracle in this life, but this life is not the end of things. In the meantime, reach out to others who are hurting with the love and compassion God supplies.

BOTTOM LINE

The compassion Jesus showed for the hurting reveals a heart that cares deeply about every loss you have suffered and every grief you endure. Let that sink in.

Moment of Strength: 2 Corinthians 12:1-10

WHAT IS GOD REALLY LIKE?

The Son radiates God's own glory and expresses the very character of God.
Hebrews 1:3

LOOKING INTO A VAST, silent, star-filled sky, countless souls have wondered, "What is God really like? Does He understand me? Does He care? Is He forever disappointed with me? Mad at me? Can He ever smile on me? Does He like me? How can I know when I can't see Him with my eyes, touch Him with my hands, or hear Him with my ears? Do I just take my best guess? Imagine? How will I ever know?"

Today's passage says that Jesus "expresses the very character of God." If you want to know what God is like, look at Jesus. More than all the prophets who have ever lived, Jesus has made God understandable. Because of His great love for us, He willingly endured unimaginable suffering on the cross to secure our salvation. The Cross shows the depths of God's love for us in the clearest way possible.

We sometimes create an artificial disconnect between Jesus and the Father. This is especially true for men who had an angry, abusive, absent, or emotionally distant father. In our minds, we can understand that God is committed to us, but we may feel an emotional connection to Jesus (a "big brother" role) while we feel distant from God in His Father role. But the heart of the Father and the heart of Jesus beat as one. If you want to get to know God, get to know Jesus, who said, "The Father and I are one" (John 10:30).

BOTTOM LINE

Jesus is the revelation of God. He shows us what the Father is really like. Ask God to help you see Him clearly.

Moment of Strength: John 17

HOLDING ON TO HOPE

Go back to your family, and tell them everything God has done for you.
Luke 8:39

THE TORTURED SOUL WAS demon-possessed, driven to madness, and living naked among the tombs. Try to visualize it. Watch him scramble over the stones. Hear him scream in the darkness. Feel the cold night rain lash on his bare skin. Look into the marred, tear-streaked face of despair. It is hard to imagine a worse fate. But the man did not suffer in isolation. His parents lived with the unique pain that is borne by those who watch helplessly while their child suffers.

Into the middle of that horrific drama stepped Jesus. A word from the Son of God brought spiritual healing and deliverance to the beleaguered man's mind. And then Jesus spoke a parting word of restoration: "Go back to your family, and tell them everything God has done for you."

It is in the heart of God to heal wounded souls and reunite families. That is why hope should still burn brightly for every grieving parent who has been praying, perhaps for years, for a lost and seemingly hopeless child. There are no pat answers, secret formulas for success, or guarantees. We cannot discern the complex interplay between fallen human will and the ways of God. We cannot understand why things happen the way they do. But we can know that the heart of our Father is good, and we can continue to hope and pray, trusting that He knows what He is doing and is faithful to us.

BOTTOM LINE

Keep bringing your pain to God, and humbly ask Him to intercede. And when nothing else makes sense, trust the heart of God.

Moment of Strength: Isaiah 59

TRULY PUTTING HER FIRST

Love . . . does not demand its own way.
1 Corinthians 13:4-5

GIVE-AND-TAKE IS fundamental to a healthy marriage. It is perfectly fine and healthy to be open about what you want. It is neither fine nor healthy to stubbornly insist on your own way. Today's passage reminds us that love is not selfish. The application of this Scripture is wide and covers every aspect of your marriage.

Here's a simple example: where to go out for dinner. We can voice a preference ("Hon, I feel like Italian food") while also inviting her preference ("What sounds good to you?"). Couples with a healthy relationship routinely negotiate, take turns, and defer to each other in all sorts of ways. But what about the big stuff?

What is a Christ follower to do when the issue is far more momentous than where to eat or where to go on vacation? Tom is offered a big promotion with far more pay and opportunity if he accepts a position in a major city. He wants to seize the chance. His wife can't imagine making the kids leave their school, their friends, their great youth group, and the sense of community in the small town they have lived in for the past decade. He sees all the advantages; she feels all the drawbacks. Tom's inner jerk urges him to make a unilateral decision, to act selfishly rather than out of love. God's way is for him to lovingly, painstakingly, prayerfully work through the decision together with his wife.

BOTTOM LINE

Jesus put others first, and He wants us to do the same. Are there areas in your life where you sense God is asking you to put your wife first?

Moment of Strength: Galatians 5:13-15

LIVE INTENTIONALLY

Work willingly at whatever you do, as though you were
working for the Lord rather than for people.
Colossians 3:23

SOMETIMES, we guys just like to take life easy and relax a little bit. There's nothing wrong with that—as long as we're careful not to become complacent or indifferent about the things that matter most. Indifference is not how God feels or responds to us, and it's not how He wants us to feel or respond to others. He wants us to live life intentionally, putting first things first.

To live intentionally, a man has to know what he believes, and he has to hold to his beliefs with great conviction. That comes first. We develop the mind of Christ by reading Scripture regularly and prayerfully. By God's grace, this strengthens our faith, and when we're firm in our faith, we're able to share our beliefs with others much more effectively. This is God's plan. He pours into us so that we can pour into others.

No matter where you work, you are an ambassador for Christ (2 Corinthians 5:20). Part of living intentionally is doing your work for the glory of God and the good of others. With the right mind-set, all your work takes on eternal significance.

Finally, in the passage known as the great commission (Matthew 28:18-20), Jesus tells us to spread the gospel all over the world and to make disciples of all nations. Intentional living includes being actively involved in God's great mission.

BOTTOM LINE

Begin praying and planning how you can live more intentionally.

Moment of Strength: Matthew 9:35-38

BE A MAN OF INTEGRITY

People with integrity walk safely, but those who
follow crooked paths will be exposed.
Proverbs 10:9

AMONG ALL THE MEN IN THE BIBLE, who better exemplifies integrity than Job? God said there was not another man on earth with Job's integrity. Job feared God, turned away from evil, resisted Satan's temptations, and maintained his integrity even when his friends turned against him and his wife begged him to curse God.

We hope we're never tested as Job was. All of his children died in a windstorm; all of his animals (i.e., his wealth) were stolen or killed; all of his servants were murdered. In other words, he suffered severely. Maintaining integrity was no easy thing for Job, and it isn't for us, either.

What does it look like to be a man of integrity today? How do we show that we fear God? By trusting and obeying in the power of the Spirit. How do we turn away from evil? By loving God more than the things of this world. And that happens as we learn to rest in God's great love for us.

How can you resist temptation? Spend time daily in God's Word, striving to maintain a clean mind and a pure heart. Run from anything that would endanger your marriage or your family. Have other guys in your life who love you and help you stay honest in all your relationships and responsibilities.

Integrity doesn't just happen. We need a plan to ensure that we're living lives of integrity.

BOTTOM LINE

What plan do you have or will you put in place to be a man of integrity? Ask God to guide you in becoming a man of integrity.

Moment of Strength: Job 1:6-22

LIFE INSTRUCTIONS

O people, the LORD has told you what is good, and this is what he requires of you:
to do what is right, to love mercy, and to walk humbly with your God.
Micah 6:8

IF EVER THERE WAS A SINGLE VERSE OF Scripture that lays out a brief summary of how Christians should live their lives, it's Micah 6:8. These few short phrases contain a blueprint for virtually every conceivable circumstance we could face. Take this verse, memorize it, and most importantly, put it into action.

What does the Lord require of you? First, you're to do what is right. Maybe there's a business deal you've been mulling over that just doesn't seem quite fair to the other side. Maybe you got pulled over for speeding, and rather than argue with the officer, you accepted the ticket. It was, after all, your foot on the gas pedal.

What does it mean to love mercy? Mercy is not receiving the judgment we deserve. Mercy is what God shows us every day. So we are to love mercy and show it to others. Maybe your wife wrecked the car. Maybe your son got a bad grade in algebra. You show them mercy because you have been shown mercy by God.

Finally, walk humbly with your God. Everything you've ever accomplished has been at God's good pleasure. On the flip side of that coin, He has carried you through every dark moment you've ever experienced. Through the good times and the bad, God has lovingly been there for you. How incredible is that? Really, the only way you can do anything at all is by His grace, so humility is the proper attitude.

BOTTOM LINE

Micah 6:8 is a beautiful verse and a great way to live our lives. So do what is right, love mercy, and walk humbly with God.

Moment of Strength: Deuteronomy 10:12

WONDERFULLY MADE

Thank you for making me so wonderfully complex!
Your workmanship is marvelous—how well I know it.

Psalm 139:14

THE CALL FROM JESSE'S TEACHER came out of the blue. No matter what she tried, she said, Jesse would not—could not?—complete his work. He wasn't being ugly or disrespectful. He was simply taking forever to get anything done. His dad wound up spending time at school, observing so that he and the teacher could figure out what to do next.

Jesse has Asperger's syndrome. It's been a wild ride to say the least. But then there are moments like this one: Not long after the incident at school, Jesse came home from his weekly piano lesson with a book of Tchaikovsky compositions. Within minutes, he was playing the intro to the "Nutcracker March" almost perfectly.

Jesse has left his parents scratching their heads more than once, but they also know that there are other parents of special-needs children who have greater challenges than they do. Although Jesse isn't wired like a lot of other people, he's otherwise perfectly healthy. How can his parents complain when he's able to walk, talk, and tell the silly jokes he loves to tell?

If you're the parent of a special-needs child, please know that you're not alone. There is hope and help to be found in any number of resources. You discovered long ago that you don't have all the answers, and that's a hard place to be. Consider it an opportunity to lean on Christ that much more.

BOTTOM LINE

Being the parent of a special-needs child is challenging to say the least, but it's also a chance to rely on God. He is always more than enough.

Moment of Strength: Psalm 139:15-18

AMBASSADORS OR UNDERCOVER?

You are the salt of the earth. But what good is salt
if it has lost its flavor? Can you make it salty again?
It will be thrown out and trampled underfoot as worthless.
Matthew 5:13

IT CAN BE TRICKY THESE DAYS TO be a bold Christian in the workplace, so many of us tend to keep our faith undercover. Maybe we don't want to be known as religious nutcases, or perhaps we believe that religion's not an appropriate topic of conversation at work. It could be that we lack the confidence to answer any questions or rebuttals, so we let fear keep us from speaking up. Whatever the reason, we stay mum when someone shares a struggle, brags about a sin, or shares their belief in some ideology not centered on Jesus. We have in our hearts the solution that others need, but we keep it under wraps until we're in "safe company."

Jesus taught that we're to be salt and light in the world. Salt by itself doesn't nourish or satisfy a need, but it makes one thirsty for the water that does satisfy. Likewise, light by itself doesn't solve a situation, but it enables us to see the right path. Both salt and light have a positive effect on their environments; they are not neutral. Light can't blend in with the darkness around it, and salt that isn't salty . . . well, Jesus said it's useless. Paul tells us in 2 Corinthians 5:20 that we are "Christ's ambassadors." That means we represent Him and speak up for His interests. Keeping quiet when the world around us needs God's comfort and direction is like putting a light under a basket—it doesn't make sense.

BOTTOM LINE

Don't hide your light or lose your saltiness. Ask God to give you discernment and courage.

Moment of Strength: 2 Timothy 2:15

SMART BUYING

True godliness with contentment is itself great wealth.
1 Timothy 6:6

IN ADDITION TO TRADITIONAL ADVERTISING, there are many services today offering deep discounts to restaurants we like, services we want, and trips we want to take. These services can be a great way to save money, but we need to make sure we're using them wisely. We can tell ourselves that we're only buying coupons to places we would go anyway, but it can be easy to overestimate just how often we would normally go to those businesses and how much we would spend while we're there. If we're not careful, we may end up spending more than we would otherwise and may have to adjust our plans to use a coupon before it expires. All the while, we think we're being smart and saving all kinds of money as we take advantage of the great deals that keep coming and coming and coming.

Keep in mind that businesses offer great sales in order to make money, not to do consumers any favors. There's nothing wrong with that, but we need to make sure that we're being good stewards of our finances and making wise purchases. So before you automatically take advantage of the next great deal, stop and think and pray. Ask yourself if you really need what's being offered. Ask God to give you wisdom. Then make the best decision you can.

BOTTOM LINE

Beware of the ways that coupons and special offers may be feeding your desire for more. Ask God for the wisdom to know what's a wise purchase for you.

Moment of Strength: John 6:32-35

BARELY LIVING

When Jesus saw him and knew he had been ill for a long time, he asked him,
"Would you like to get well?"
John 5:6

THE MAN IN JOHN 5 WHO HAD been an invalid for thirty-eight years was alive, no doubt, but you might argue whether he was really living. Not only was he sick, but he also didn't have any friends to help him (John 5:7). Finding the man in this state, Jesus asked him what might seem to be an obvious question: "Would you like to get well?" Notice that Jesus asked whether the man wanted to *get* well rather than *be* well. Jesus healed the man immediately (so he could be well physically), but His greater concern was for the man's spiritual condition. That's why Jesus sought the man out later and found him in the Temple. We read there that Jesus addressed the man's sin problem so that he could get well spiritually.

Don't misunderstand—we don't earn our salvation. If we could reconcile ourselves to God on our own, it wouldn't have been necessary for Jesus to leave His home in heaven the first time. But we can't, so He came, and now we have a choice of how to live. If you've been feeling down-and-out, by God's grace it's time to get up. He provides everything we need to be free of what holds us in bondage. Picking up your mat means taking responsibility for your life and working to remove those things in your life that have crippled you spiritually. It also means walking with God again in the freedom and power that He provides.

BOTTOM LINE

Don't settle for barely being alive when God's will for you is to thrive abundantly in the new life you have in Christ. What's holding you back?

Moment of Strength: John 10:10

NOT IN THE MOOD

The man who finds a wife finds a treasure, and he receives favor from the LORD.
Proverbs 18:22

ONCE UPON A TIME, early in your marriage, physical intimacy was a big part of your relationship. You didn't need an excuse. Nowadays, you need a battle plan executed with the precision of a four-star general to have any hope of a romantic interlude.

It's been too long, right?

"We get off work at 1700 hours, and Susie needs to be at her piano lesson by 1900 hours. You drop Bobby off at his soccer practice at 1915 hours. We need milk and a few other things, so I'll swing by the grocery at 1930. We'll meet at the house right after that. Ready—go!"

That's an exaggeration, but life can seem that way sometimes.

Sometimes, no matter how hard you try, the avalanche of responsibilities you face will not allow you and your wife to be alone together in the same place at the same time. Other times, she might be dead tired and just not in the mood. You might be worn to a frazzle and not in the mood either. Who knows?

Don't let busyness drive a wedge between the two of you. Your wife is still a treasured gift from God, and she's still the best friend you've ever had, by far. Always let her know how much she means to you, with no expectation of it leading to anything else. Physical intimacy is an important part of marriage, but it's far from the only part.

BOTTOM LINE

Physical intimacy with your wife is awesome, but when life's distractions and responsibilities come between you, don't let them crush your relationship.

Moment of Strength: Genesis 2:18-25

HALF BAKED

Amaziah did what was pleasing in the LORD's sight, but not wholeheartedly.
2 Chronicles 25:2

SOUNDS LIKE A WEIRD DREAM, doesn't it? It's definitely not the way to live. But think a little deeper—do you ever give God or your wife halfhearted devotion?

Amaziah's kingship was a nightmare, and one reason was his tendency to worry. He was constantly worried about what others thought about him, and he sought to please everyone. When we worry, we show God halfhearted devotion. Excessive worry is a lack of trust in God and His Word. It's also a sin.

The danger of being a halfhearted Christian is that we can look okay on the outside but be empty on the inside. Though we may think we've got everyone fooled (including ourselves), God won't be fooled by our halfhearted commitment. An occasional dalliance with online flirting, porn, or a bar with the boys after work may not seem like a big deal, but those things undermine your relationships with God and your wife. God wants you to be fully committed. And so does your wife.

The best way to love your wife is to love God with wholehearted devotion. Only when you've given your first love away to God will you have a heart filled up with love for your wife. Anything else is just half-baked and not worth much.

BOTTOM LINE
Love your wife best by loving God first.

Moment of Strength: Revelation 2:1-7

WHO DROPPED THE BALL?

Again he said, "Peace be with you.
As the Father has sent me, so I am sending you."
John 20:21

IN 1916, GEORGE ALLEN HAD the dubious distinction of playing halfback in a record-setting football game, when Cumberland College lost to Georgia Tech 222–0. Georgia Tech's coach was John Heisman, the namesake of the Heisman Trophy. As the score mounted, Cumberland College became dramatically demoralized. Then, on one of the few plays when Allen's team had the ball, the ball was snapped to the quarterback, who immediately fumbled it. Tech's linemen were charging in, the ball was bouncing around the backfield, and the quarterback screamed at Allen, "Pick it up! Pick it up!" Allen took one look at those charging linemen and shouted, "Pick it up yourself! You dropped it!"

That's a lot like us, isn't it? We want to place the blame and the responsibility on someone else.

Jesus gave us the responsibility and privilege of sharing His message with others. Note the word *you* in this verse. The charge was given to every follower of Jesus, not just to pastors and missionaries. This is our responsibility, each one of us. It is not optional. We can't pass it off, delegate it to someone else, or pay someone to do it for us. You and I are to communicate the message of Jesus. We have the honor of being His witnesses to a lost world.

Let's pick up the ball of the gospel and run with it. Many people will be glad we did.

BOTTOM LINE

Look for the divine appointments God has for you today to share His story.

Moment of Strength: Romans 10:14

THE COMMAND TO LOVE

The most important commandment is this: "Listen, O Israel!
The LORD our God is the one and only LORD. And you must love the
LORD your God with all your heart, all your soul, all your mind, and
all your strength." The second is equally important: "Love your
neighbor as yourself." No other commandment is greater than these.
Mark 12:29-31

A MAN WAS IN NEED OF CLOTHES, especially coats and blankets for the winter. Another man saw the need and wanted to help. He sent word out to others for help. Many people responded by donating clothes, coats, and blankets for the needy man.

Another man was soon to be released from jail. Separated from his family, he needed a coat, a meal, a night's lodging, and a bus ticket to return home to his parents. A Sunday school class provided the funds, and two men from the class picked the man up from jail, gave him a coat, took him out for dinner, got him to a hotel, and purchased a bus ticket for him. Both acts of generosity and service were examples of loving your neighbor as you would want to be loved. Even better, it's what Jesus commands us to do.

With the words "as yourself," Jesus is not advocating self-love; rather, He is showing us how to love others. We should love them as we would want to be loved. There are all kinds of ways that we can show love for others. Buy lunch for a single parent. Call a shut-in to encourage her and pray for her. Babysit for a neighbor. Pray for five people you know who are hurting. Volunteer in a community soup kitchen. Mentor a student or young man who could use some direction. Ask the Lord to open your eyes to the needs all around you.

BOTTOM LINE

What are some practical ways you can serve others the way you would want to be served? Ask God to give you ideas and a willing heart.

Moment of Strength: Matthew 7:12

LEADING, FOLLOWING, WATCHING

You should imitate me, just as I imitate Christ.
1 Corinthians 11:1

THE APOSTLE PAUL would have fit well into today's corporate structure. He could've written books on leadership, winning, perseverance, and vision. Paul's motor had a different gear—he was compelled to preach the gospel (1 Corinthians 9:16). And he worked to lead churches and disciple younger believers such as Timothy.

The best leaders are also great followers. Though by all appearances Paul had a strong personality, he also could have written books on humility, submission, and service. When he first came to know Christ, he spent time being taught by Peter (Galatians 1:18). Above all else, Paul wanted to follow Christ (Philippians 3:10-14). It has often been said that the world has never seen one man completely sold out to Jesus—yet Paul came as close as anyone ever has.

Paul also knew when to get out of God's way. He had great wisdom from the Lord and knew that he ultimately had to hide behind the Cross of Christ and let others see Jesus, not him. In his second letter to Timothy, he acknowledges that it was time for him to exit stage right (2 Timothy 4:6) and let another generation lead. Great followers are sensitive to God's leading and know when it's time to step aside. May God give you the strength to imitate Jesus and recognize His guidance in your life.

BOTTOM LINE

Find a leader to follow and a follower to lead. Above all, make sure that you're following Jesus yourself and listening to His voice.

Moment of Strength: 2 Timothy 2:2

LEAVING A LEGACY

Now that I am old and gray, do not abandon me, O God. Let me proclaim your
power to this new generation, your mighty miracles to all who come after me.
Psalm 71:18

EVERY MAN SHOULD occasionally turn off the TV to get a sober hold on reality, and there is no better way to do this than to stroll through a cemetery. Since mortality occurs in 100 percent of the male population, it's good to be reminded that we spend a very short time on this earth.

But thanks to Jesus, death is not the end of the story. Our lives on earth can still speak volumes to those who come after us. The cold, hard headstone need not be the only memorial of our existence.

The church of St. Michael's in Lyndhurst, England, dates back hundreds of years. At one point, the cemetery around the church fell into disrepair, and headstones were broken and scattered. Then church leaders repositioned the headstones as steps along the footpath leading up the hill to the church. In this way, all who go to worship there are assisted by those who have gone before them.

How can the memory of your life aid others in their eternal climb? Concern yourself more with character than comfort. Don't go to the grave with your best work still in you. Strive to give more than you take. Use your time wisely. Center your life on God and His Word. In doing so, you will proclaim God's power to the next generation, and you will leave a lasting legacy of His work in your life.

BOTTOM LINE

Start living and leaving your future legacy today. If you haven't done so
already, prayerfully create a life plan that can help keep you focused.

Moment of Strength: Hebrews 11:1-4

WORKING MUSICIAN?

[Some] served as singers at God's Temple. Their daily responsibilities
were carried out according to the terms of a royal command.
Nehemiah 11:22-23

SOMETIMES, church artists have gotten by on their giftedness and haven't been as quick to meet the needs of others as they could have been. In Nehemiah's day, the king established a policy that the musicians would have daily tasks in God's house in addition to leading worship. Singer by night, janitor by day!

Scripture also reminds us of the example of Bezalel (Exodus 35), a gifted artist who was filled with the Holy Spirit in wisdom, understanding, and knowledge. He had teaching gifts. Ultimately, the gift of music is simply a means to another end—it gives one the opportunity to serve.

If you are a church musician, make sure that you see yourself as part of the entire church and not just as a specialist called in to perform. After all, you aren't more talented than others, really; it's just that your gifts are more on display, while the gifts of others are not as visible. You are still called to serve others, and often that doesn't have anything to do with your music.

If you're not a musician, don't let one bad encounter spoil your impression of artists. Accept them into your circle, even if they see life differently than you do. Musicians and other artists can help us interpret what God is saying to us, and help us get in touch with the emotional part of our lives that God created for His glory.

BOTTOM LINE

The church needs worship leaders who serve. It also needs the body of Christ
to embrace the artists among us.

Moment of Strength: Exodus 35:30-35

LONELY IS THE SADDEST WORD

Jacob left Beersheba and traveled toward Haran.
Genesis 28:10

LONELINESS IS NO ONE'S FRIEND but is everyone's acquaintance. Loneliness eats at your insides and brings a vacuum of emptiness. It creates a gnawing hunger of wanting to belong, to be understood, and to be loved. You can have a million friends and still be lonely. Loneliness is not the absence of people; it is the absence of intimacy. Loneliness doesn't come from being alone; it comes from feeling alone.

That was how Jacob felt. He was a man on the run. He cheated his brother, Esau, out of his birthright, and Esau threatened to kill him. Jacob left Beersheba with his birthright and the blessing and little else. He was a fugitive, he was alone, and he was depressed. The place where he found himself—a desolate, lonely place—was a picture of his barren heart. It was a place of dashed hopes and dreams.

There are some things you can do when you are feeling alone. Find a friend. Get in a group. Get out of the house. Do something new. Forgive those who have hurt you. Spend time with God. Read a good book. Help someone who is less fortunate than you. And remember, you are never truly alone. The Lord is with you, and He loves you.

BOTTOM LINE

Everyone experiences loneliness from time to time, but no one has to stay lonely. God promises to always be with us (Psalm 34:17-19).

Moment of Strength: Hebrews 13:5

AN UNDERDOG'S HEALING

"Don't be afraid!" David said. "I intend to show kindness to you. . . ."
Mephibosheth bowed respectfully and exclaimed, "Who is your servant,
that you should show such kindness to a dead dog like me?"
2 Samuel 9:7-8

MEPHIBOSHETH SAW HIMSELF not only as a dog, but as a dead dog. This was understandable, given the strikes against him. He was an orphan and the last survivor of a deposed dynasty. He had lost his family's wealth and prestige. Even more, he was permanently crippled from a childhood accident. In a culture that often saw handicaps as a divine curse, it's no wonder Mephibosheth held such a low opinion of himself. All the voices in his head whispered his unworthiness. The mental scripts he played and replayed made him nothing but a dead dog. It took a royal offer of indescribable grace to heal his broken sense of self and restore his royal identity.

King David summoned Mephibosheth with one simple goal in mind: to show him God's kindness (2 Samuel 9:3). The Hebrew word for kindness, *hesed*, indicates freely given love and grace. The book of 2 Samuel teaches that if we want to know what God's grace looks like, we can look at how David treats Mephibosheth.

What did that look like? (1) A summons out of nowhere, just as God called us when we were unworthy; (2) an unexpected embrace—like the father embracing the Prodigal Son; (3) a restoration of what was lost; and (4) a seat at the king's table forever. Though God never healed Mephibosheth's damaged body, He restored his broken soul.

BOTTOM LINE

When God saves us from sin, He delivers us from brokenness, as well. Are there areas of brokenness in your life that need the Father's healing? Ask Him for it.

Moment of Strength: 2 Samuel 9:1-13

A MUST-HAVE TOOL

*I was a skilled craftsman beside Him. I was His
delight every day, always rejoicing before Him.*
Proverbs 8:30, HCSB

WHAT IS THE ONE TOOL you can't live without? Some might say their table saw, whereas others would fight you if you tried to take away their battery-operated drill. So what's a key tool for an apprentice of the Master Carpenter? It's wisdom.

When God created the heavens and the earth, wisdom was a crucial tool on His belt. When He formed the heart of the giraffe, the legs of the cheetah, and the fins of the killer whale, He used the wisdom tool. And when He breathed life into Adam and Eve, knowing what it would cost Him to restore the relationship with humanity once they sinned, His wisdom put the finishing touches on creation.

Hakam is the Hebrew word for wisdom. It carries the idea of "living skillfully." Where our knowledge of God intersects with and influences the way we live our lives, at that point we can be said to possess wisdom. Wisdom is knowledge of God that leads to right living. It's that must-have tool that you'll reach for every day. It will become well-worn with time, yet it will never become dull. In fact, it grows sharper and stronger the more you use it, if you make the effort to obtain it.

So how do you get wisdom?

Ask for it (James 1:5), live with a healthy fear of God (Proverbs 1:7), and meditate on God's Word (Psalm 1:1-2). You'll wonder how you ever got along without it.

BOTTOM LINE

Ask God to give you wisdom that will affect you for the rest of your life. And ask Him to give you the desire to keep growing in wisdom.

Moment of Strength: Proverbs 8:27-36

ACCEPTING OUR LIMITATIONS

The LORD is like a father to his children, tender and compassionate to those who fear him. For he knows how weak we are; he remembers we are only dust.

Psalm 103:13-14

THE PRESSURES WE FACE AS men are enormous and can sometimes be overwhelming. Most of us are expected to balance the often competing roles of husband, father, provider, disciple, and friend. The expectations concerning our performance in each of these roles can reach a kind of merciless perfectionism that leaves us intolerant and harshly judgmental of anything less than what we consider our very best. We burn ourselves out because there is always something that needs to be done or needs to be done better.

As great as it might be to live a life without any limits, it simply cannot be done. Thankfully, God has no trouble remembering that "we are only dust." He has compassion on us in our limited human capacity. Though we often forget this basic fact of our creation, God has a way of constantly reminding us that we are needy and that we can't make it on our own.

Rather than attempting to deny our limitations, we must learn to accept that we are His creation and that He has a long history of working with those who have limited resources. How is God reminding you of your complete dependence on Him today? Recognizing our weakness is actually a great blessing. It's much better to live according to reality than to deny the truth and exhaust ourselves attempting to do more and be more than God has intended.

BOTTOM LINE

Our limitations are not a surprise to God. Ask Him to help you learn how to accept your limitations and rest in Him.

Moment of Strength: Psalm 46:10

THE HOUSE OF THE LORD

*How lovely is your dwelling place, O Lord of Heaven's
Armies. I long, yes, I faint with longing to enter the
courts of the Lord. With my whole being, body and soul,
I will shout joyfully to the living God. . . . A single day in
your courts is better than a thousand anywhere else!*
Psalm 84:1-2, 10

IT HAD BEEN FOUR DAYS SINCE Bryan's wife had left for a weeklong trip. At
home, while his wife was away, he had to juggle work, taking care of their two
small children and their dog, and all the other little things that his wife did to
make the family and household run smoothly. At the beginning of the week,
he was really excited for her to go on her trip. But about halfway through,
he could not wait to have her back. After only a few days of her being gone,
a longing was growing in Bryan's heart to be in the presence of his wife and
have her back at home.

In Psalm 84 a similar longing develops for the presence of God. In the
Old Testament, the presence of God was localized in the Temple. If people
wanted to experience God's presence, they went on a journey to Jerusalem.
As they traveled, their anticipation and expectation grew. Upon arriving in
Jerusalem and entering into the Lord's presence in the Temple, the heart of
the sojourner would be filled with joy and happiness.

However, for Christians today, no journey is necessary to experience the
joy of God's presence. There is no leaving, no reunion. Through the Holy
Spirit, God's presence dwells in us always, never to be taken away. As Jesus
said to the disciples before He left, "I am with you always, even to the end of
the age" (Matthew 28:20).

BOTTOM LINE

*The pleasures of God are constantly available for those who live in the
presence of God.*

Moment of Strength: Psalm 84

A DIFFERENT GOSPEL

I am shocked that you are turning away so soon from God, who called you to himself through the loving mercy of Christ. You are following a different way that pretends to be the Good News but is not the Good News at all.

Galatians 1:6-7

THE GOSPEL COMES TO us with revolutionary, life-changing power. Paul says it is the power of God (Romans 1:16). It simultaneously demolishes human pride and despair. It produces joy, freedom, courage, hope, purpose, and passion. It is given to us completely free of charge. We don't have to qualify to receive it—in fact, we cannot qualify to receive it. It does not operate according to human logic or wisdom. Rather, it operates according to God's wisdom.

The gospel is good news—the best news ever. It is the message of God's grace based on the historical events of Christ's life, death, and resurrection. As such, it is objective, not just a theory someone dreamed up. It produces experiences, but it is not an experience. The gospel is the unchanging, reliable, and foundational news that Christ died for our sins to bring us back to God. And yet we're tempted to depart from it. We're tempted to look for something more or different. But according to Paul, we look in vain because there is no gospel other than the one that has been delivered to us once and for all.

Drifting from the gospel is a serious matter because it diminishes God's glory and damages our faith. God is glorified in the gospel as no one else is. His matchless grace is on full display. And the gospel sets us free like nothing else can. So hang on to the gospel with all you've got. It's the best news ever.

BOTTOM LINE

The gospel is not something to take for granted; it's something to be upheld, delighted in, and shared. Ask God to give you a greater love for the gospel.

Moment of Strength: Galatians 1:3-5

TAKING THE LONG VIEW

That is why we never give up. Though our bodies are dying,
our spirits are being renewed every day. For our present
troubles are small and won't last very long. Yet they produce
for us a glory that vastly outweighs them and will last forever!

2 Corinthians 4:16-17

THE APOSTLE PAUL SAID his trials were momentary, light, small troubles. Do these sound like small troubles to you?

> Five different times the Jewish leaders gave me thirty-nine lashes.
> Three times I was beaten with rods. Once I was stoned. Three times
> I was shipwrecked. Once I spent a whole night and a day adrift at
> sea. I have traveled on many long journeys. I have faced danger
> from rivers and from robbers. I have faced danger from my own
> people, the Jews, as well as from the Gentiles. I have faced danger
> in the cities, in the deserts, and on the seas. And I have faced danger
> from men who claim to be believers but are not. I have worked hard
> and long, enduring many sleepless nights. I have been hungry and
> thirsty and have often gone without food. I have shivered in the cold,
> without enough clothing to keep me warm.
> 2 CORINTHIANS 11:24-27

And Paul wasn't finished.

We may not have to face the severe trials that Paul did, but just the same, we can begin to lose hope as the accumulation of a thousand small trials takes its toll and as life becomes wearisome.

By God's grace, Paul was able to view his trials as temporary—which they were—and as not that big of a deal compared to eternity. This perspective certainly didn't come to Paul easily or automatically. Like us, Paul needed to learn to value the things of God so highly, to give them such weight, that everything else would pale by comparison. How about you? Who or what do you care about most?

BOTTOM LINE

Thank God that this life isn't all there is! When we live for the next life, we discover that things here aren't so bad. Live today with eternity in mind.

Moment of Strength: 2 Corinthians 4:7-18

WORTH REMEMBERING

O Lord my God, you have performed many wonders for us.
Your plans for us are too numerous to list. You have no equal.
If I tried to recite all your wonderful deeds,
I would never come to the end of them.

Psalm 40:5

WANT TO BOOST YOUR FAITH? Want to see God better and thereby see everything else better, including your current situation? Try this. Go back to the beginning of your walk with God and write down all the key times when you can remember His activity in your life. Make an extended journal entry of His faithfulness to *you* in *your* life. Recall how many times and ways He delivered you when it seemed that deliverance was an impossibility. You may discover yourself resonating with some lyrics in the famous hymn "Amazing Grace":

Through many dangers, toils and snares,
I have already come;
'Tis grace hath brought me safe thus far,
And grace will lead me home.

Recalling God's faithfulness to you during your life can be an enormously helpful faith-building exercise. Perhaps you're one of those people who periodically goes back and reads past journal entries in order to see God's hand in answered prayers and providential happenings. But even if you're not, there's another way to boost your faith that's just as powerful, if not more so. It's reading the Bible! Romans 15:4 says: "Such things were written in the Scriptures long ago to teach us. And the Scriptures give us hope and encouragement as we wait patiently for God's promises to be fulfilled." And Hebrews 11, of course, gives us the "hall of faith," which is all about God's faithfulness.

BOTTOM LINE

We need to remember God's faithfulness to us. Look for God's activity in your own life and in the lives of other saints, past and present.

Moment of Strength: Psalm 136

PRAYING WITH CONFIDENCE

Let us come boldly to the throne of our gracious God.
There we will receive his mercy, and we will find
grace to help us when we need it most.

Hebrews 4:16

WE'RE TOLD IN TODAY'S VERSE that we *can* and *should* "come boldly to the throne of our gracious God." But doesn't that seem a little presumptuous on our part? After all, maybe we haven't exactly been doing a bang-up job of living the Christian life lately. So who are we to come *boldly* to God's throne? Wouldn't a humbler approach be more appropriate? Shouldn't we get our act together a little more before we come knocking on God's door, shamelessly asking Him to bless us and provide what we need and want?

We may not consciously think any of this, but deep down inside, this is how we often operate.

Why *don't* we come to God boldly in prayer? Because we don't think we can. In some translations, there is actually a "therefore" at the beginning of Hebrews 4:16, and what precedes it is this passage: "So then, since we have a great High Priest who has entered heaven, Jesus the Son of God, let us hold firmly to what we believe. This High Priest of ours understands our weaknesses, for he faced all of the same testings we do, yet he did not sin" (Hebrews 4:14-15).

We can come boldly because we come in the name of our sinless, sympathizing High Priest, the Lord Jesus Christ. His merit is our merit. His record is our record. His privilege is our privilege, too. So come boldly. Come like a child. Come like *God's* child. Because you are.

BOTTOM LINE

Prayer is our great privilege and opportunity. When we come boldly to God,
we're promised mercy and grace, not judgment. So pray like you mean it!

Moment of Strength: Matthew 7:7-12

PARENTING HONESTLY

*Direct your children onto the right path, and
when they are older, they will not leave it.*
Proverbs 22:6

FRANK WASN'T PREPARED FOR the question that Blake, his nine-year-old son, casually threw out as he passed the rolls at dinner. The question focused on specific events that had led to the divorce of the parents of Blake's friend Will in the previous year. Frank, nervously glancing across the table at his wife, Sheryl, took a deep breath and, although he was a bit uncomfortable, began to answer Blake's questions openly, honestly, and in a manner that was age-appropriate for Blake and his siblings.

Honesty is one of the first attributes that we teach our children. Telling the truth is essential to establishing the trust that supports all relationships. Though we most often think about honesty from the perspective that our kids need to be honest with us, we must realize that trust can also be undermined when we aren't completely honest with our kids. Let's face it: The world we live in can be a very dark and scary place. In an effort to protect our kids, it is very tempting to shield them from hard things.

But what is more frightening for a child: to have a parent lovingly tell them the truth about the broken world that we live in, or to discover through experience that the world portrayed by their parents doesn't match their reality? Are there any ways in which you are being dishonest with your children in an effort to protect them?

BOTTOM LINE

Our children need us to prepare them for the realities they will face in the world. Ask God to give you the wisdom and courage to do this well.

Moment of Strength: Ephesians 4:25

FORGIVENESS IN MARRIAGE

*Since God chose you to be the holy people he loves, you must clothe yourselves
with tenderhearted mercy, kindness, humility, gentleness, and patience.
Make allowance for each other's faults, and forgive anyone who offends you.
Remember, the Lord forgave you, so you must forgive others.*
Colossians 3:12-13

SCOTT DIDN'T KNOW WHAT TO DO. Only eight months into marriage, he and his wife were fighting more and more and seemed to be getting along less and less. Their blissful engagement and honeymoon were a distant memory, and he often found himself wondering whether or not he'd made a mistake and married the wrong person.

"If I had married the girl God wanted me to marry," he reasoned, "then surely marriage wouldn't be this hard."

But marriage is hard work because, among other things, it exposes us. Though it is relatively easy to manage or hide our insecurities and weaknesses when we live alone, marriage forces us into such close community with our spouse that hiding our brokenness becomes nearly impossible. We don't like the vulnerable feeling of being exposed, so we may get irritated with our wife and focus on her sinfulness rather than dealing with our own.

The fact is, marriage is a work in progress. Acknowledging and exposing the brokenness and sin in yourself and your wife can help you both to see your desperate need for Christ and to experience His grace. When we are aware of our weakness, we will feel more compelled to run to Christ for perspective and help.

Awareness of our own brokenness makes it easier to forgive as we have been forgiven, and all good relationships are sustained by forgiveness.

BOTTOM LINE

Christ's love can shine brightest in the presence of our failures and shortcomings. Ask Jesus to help you to forgive as you've been forgiven.

Moment of Strength: Ephesians 5:25

ALL IN

My life is worth nothing to me unless I use it for finishing the
work assigned me by the Lord Jesus—the work of telling others
the Good News about the wonderful grace of God.
Acts 20:24

IF WATCHING POKER ON TV sounds like as much fun as watching the grass grow, you probably share the majority opinion. However, poker has appeared regularly on television since the late 1970s. And beginning in 2002, Texas Hold'em tournaments have been getting high ratings. (But we're not advocating or condoning gambling in any form.)

The most dramatic part of a Texas Hold'em match is when one of the players decides to go all in. He pushes all his chips to the middle of the table, willing to risk everything.

When we faithfully follow Jesus Christ, our lives are not a gamble. We're already winners. Yet many of us nibble at the edges of a relationship with Him with "little bets." We'll throw in a few chips with God but keep many of our talents piled up next to us. We play not to lose, rather than to win big.

Instead of our trying to stay in control, God wants us to go "all in" for Him. Without God, our lives are worth nothing. That's what Paul concluded about his own life. By going all in with God, you're guaranteed to get a "royal flush" ministry—*royal* because you're serving the King of kings, and *flush* because your life will be flush with opportunities to glorify Him. That's what life is all about. So play to win with your life. Paradoxically, that means losing your life for the sake of Jesus and the world-changing good news that God loves us.

BOTTOM LINE

When you take a risk with God, it's no risk at all. You can only win. So trust God and live your life to the fullest for Him.

Moment of Strength: Deuteronomy 10:12-13

GIVING YOUR BEST

*Never sacrifice sick or defective cattle, sheep, or
goats to the LORD your God, for he detests such gifts.*
Deuteronomy 17:1

FOR MANY OF US, giving involves writing a check to our church or to a ministry that we support rather than giving a sheep or an ox to our local clergyman. As long as the check clears, we might consider that there's nothing "sick or defective" in our offering, right?

Not necessarily. Just because we don't approach God through the Old Testament system of animal sacrifices doesn't mean that the checks we write today are always pleasing to Him. As with everything else in the Christian life, obedience in giving is a matter of the heart. When we see that everything we have comes from God, including our ability to work and earn income, we become grateful, and grateful people are generous.

There are many Scriptures that prompt us to examine our hearts in giving, but Deuteronomy 17:1 focuses on the quality of what we give. Like the Israelites of Moses' time, we often tend to serve ourselves first and give only the leftovers to God. Or perhaps we give to God first, but only an amount that leaves us with enough to satisfy ourselves. In either case, we disguise self-serving motivations as obedience. What God wants from us instead is a gift that honors Him as the provider of all we have and that demonstrates our trust for all we will need for tomorrow. When we learn to trust at that level, the grip on our paychecks will loosen, and our giving will look more like an act of worship and thanksgiving, as it should be.

BOTTOM LINE

Our giving is a reflection of our faith. Are you in the habit of giving prayerfully and generously?

Moment of Strength: Matthew 6:28-33

A PROPER RESPONSE

*Honor the LORD with your wealth and with the best part
of everything you produce. Then he will fill your barns
with grain, and your vats will overflow with good wine.*
Proverbs 3:9-10

IMAGINE THIS: You don't have a job. Your family has eaten macaroni and cheese five nights a week for the past month. Then a kindhearted friend shows up with a box full of food and a huge ham. He helps you and your wife prepare the feast, then joins your family at the table for a meal you'd never have had if not for him. After serving yourself the best part of everything, you put the rest away to save for tomorrow's meal, then scrape what's crusted to the sides of the dishes and serve that to your benefactor. That's his portion—your "thank you" to him. Not a very gracious way to respond to such great generosity, is it?

Ridiculous, isn't it? Rude, ungrateful, unthinkable. But is this a picture of how we thank God for all He has given us? We need to recognize that God is the source of all that we have. If not for His provision and grace, we would be in a state of physical and spiritual poverty without hope of a way out. Our response to His provision, then, should be to take pleasure in giving Him the choice portions of the "meal" He has given us. He created it, He gave it, and He deserves it. Let that be our heart in giving back to Him.

This mind-set doesn't come all at once; and in the meantime, God is gracious and patient with us. Ask Him to increase your faith and show you ways to share your resources, time, and efforts.

BOTTOM LINE

Delight yourself in sharing all that God has freely given to you. Share it with Him and share it with others.

Moment of Strength: 2 Corinthians 8:7-12

PROPER ADVICE

*"What sorrow awaits my rebellious children," says the Lord.
"You make plans that are contrary to mine. You make
alliances not directed by my Spirit, thus piling up your sins."*
Isaiah 30:1

To whom do you go to for advice and counsel when making big decisions at work or in your personal life? If you're like most men, you go to someone with expertise, whom you respect and who has experience in situations and environments like yours. These are all great qualifications for someone we would take advice from, but there are two more criteria we should include on our list: whether our counselors have an active relationship with God and whether they have a discipline of seeking God in their decisions. When we leave God out of the picture, we're asking for trouble.

Proverbs is full of warnings against relying on human wisdom. Not only might we find ourselves on the wrong path, we very likely will find ourselves moving with the wrong motivation. Thankfully, Scripture also shows us how to recognize true wisdom and gives great assurance to those who pursue it. The next time you want to seek advice on a matter, make sure you find someone whom you can trust to pray with you over the decision and then seek God's wisdom with you. Whatever choices you might be required to make in the course of a day, God has a particular one in mind for you. You may well miss that option if you're not seeking Him yourself and if you're using society's definition of "wise counsel" instead of God's.

BOTTOM LINE

Be deliberate about seeking advice from those you can trust. Ask them to pray with you about the matter. Let God direct you with His wisdom.

Moment of Strength: James 3:13-18

HE IS NOT LIKE ME

"My thoughts are nothing like your thoughts," says the LORD.
"And my ways are far beyond anything you could imagine."
Isaiah 55:8

THERE IS SOMETHING unsettling about the "otherness" of God. He is so unlike us on so many levels that the very idea of understanding Him can seem preposterous. For starters, He is unimaginably powerful. He can speak a solar system into existence without breaking a sweat. He is also utterly good, while we are painfully aware of our maddening propensity to embrace the darkness.

The writings of Isaiah paint a sweeping portrait of an unspeakably powerful being who declares that His ways and thoughts are above and beyond us. So given what God says about Himself, can we even begin to get a grasp on the Lord of the universe?

We can, not because we are inherently capable but because God has gone to extreme lengths to demystify Himself for us. Not content to simply reign over us as a distant Sovereign, God took the breathtaking step of becoming one of us. And then He took the full force of the punishment that was due us for our sin.

The life and death of Jesus reveal the depth of God's love for us. In Jesus, God actually shares our humanity. He really "gets us" because He was truly one of us. In light of who God is, it is completely appropriate to stand in awe. But we do not stand at a distance. Jesus bridged the gap. He has revealed the heart of the Father to us, and it is overwhelmingly good.

BOTTOM LINE

God has revealed Himself through His Son. Make sure you're viewing God through the lens of Jesus as revealed in Scripture.

Moment of Strength: John 10:14

WHY GLORIFY GOD?

*In their righteousness, they will be like great oaks
that the LORD has planted for his own glory.*
Isaiah 61:3

GOD TALKS—A LOT—ABOUT His people glorifying Him. He repeatedly calls us to praise Him. On one level this can seem kind of jarring. Why does God require us to tell Him how awesome He is? A quiet little part of our souls may ask, *Does He have ego needs or something?* It can feel a bit awkward to read these commands to glorify God.

But if we think about it, the call to glorify God really is a call to align ourselves with reality. It is a mandate to embrace the truth. Glorifying God is simply the rational response to who He is. When you see the Grand Canyon, it takes your breath away. It is an utterly appropriate response to ooh and aah and stare in slack-jawed wonder. Glorifying and praising God is a version of oohing and aahing at a supernatural wonder.

Awestruck adoration is what happens when we begin to see what a grand, kind, merciful, and powerful God we serve. Because He created all things and is greater than everything He spoke into existence, what could possibly be more amazing than God? And then He became one of us, died for us, and secured our salvation. To speak the truth about God, meditate on His character, and dedicate our lives to His service is to glorify Him. It isn't that He needs to keep hearing how amazing He is. It's that we need to keep remembering it!

BOTTOM LINE

Humans are fickle, easily distracted, and prone to embracing lies over truth. Glorifying and praising God reorients us to reality.

Moment of Strength: Psalm 145

MARRY INSIDE THE FAITH

Swear by the LORD, the God of heaven and earth, that you will not allow my son to marry one of these local Canaanite women.

Genesis 24:3

IT WAS A BIG DEAL TO Abraham that his son married in the faith. And it should be a big deal to fathers today. The New Testament carries this explicit warning: "Don't team up with those who are unbelievers" (2 Corinthians 6:14). As fathers, we need to talk to our kids about the heartbreak and folly of marrying a person who does not follow Jesus. Wisdom dictates that we have this conversation before our kids find themselves falling head over heels for someone who is not a Christian. Young people are especially notorious for letting feelings trump all else. Talking your son or daughter out of a relationship is exponentially more difficult than convincing them to not date an unbeliever in the first place.

Young people often harbor hopes that the non-Christian they are dating will convert. And they can likely point to a situation where it worked out for someone else. If you have a child in that boat, gently pose the question, "But what if they don't? Would you want to go through life with no spiritual connection to your mate? How will your children be raised? Is that really fair to your kids?" Open a Bible and show them Paul's warning about marrying an unbeliever. Ask them to talk to God about it. You cannot prevent your children from making a bad decision, but you can do your best to guide them.

BOTTOM LINE

The Bible is clear that God wants His children to marry only someone who is also a child of God. Explain that to your kids before they begin dating.

Moment of Strength: 2 Corinthians 6:14-18

ALL MEN CAN BE FATHERS

I am writing to Timothy, my true son in the faith.
1 Timothy 1:2

THE APOSTLE PAUL WAS not a father, but he had many spiritual children. Both Timothy and Titus were led to Christ by Paul, and he affectionately referred to both of them by the term "my true son." One of Paul's "true sons" was a man named Onesimus, a runaway slave who was the main subject of the epistle to Philemon. Paul's love for Onesimus was captured in these words: "[I], Paul, an old man and now also a prisoner for the sake of Christ Jesus . . . appeal to you to show kindness to my child, Onesimus. I became his father in the faith while here in prison. Onesimus hasn't been of much use to you in the past, but now he is very useful to both of us. I am sending him back to you, and with him comes my own heart" (Philemon 1:9-12).

Whether or not you have children of your own, you can be a spiritual father. If God uses you to lead another person to faith in Christ, you have played a role in birthing a new life into the church. Many men long for a father/son relationship but are childless or even estranged from their own kids. Whether you lead someone to Christ or play a mentoring role to a new believer, rich and rewarding relationships can be found in the family of God.

If you long to be a spiritual father, pray for God to fulfill that dream, and begin to actively look for opportunities. A lot of young men are desperate for some guidance and encouragement from an older, more mature Christian man. You can be an answer to prayer.

BOTTOM LINE

Whether you are married, widowed, single, or divorced, you can play a fatherly role in the life of a younger Christian. Pray for opportunities.

Moment of Strength: Philemon 1

NOT AFRAID

Don't be afraid, for I am with you. Don't be discouraged,
for I am your God. I will strengthen you and help you.
I will hold you up with my victorious right hand.
Isaiah 41:10

AT THIS TIME OF YEAR, it's hard to ignore all the scary stuff on TV, at the movies, and filling store shelves. In the United States, Christmas and Easter are still the most lucrative holidays, but Halloween is gaining fast. More than $8 billion will be spent this year on candy, costumes, and decorations.

Researchers say that one of the reasons people like feeling scared is that deep down they know there's no real danger (the exception, of course, is feeling scared in a life-threatening situation). It's more a sense of excitement than fear.

Instead of getting caught up in the macabre, grotesque, and scary this time of year, God wants us to focus on Him (just like at every other time). He doesn't want us to live in fear. Jesus came to set us free from fear. In John 14:27, Jesus says, "I am leaving you with a gift—peace of mind and heart. And the peace I give is a gift the world cannot give. So don't be troubled or afraid."

Because God is with us, we have no reason to fear. We may have moments of trepidation, but deep down we should know that with God on our side, we can live courageously. So when you face fear, stand out by living fearlessly. Be courageous. Be bold. Be excited. Make a difference for God. And maybe even celebrate Reformation Day instead!

BOTTOM LINE

Fear causes us to live small lives and miss out on opportunities that God brings our way. Ask Him to help you live fearlessly.

Moment of Strength: Psalm 118:6

ON THE RIGHT TRACK

Serve only the LORD your God and fear him alone.
Obey his commands, listen to his voice, and cling to him.

Deuteronomy 13:4

RODEL HAD NEVER BEEN TO ALASKA. So when some buddies invited him to go elk hunting in the Last Frontier, he jumped at the chance. Freshly fallen snow greeted him on the first morning of his hunt. Everybody decided to split up and meet later. Almost immediately, Rodel found elk tracks. He followed them for what seemed like miles. Growing tired, he decided to head to the rendezvous point. He arrived first, but soon one of his hunting buddies found him.

"Did you see it?" the friend asked.

"No, but I followed the elk tracks for miles," Rodel answered.

"No, not the elk," his friend said. "There was a bear following your tracks."

As Christians, we're called to follow Christ. Deuteronomy 13:4 commands us to follow, worship, and remain faithful to the Lord. But as we focus on our goal to follow in Christ's tracks, we can't lose sight of the fact that we're being watched as well.

Satan is more dangerous than any bear. Scripture compares him to a lion waiting to devour us (1 Peter 5:8). He wants to get us off God's path and render us ineffective for the Kingdom. He'll stop at nothing to hinder our progress. As Christ followers, we need to remain focused. Follow God, but be alert to an enemy who wants to get you off track.

BOTTOM LINE

Think of two things you can do to stay more on track for Christ.

Moment of Strength: James 4:7

PRAYING FOR PEOPLE IN POWER

I urge you, first of all, to pray for all people. Ask God to help them;
intercede on their behalf, and give thanks for them.
1 Timothy 2:1

AMERICANS LOVE TO VENT about politics, and these days it's easier than ever to unload. Talk radio can range from informative and entertaining to bombastic and goading. Politics can also raise your blood pressure as yet another outrageous act by an elected official is revealed or a bad policy is dissected. Some elected officials are actually noble statesmen. Some are ridiculous. Some are criminals who get indicted and sent to prison for corruption. It is perfectly fine and quite biblical to be angry at evil, but today's passage reminds us to pray for those who are in authority. Even if they are wrong. Even if they are self-serving. Even if you can't wait to vote them out.

The fact that we get to collectively hire or fire our leaders at the ballot box does not absolve us of the responsibility to intercede for them. Praying for people you don't like very much is actually a very healthy and biblical thing to do. It is good for them and good for you. A little bit of your own self-righteousness dissipates when you pray for people you don't like. Just think—wouldn't it be great if leaders who weren't Christians found Jesus as a result of your prayers? Pray for that. Pray that they would tell the truth, make the right decisions, take the long view, and put the national interest above self-interest. Venting is a poor substitute for prayer.

BOTTOM LINE

You have a First Amendment right to criticize politicians. But you have a
divine call to pray for your leaders.

Moment of Strength: Matthew 22:15-22

AN ACCEPTABLE GIFT

When it was time for the harvest, Cain presented some of his crops
as a gift to the LORD. . . . But [God] did not accept Cain and his gift.
This made Cain very angry, and he looked dejected.

Genesis 4:3, 5

THE STORY OF CAIN AND ABEL IS well-known and tragic. It begins with two brothers born to Adam and Eve. Given the personal relationship and face-to-face interaction their parents once enjoyed with God in Eden, you would think these brothers would want to please God.

Nevertheless, Cain gave an offering that displeased God. The Bible notes that Abel offered the firstborn and the fat portions (the best), but all we know about Cain's offering is that he eventually gave "some of his crops." Cain knew what God wanted, yet apparently he chose to give just a token offering.

Notice also that it wasn't just Cain's offering that displeased God; it was Cain himself. God was the true source of Cain's harvest (Mark 4:27), yet Cain didn't display an attitude of thanksgiving or true worship. He simply went through the motions. The rest of the story tells how Cain's selfish disregard devolved into further sin, just as sin can do for us today.

God isn't fooled by our actions. He knows the attitude of our hearts when we pray, read, sing, and tithe. He looks with favor on those who truly worship Him, but He is not pleased when we merely go through the motions.

BOTTOM LINE

Before giving or serving in church, pause to consider why and how you're doing it. Let thanksgiving and true worship be your motivation.

Moment of Strength: 2 Corinthians 9:6-11

LEARNING TO REST

Seek the Kingdom of God above all else, and live righteously, and
he will give you everything you need. So don't worry about tomorrow,
for tomorrow will bring its own worries. Today's trouble is enough for today.
Matthew 6:33-34

"BUT DAD, YOU PROMISED. All the other dads are going to be there."

Robert's heart sank. He had done it again. Another client crisis meant he would be working late again tonight and wouldn't be able to attend his son's first wrestling match of the season. The disappointment in his son's voice felt like a baseball bat to the midsection.

Lately, Robert's clients seemed to be "in crisis" more often, which meant more hours and more late nights. Robert could see that this was beginning to create a crisis at home as he became increasingly disconnected from his wife and children.

As men, what we do, how much we are able to accomplish, and how successful we are at work can often form the foundation of our sense of identity. Everywhere we turn, the message is loud and clear: The more we do, the better we are. So we begin to worship at the altar of busyness and work. The result? We become irritable and unhappy in our busyness.

When success and accomplishments become the basis of our identity, deep insecurity is the result. There is always more work to be done and more success to be gained. The idol of work, like any idol, will always fail to satisfy the deep longings of our heart.

After His work of creation, God rested. He has also commanded that we take time to rest. Are you currently justifying the idol of busyness?

BOTTOM LINE

God intends for us to keep work and rest in proper balance in our lives. Ask Him to help you.

Moment of Strength: Ecclesiastes 3:1

AN EMISSARY OF GOD

Whom should I send as a messenger to this people? Who will go for us?
Isaiah 6:8

IT IS QUITE AMAZING THAT the all-powerful God of the universe, with legions of angels at His disposal, has chosen to use human beings as His ambassadors. Isaiah was just a guy—a mere man. Not unlike us. But he was summoned to the courts of heaven and received his appointment. No angel accepted the invitation, for it was not extended to them.

The Lord seeks men as His messengers. God is still posing the question, "Who will go for us?" It's not that any of us are naturally qualified for the job; it's that God's calling makes us qualified. He is able to use ordinary people to accomplish extraordinary things in the world. In this, He is glorified.

For every man seeking a significant role in the world, "Ambassador for God" surely fills the bill. You do not have to relocate to a foreign land to be part of God's mission. Indeed, missionaries such as the apostle Paul were rarities in the early church. A relative few were sent out. The normal practice was for believers to shine in the corner of the world where God had already placed them. Who will have the high honor to represent Jesus in your workplace, your neighborhood, your classroom, your club, or your gym? You are uniquely placed and qualified to show the love and grace of God in your sphere of influence. God can and will use you as you take up your commission.

BOTTOM LINE

The Lord has made you an ambassador for His Kingdom. See yourself as called and qualified.

Moment of Strength: 2 Corinthians 5:16-21

PRISON MINISTRY

*"When did we ever see you sick or in prison and visit you?" And the
King will say, "I tell you the truth, when you did it to one of the least
of these my brothers and sisters, you were doing it to me!"*
Matthew 25:39-40

DURING HIS LIFETIME, Chuck Colson certainly advanced prison ministry by light-years. Himself a convicted felon, Colson came to know Christ, and his life's purpose was irrevocably changed. He founded Prison Fellowship, a ministry that has shared God's love with hundreds of thousands of convicts all around the world. It's reaching out to "the least of these."

What about you? Read the verse above again. Have you ever carried out the mandate of this Scripture? Have you ever even thought about it?

Set aside what you've seen on TV shows and in the movies. Prison ministry isn't a replay of scenes from *Escape from Alcatraz*. Most of the men you would visit are extremely thankful and cordial. Many are eager for fellowship and prayer with a Christian brother. They're not looking for legal advice or a handout. They are simply Christian brothers in need of some love and encouragement. Your ministry is to walk with Jesus and bring Him through the gates with you. In doing so, you will bring these men the encouragement they need to keep focusing on the Lord and relying on His grace in their times of struggle.

There is a beautiful point when the Jesus inside you reaches out to the Jesus inside them and a connection is made. For a holy moment, all that is seen is Jesus. When you serve the needs of the least in our society, you do it as unto the Lord.

BOTTOM LINE

Pray for an obvious opportunity to serve the least in our society. Then, as soon as God provides, do it!

Moment of Strength: Matthew 25:31-46

KNOWING PEACE

*May grace and peace be multiplied to you through
the knowledge of God and of Jesus our Lord.*
2 Peter 1:2, HCSB

PEACE IS TALKED ABOUT throughout Scripture, but how real is it in our lives? Where's the peace when we're at odds with our boss or our spouse, or when we're dealing with a job loss or serious illness? It's easy to get confused, discouraged, or anxious if we're expecting God to deliver us from pain and hardship. That's because He doesn't give us peace as the world gives (John 14:27). In fact, Jesus tells us to take up our crosses and follow Him (Matthew 16:24), which seems contradictory to an easy and comfortable notion of peace.

There's nothing wrong with wanting stability and prosperity in our lives, but we misinterpret Scripture when we claim those as promises from God. Consider that the apostle Paul's life was filled with shipwrecks, beatings, imprisonment, and betrayal (2 Corinthians 11:23-28); yet he apparently experienced peace, and he encourages us to do the same (Philippians 4:6-7). God's peace isn't about our circumstances; it's about being aligned with His will and understanding how He wants to use our circumstances for His glory. It involves a choice on our part to trust God and follow Jesus.

The key is knowing Jesus personally. This comes through intentional and consistent time in His Word, heartfelt prayer, and obedience to what we know He wants of us.

BOTTOM LINE

Perhaps you've seen the following bumper sticker: "No Jesus = No Peace. Know Jesus = Know Peace." That invitation is extended to us moment by moment.

Moment of Strength: Isaiah 26:3

PICKING ON OTHERS

Do not judge others, and you will not be judged.
Matthew 7:1

ASK SOMEONE WHY THEY don't go to church, and often their response is "I don't want to feel judged by others." And let's be honest—it can be tempting to judge others because it takes the focus off our own shortcomings and need for grace. When we do that, though, we hurt our witness and open ourselves up to charges of hypocrisy. As recipients of lavish grace from the Father, we ought to be people known for grace, not judgment.

The words of Jesus are simple and concise: "Do not judge." But this is not a reference to being a discerning Christian. Scripture repeatedly counsels us to evaluate carefully and choose between good and bad. Instead, Jesus warns us here about hypocritical judging in a self-righteous way.

If we foster a critical spirit toward others, we will reap what we sow. Our motivation in judging others usually isn't a loving concern for their lives. Often, we judge in order to narrow our field of comparison, to make ourselves look better than we really are.

Often, God allows us a privileged peek at people's failures, not so that we can feel holier-than-thou and dismissive but so we can pray for those people and consider how we can show them mercy. The next time you are tempted to pick on someone else's faults, ask yourself this question: How did *I* get into the Kingdom?

BOTTOM LINE

Ask God to temper your judging, and turn up the heat on your loving.

Moment of Strength: 1 Peter 5:5-7

THE SECRET OF CONTENTMENT

I have calmed and quieted myself, like a weaned child who no longer cries for its mother's milk. Yes, like a weaned child is my soul within me.

Psalm 131:2

LEADERSHIP IS COSTLY. It requires imagination and courage. It involves managing crises, sorting out confusion, and handling conflict. And it's no different when you walk into your house—you're the spiritual leader of your family. When do you rest?

A long life of leadership can actually lead to stress addiction. For some, the thrill of the hunt—the adrenaline rush of closing the deal—brings a measure of satisfaction. But it never lasts. In the midst of struggle and heartache and stress, how do you care for your own heart? Porn, food, and alcohol are ways that some men "self-soothe." These things will alter our minds and may give a temporary sense of comfort. But they are not honorable.

Political and military leaders know stress, and King David certainly had his fill of it. In between military campaigns against the Philistines; dodging his would-be assassin, King Saul; and a personal scandal that rocked his world, David learned how to comfort his soul. We can learn the secret from him.

David said that he calmed and quieted himself "like a weaned child who no longer cries for its mother's milk." In other words, he cultivated a quiet heart by resting in the Lord's presence. We, too, can learn the secret of contentment. We can turn from dishonorable comforters to "the source of all comfort" who "comforts us in all our troubles" (2 Corinthians 1:3-4).

BOTTOM LINE

Ask God to help you find honorable ways to rest in Him alone.

Moment of Strength: Psalm 131

SEEING SOMEONE IN THE STORM

Jesus spoke to them at once. "Don't be afraid," he said.
"Take courage. I am here!"
Matthew 14:27

IN ITS MOST COMMON FORM, fear is an internal warning mechanism that signals danger nearby and warns us that we had better do something about it. The intensity of our fear is often in direct proportion to the immediacy of the danger.

In the ancient Greek language, the word for *fear* meant "flight." Think of pheasants being flushed from their nesting areas and taking flight because they have been frightened by the approaching danger of a hunter. Or think of a soldier in battle fleeing the enemy while under fire.

Simon Peter was fearful in a boat on the Sea of Galilee. He and his buddies were sailing across the sea, per Jesus' request, when a tumultuous storm came raging upon them. The Gospels recorded the place (the Sea of Galilee), the time (the fourth watch of the night, 3:00–6:00 a.m.), and the conditions (a storm) to remind us that Jesus often comes when we need Him most.

Jesus' words calmed their emotions and relieved their fear. Peter wanted more, asking to come to Jesus on the water. Though the water was dark and dangerous, that was where Jesus was, so that's where Peter wanted to go for safety. It took courage to do that. For Peter's fear to be relieved, he had to get out of the boat and go toward Jesus. The requirements have not changed. If you're afraid—and we all are sometimes—take your fear to Jesus.

BOTTOM LINE

Courage gets us out of our boats. Faith holds us up. Walking on the water hinges on whether we focus on the Savior or on our storms.

Moment of Strength: Psalm 56:3

THE NEED FOR REAL FRIENDS

Jonathan made David reaffirm his vow of friendship again,
for Jonathan loved David as he loved himself.
1 Samuel 20:17

EVERY PILOT NEEDS A WINGMAN. Every camper needs a buddy. Batman had Robin. The Lone Ranger had Tonto. Butch Cassidy had the Sundance Kid. Two are better than one. Survival in this world is tough—whether the challenge is physical, mental, emotional, or spiritual. You need someone to help you along the tough road ahead.

Never go into battle alone. You don't need a lot of money or equipment, but you do need a friend.

A real friend walks in when everyone else walks out, brings out the best in you, doesn't think you've done a permanent job when you make a fool of yourself, knows you as you are, understands where you have been, accepts who you've become, and gently challenges you to become better.

Do you have someone like that in your life? Someone like Jonathan was for David and David was for Jonathan? They were real friends. They were buddies. They needed each other. They stood beside each other. These men demonstrated mutual acceptance despite differing backgrounds. Promise, not performance, characterized their friendship. Jonathan did not have to do favors for David, and David wasn't expected to kill more giants to remain Jonathan's friend. Their friendship reached a depth of intimacy and trust that few relationships experience.

Who's your Jonathan?

BOTTOM LINE

We need friends for a healthy, happy life. Without them, we sentence ourselves to less than the best. Seek good friends, and seek to be a good friend.

Moment of Strength: Proverbs 27:10

WHEN WE JUST DON'T GET IT

You hypocrites! Isaiah was right when he prophesied about
you, for he wrote, "These people honor me with their lips,
but their hearts are far from me. Their worship is a farce,
for they teach man-made ideas as commands from God."
Matthew 15:7-9

THE ENGLISH WORD HYPOCRITE HAS its origins in the world of ancient Greek theater. On the stage, an actor lays aside his true identity and assumes a false one. He is no longer himself but is someone in disguise, impersonating someone else. In the theater, no harm or deceit comes from actors playing their parts. The audience, having come to watch the drama, is not taken in by it.

The religious hypocrite, on the other hand, deliberately sets out to deceive people and is often deceived himself. He is like an actor in that he's pretending, yet he is quite unlike an actor in that he takes a real religious practice and turns it into what it was never meant to be. He does his good deeds, his religious activities, to be seen by people in order to win their applause.

Jesus often accused the Pharisees of hypocrisy. He loved them, but He detested their practices. They disgraced the Temple, the Scriptures, and the Jewish faith—all in the name of God.

Hypocrisy strikes a raw nerve because it is antithetical to what Jesus professed. True Christianity is about authenticity—a genuine relationship with God, loving relationships within the faith community, and sincere actions by Christ followers.

Hypocrisy is offensive because it pretends to be authentic, but isn't. Consequently, it damages Christianity like nothing else.

BOTTOM LINE

Jesus wants His followers to focus on internal reality over external appearances, on attitudes above actions, and on grace over works.

Moment of Strength: Psalm 26:4

WORK HARD AT RESTING

There is a special rest still waiting for the people of God.
For all who have entered into God's rest have rested from
their labors, just as God did after creating the world.
So let us do our best to enter that rest. But if we disobey God,
as the people of Israel did, we will fall.

Hebrews 4:9-11

WE ARE A TIRED PEOPLE. For many, workaholism is no longer merely a symptom; it is a way of life. In our work-driven culture, we often deplore drug and alcohol addicts but promote and admire work addicts. William McNamara, the late Carmelite monk who wrote several books on contemplative living, once said, "Possibly the greatest malaise in our country today is our neurotic compulsion to work."

Burnout, overwork, and nervous breakdowns were not part of God's plan and design for us. An antidote exists—*rest*. Rest was not meant to be a luxury, but it is a necessity for growth, maturity, and health. God intended rest to be a blessing for us!

The writer of Hebrews speaks of something better than a day off or a vacation or taking a break. He called it *God's rest*. Note the personal and possessive pronoun: *God's*. God rested from His creation work. He did not rest because He was tired. He rested because He had completed His work. In doing so, He provided an example for us to follow. His rest can be ours, too.

How? Rest is prioritizing a block of time on a regular basis to keep all of life in proper perspective, in order to remain free of burnout and breakdown. Rest is the check and balance to a busy life. It is like an oil change for your car, your lunch break at work, or the halftime break at the football game. Find God's rest and you will find balance and renewed life.

BOTTOM LINE

The old proverb says it best: "If we don't come together, we will come apart."
Rest is as spiritual as praying and reading the Bible. Have you learned to rest?

Moment of Strength: Exodus 20:8-11

FOCUS OF A FOLLOWER

Run with endurance the race God has set before us.
Hebrews 12:1

THE GUYS WERE EAGER TO get to the hunting lodge for a weekend in the woods. Eric and Shawn were the two drivers, with Eric in the lead because Shawn didn't know the way. Everything was going great until Shawn got caught up in a conversation with one of his passengers and didn't notice that Eric was taking the off-ramp to a different highway. After driving for miles trying to "catch up," Shawn finally had to admit he was lost and pulled over to call Eric on his cell phone.

When we're headed somewhere and don't know the way, we must pay close attention to our leader or we may never reach our goal. Spiritually, it is imperative that we keep our eyes on the one we're following—Jesus. Remember the story of Peter walking on water? When Peter wanted to do what Jesus was doing, Jesus told him, "Come!" (Matthew 14:29, HCSB). The minute Peter took his eyes off Jesus and looked at the water, he began to sink.

To make sure we stay on the right spiritual path, we have to recognize Jesus by knowing Him through His Word, by keeping our eyes and hearts focused intently on Him, and by avoiding all the distractions and pitfalls that could get us off the path. We're in a race, and the only way to run well is to keep our eyes fixed on Jesus.

BOTTOM LINE
Focus on Jesus so your life will stay on the right path.

Moment of Strength: Matthew 14:22-33

THE SEARCH IS ON

Commit your actions to the LORD, and your plans will succeed.
Proverbs 16:3

WITH ALL THE TURMOIL IN the economy over the past several years, some men have lost their jobs to workforce reductions or companies going out of business. Other guys have entered the job market because they just need a change and are looking for a new career.

No matter what your situation is, take some advice from King Solomon. In Proverbs 16:3, he says, "Commit your actions to the LORD, and your plans will succeed." That's a pretty bold promise. But God can accomplish amazing things and open up unexpected opportunities. Let your faith in His power and faithfulness give you hope. If you're searching for a new job, look for areas where God has gifted you. Focus on quality jobs that you'd enjoy instead of sending résumés to everybody. Sometimes an unwanted change results in a great new opportunity.

The current economy can sometimes make a job search seem hopeless. Fuel your hope by talking with other men. Ask your friends and men in your Bible study group to pray for you. Use social networking to communicate your desire for a new job to other friends and acquaintances. When you get God's people involved, you may be surprised by what can happen. Above all, remember that your worth does not come from your job. Your worth comes from the Lord. And in His eyes, you're priceless, regardless of the work you do.

BOTTOM LINE

If you're currently in a job search, look for God in the process. He could be leading you to something totally unexpected.

Moment of Strength: Proverbs 3:5-6

MY FORTRESS

I will say to the LORD,
"My refuge and my fortress, my God, in whom I trust."
Psalm 91:2, HCSB

YOU'RE TIRED. It seems as if the whole world is closing in on you, and there's not a thing you can do about it. You barely have enough to cover the bills. The "check engine" light is on in your car. You haven't been feeling very well. You and your wife had an argument. Your kids are driving you crazy. To make matters worse, a lot of things people say that might help you relax really don't work. Yoga? C'mon. You've got to be kidding. Your body just doesn't bend that way anymore. The self-help books that made somebody a bazillion dollars all seem to say the same things.

You need help, but you don't really know where to turn. Consider this. Several times in the Bible, God is referred to as our fortress. We think of a fortress as a source of impregnable protection, of safety and security. No matter what might be taking place outside those walls, we can be at peace within. For us, God is all of those things. Under His care and protection, we can have the ultimate sense of security.

Nowhere does Scripture promise us a carefree life once we become Christians, but what we do have is the ability to endure hardships, because God is with us. He is there. He always has been and always will be with us. Our God is a mighty fortress of comfort and strength.

BOTTOM LINE

God is the ultimate fortress, in whom we can have an everlasting sense of peace and security. Will you place your complete trust in Him today?

Moment of Strength: Psalm 18:1-6

BAR CODES

Stop judging according to outward appearances;
rather judge according to righteous judgment.
John 7:24, HCSB

ON JUNE 26, 1974, Clyde Dawson of Troy, Ohio, placed a ten-pack of chewing gum on the conveyor belt at Marsh's Supermarket, and cashier Sharon Buchanan did something that had never been done before—she scanned the gum, and the UPC bar code rang it up for sixty-seven cents. That pack of gum is in the Smithsonian today, and you can no longer buy a ten-pack for only sixty-seven cents.

Bar codes track, identify, and evaluate all kinds of products. With one swipe, they record purchases, update inventory, add the sales tax, and even wish you a nice day! They provide an efficient shortcut for doing business. But when we use shortcuts with people to assess their value and place, we can do some real damage. Anytime we fall back on stereotypes, prejudices, or age discrimination, we improperly evaluate people who are of great worth to God. Judging others by their outward appearance will never be an appropriate shortcut through life.

Jesus was judged and evaluated incorrectly by the people in His day. Isaiah said of Him before He was born, "He didn't have an impressive form or majesty that we should look at Him, no appearance that we should desire Him" (Isaiah 53:2, HCSB). Thankfully, God judged Him worthy to be our atoning sacrifice.

BOTTOM LINE

Ask God to help you view people as He does—His much-beloved creations.

Moment of Strength: 1 Samuel 16:7

THE BODY OF CHRIST

For as the body is one and has many parts, and all the parts of that
body, though many, are one body—so also is Christ. . . . But now God
has placed each one of the parts in one body just as He wanted.

1 Corinthians 12:12, 18, HCSB

IMAGINE THIS SCENARIO: A typical Sunday morning at church involves arriving casually late, slipping in and out unnoticed and undisturbed, then discussing on the way home whether or not you "got anything out of the service."

We're all at different points in our spiritual journey, but Paul tells us in 1 Corinthians 12 that every follower of Christ is called to be actively engaged in the life of His body. Just as a body has different parts with different functions, so does the family of God's people. Every believer is called and gifted by God to serve in a specific and unique role. Each role is vitally important.

When all of these different parts come together in unity, something beautiful happens. In a symphony, when all of the different instruments work in harmony, beautiful music is the result. In the same way, when all the different parts of Christ's body work together, we beautifully reflect the fullness of God to the world.

Each member is needed and valued by the whole. We have the responsibility to discover our God-given gifts so that we can give them back to God as an offering of worship and gratitude. We experience God in all His fullness when our engagement with His body isn't defined by a consumer mentality but is characterized by faithful participation and service.

BOTTOM LINE

As individual members of the body of Christ, we experience and reflect the
fullness of God when we join together and become whole. Which part are you?

Moment of Strength: 1 Corinthians 12

SEEING THINGS ARIGHT

Joseph replied, "Don't be afraid of me. Am I God, that I can punish you?
You intended to harm me, but God intended it all for good. He brought
me to this position so I could save the lives of many people."
Genesis 50:19-20

JOSEPH'S BROTHERS RESENTED him because their father treated him specially. So when the opportunity presented itself, Joseph's brothers got rid of him—they sold him into slavery. It's hard for us to grasp, but they placed little value on human life, even the life of their own brother.

Years later, when the brothers had to go to Joseph for food during a great famine, they were terrified that he would want revenge. They remembered how badly they had treated him and how they had lied to their father. But despite the painful journey it took to get to that point, Joseph could see God's hand in all that had happened, and he wasn't bitter or vengeful.

Our perspective is often skewed by what we consider most important to us at the moment. If Joseph had viewed revenge against his brothers as most important, he would have reacted differently, and he likely would have missed the big picture of what God was doing through him. Like Joseph, we need to always remember the sovereignty of God. He is in control, and He is good. That's the right perspective to have.

When facing a troubling situation, try to look at the circumstances with eyes of faith—maybe a redemptive outcome will emerge from a seemingly bad situation. God is able to bring good out of bad in ways we never could have imagined.

BOTTOM LINE

God is up to good, we can be sure of that. Trust Him to work things out in the best possible way, in His perfect timing.

Moment of Strength: Genesis 50:15-21

MAN IN THE MIDDLE

After three days, they found Him in the temple complex sitting among the teachers, listening to them and asking them questions.
Luke 2:46, HCSB

IN LUKE 2:41-52, we find Jesus "in the middle." No longer the baby of Bethlehem, not yet the Christ at Calvary. Like all twelve-year-olds, He was no longer a small child, but not yet a fully grown adult. When Mary and Joseph finally found Him after He went missing from their homeward bound caravan, they discovered Him in the middle of a group of teachers, listening and learning.

When the family returned to Nazareth, Jesus continued to be obedient to His parents, and He "increased in wisdom and stature, and in favor with God and with people" (Luke 2:52, HCSB). This gives us a clue as to how we should live when we are "in the middle," when we're going through a time of preparation.

Jesus grew in wisdom, which surely involved making God's Word the center of His heart and thinking. He also grew in stature before the time was right for His preaching ministry to begin. When His ministry began, He was ready. He had matured.

At times, Jesus seemed to grow in favor with man. (It's hard not to when you feed thousands at a time and heal diseases.) But more importantly, Jesus grew in favor with God by obeying His heavenly Father all the way to the cross. It was a costly obedience that He undertook willingly "for the joy that lay before Him" (Hebrews 12:2, HCSB). Perhaps you find yourself in the middle right now—in a time of preparation and waiting. If so, keep trusting God, and keep obeying.

BOTTOM LINE

When you find yourself "in the middle," Jesus is there with you. Enjoy the journey of knowing God and resting in His timing.

Moment of Strength: Luke 2:41-52

DON'T FORGET THANKSGIVING

*Blessing and glory and wisdom and thanksgiving and honor
and power and strength belong to our God forever and ever! Amen.*
Revelation 7:12

IT'S EASY TO OVERLOOK the Thanksgiving holiday. As soon as Halloween costumes come off the store shelves, Christmas decorations go up. And the United States isn't the only Christmas-enthused culture. In the Philippines, radio stations start playing carols as early as September. Of course, they don't have a Thanksgiving holiday to celebrate there.

The original Thanksgiving festival started on December 13, 1621. The pilgrims gathered with their Native American friends to feast for three days and celebrate God's goodness and provision.

Today, Thanksgiving barely lasts through the afternoon, with some stores opening for Christmas shopping later in the day.

Sadly, it's easy for thanksgiving to get pushed out of the way in our own lives, too. We take God's blessings for granted. We believe in our abilities to "make things happen" rather than trusting God's gracious provision. We don't thank Him enough for His love and grace.

During this important season, we need to pause and be thankful. The apostle John describes a scene in which God is being worshiped with the words: "Blessing and glory and wisdom and thanksgiving and honor and power and strength belong to our God forever and ever!" (Revelation 7:12). We will be thanking God for all eternity, and the time to get started with that is today and every day of the year.

BOTTOM LINE

God deserves our thankfulness. Strive to show it to Him on a daily basis.

Moment of Strength: Psalm 100:4

JESUS AND THE MATH PROBLEM

Jesus asked, "Didn't I heal ten men? Where are the other nine?
Has no one returned to give glory to God except this foreigner?"
Luke 17:17-18

JESUS WAS THE ULTIMATE in-between person. Fully God, yet fully man. Owner of heaven, yet a pauper on earth. All-powerful, yet living in a body that grew tired. And in Luke 17, He was in between Samaria and Galilee. Between the racially mixed Samaritans and the proudly pedigreed Jews.

The ten lepers were in-between as well. They had no acceptance among God-fearing Jews, but they had no home with the Romans either. They were not allowed in the land of the living but were not yet in the grave with the dead. Then these in-between guys met the ultimate in-between guy, and He simply told them to go and show themselves to the priest.

As they went on their way, they began to notice a change. They'd been healed! Then one regained feeling in his chest, and he quickly ran back to Jesus, who had no problem with the math. There had been ten; now there was only one. "Where are the other nine?" He asked. Then He said, "Stand up and go. Your faith has healed you" (Luke 17:19).

Thanksgiving is an ego-killer, a way of admitting we have riches that we were unable to obtain by ourselves. And this is why we are told to constantly be in an attitude of gratitude. Because when you do the math, you've got a lot to be thankful for. One God in between two thieves = infinite life.

BOTTOM LINE

There is nothing you have without the grace of Jesus. Nothing. So everything you have is reason to give thanks.

Moment of Strength: Luke 17:11-19

LEARNING TO FIGHT FAIR

Some people make cutting remarks, but the words of the wise bring healing.
Proverbs 12:18

EDDIE REGRETTED THE WORDS AS soon as they left his mouth. He and his wife, Cindy, had spiraled into a huge fight over weekend plans while on their way home from the grocery store. In an effort to quickly gain the upper hand, Eddie launched into a verbal tirade that included jabs about Cindy's housekeeping and culinary skills. He mumbled a quick "I'm sorry" in Cindy's direction, but the damage had already been done.

Because each spouse brings differing perspectives, expectations, and experiences into the marriage relationship, there is no avoiding conflict and disagreements in marriage. But experiencing conflict does not mean that we have to resort to name-calling or the silent treatment. Learning to fight fair while resolving marital conflict is essential to developing and maintaining intimacy in marriage.

Pride drives our desire to be right and to win arguments at all costs, even at the expense of our spouse. Pride is one of the greatest enemies of marriage; humility is one of the greatest friends of marriage.

Are you guilty of keeping score with your wife? Is your need to be right in every disagreement causing you to dishonor her? What would it take for you and your wife to learn to fight fair? If you haven't learned how to do that, the sooner the better.

BOTTOM LINE

Conflict handled properly can fine-tune a relationship. Prayerfully humble yourself and seek to understand rather than be right.

Moment of Strength: Ephesians 5:1-2

LEARNING TO LET GO

Direct your children onto the right path, and
when they are older, they will not leave it.

Proverbs 22:6

FROM THE MOMENT OUR children are born, our job as parents is to prepare them to function in a broken world without us. This is no doubt one of the toughest challenges we will ever face. Headlines from newspapers all over our country are daily reminders that the world in which we live is a dangerous and scary place. As fathers, it is natural for us to want to shield and protect our children from harm and to make their way as easy as we possibly can.

But if we're not careful, these natural instincts, fueled by our own fears and insecurities, can cause us to be overprotective and to over-parent, thus handicapping our children. When we lose the perspective that God is ultimately in control, our fears take over, and we attempt to be everything for our children, including their savior. As a result, many kids today are growing up without the life skills necessary to make good decisions and take care of themselves.

Parenting, like everything else in our lives, is a walk of faith. And thank God that it is! God has not called us to try to control everything. What a relief. In what ways is God showing you your desperate need for Him through your children? Have you been guilty of making an idol of your children and their future happiness? Take some time to reflect on specific areas you need to release to God as they relate to your children, and then ask God to help you.

BOTTOM LINE

Though we are instrumental and vitally important in the growth and development of our children, how they ultimately turn out is not entirely up to us.

Moment of Strength: 1 John 4:18

THE GOOD FATHER: PART 1

Don't be like them, for your Father knows exactly
what you need even before you ask him!
Matthew 6:8

WHAT COMES TO YOUR MIND and heart when you hear the word *father* can define you for a lifetime. If your earthly father failed you, abandoned you, used you, hurt you, ignored you, failed to protect you, or exploited you, then you sustained a wound. That wound affects you in deep ways—especially in how you view God. It is natural that you would project onto your heavenly Father the attributes you saw in your earthly father.

Many men need to correct their deepest instincts about God the Father. He is the ideal Father. He doesn't share any of the imperfections of your earthly father.

- *He is an ever-present Father.* He doesn't abandon His children. He never becomes so preoccupied that He forgets where He put you. He never leaves you or forsakes you (Hebrews 13:5).
- *He is a patient Father.* God knows you are "only dust" (Psalm 103:14). Your weaknesses are no surprise to Him. He is "slow to anger" (Psalm 86:15, HCSB).
- *He is a steady Father.* Many earthly fathers are unpredictable. A child never knows whether "good dad" or "bad dad" will come walking through the door. Your earthly dad might have been fickle, moody, and changeable, but your heavenly Father has no bad days. "He never changes or casts a shifting shadow" (James 1:17).

BOTTOM LINE

God is the Father you've always dreamed of. Ask Him to reveal Himself to you, and read the Scriptures with that goal in mind.

Moment of Strength: Psalm 103:1-18

THE GOOD FATHER: PART 2

God never said to any angel what he said to Jesus:
"You are my Son. Today I have become your Father."
Hebrews 1:5

GOD THE FATHER IS utterly devoted to His Son, Jesus. At Christ's transfiguration, the Father declared His "delight" in His Son and commanded His followers to "listen to Him" (Matthew 17:5, HCSB). The Father "highly exalted Him" (Philippians 2:9, HCSB). He commanded the angels to "worship Him" (Hebrews 1:6, HCSB).

The Father's commitment to glorify the Son is mind-blowingly beautiful, powerful, and deep.

Even more astounding is the Father's commitment to bring "many children to glory" (Hebrews 2:10). The way God loves and fathers Jesus is the exact same way He loves and fathers you.

- *He is a forgiving Father.* Even if you've failed Him and pushed Him away and sinned against Him again and again, your Father eagerly waits for you to come home. Through Christ, He has thrown all your sins behind His back (Isaiah 38:17).
- *He is an attentive Father.* He is fully aware of all your needs. Your Father notices your smiles, your frowns, your hopes, and your dreams. He provides all you need (Matthew 7:11).
- *He is a satisfied Father.* Some men never receive their earthly father's blessing. They work unceasingly for his approval. God isn't like that. If you're His child, He finds nothing to condemn in you (Romans 8:1) and declares you blameless (Jude 1:24). You can rest in His acceptance and love.

BOTTOM LINE

It is time to disentangle your thoughts of God from the imperfections of your earthly father and to recognize Him as the Dad you've always longed for.

Moment of Strength: Galatians 4:1-7

THE "BOTTOM-LINE" MENTALITY

Look here, you rich people: Weep and groan with anguish
because of all the terrible troubles ahead of you.

James 5:1

THE SCRIPTURES WARN US against a money-only, bottom-line mentality that sees life only through the prism of our finances. James, pastor of the early church in Jerusalem, saw this worldview firsthand, as wealthy aristocrats both inside and outside the church cheated their employees and exploited the poor. James spoke prophetically about God's coming justice on behalf of victims of injustice, and he didn't mince words warning the rich against the miseries coming their way. There are certainly injustices in our society today, too, but we may not regard them with the same seriousness that the Bible does.

A gospel-centered approach to wealth puts a higher value on relationships than on money. In this worldview, wealth is simply a tool for a greater end: glorifying God and serving His people. The gospel-centered employer cares more about his employees than his bottom line. He uses his means to help the less fortunate. And he recognizes that his financial success is the result of God's grace.

This countercultural philosophy not only invites God's favor but also stands as a stark contrast to business environments that are increasingly characterized by greed. It is the gospel lived out in plain view, a signpost to the radical nature of Christ's coming Kingdom, where money doesn't rule the day.

BOTTOM LINE

Wealth makes a great tool for Kingdom work, but a very poor idol.

Moment of Strength: James 5:1-6

CHRISTIANS IN AN AGE OF GREED

Dear brothers and sisters, be patient as you wait
for the Lord's return. Consider the farmers who
patiently wait for the rains in the fall and in the spring.
They eagerly look for the valuable harvest to ripen.

James 5:7

JAMES SAYS, "Be patient as you wait for the Lord's return." Patience is a virtue in a world filled with sin and struggle. We need to maintain a long-term perspective, recognizing that God will eventually put things right, even if now there is much suffering and injustice to bear.

In James's day, as in our own, many believers were victims of a culture in which greed reigned, often at the expense of good, hardworking people. Wealthy landowners bribed corrupt judges and exploited the poor. They squeezed their employees by withholding their wages, hoarding the money for themselves. It was a disgrace.

James never condones injustice or calls believers to make peace with it. Not at all. But he does urge us to focus our gaze on heaven and find our hope in Christ's coming reign rather than in this world. The irony is that when we take such an approach, we become so freed up from the things of this world that we're actually much more effective as agents of transformation. We live as if we have nothing to lose, because ultimately we don't.

The workplace is part of our mission field. Mondays become extensions of Sunday, and we serve as emissaries of God's Kingdom. Our lives are not meant to be disjointed in any way but should be wholly devoted to God in every sphere of influence we have.

BOTTOM LINE

A Christian in the workplace is more than an employee. He is an ambassador of the gospel, on a mission for God.

Moment of Strength: James 5:7-11

WHEN INTEGRITY MATTERS MOST

Most of all, my brothers and sisters, never take an oath,
by heaven or earth or anything else. Just say a simple
yes or no, so that you will not sin and be condemned.
James 5:12

WE CAN TALK A LOT ABOUT integrity and character, but we won't really see it until we're put to the test. In James's letter to the church of Jerusalem, he encourages the people to maintain their integrity, especially while under pressure. The tough times reveal who we really are.

James was speaking mainly to the poor: the victims of a corrupt and unjust system in which the wealthy made their money by dishonest means. These powerful entities seemed unstoppable. So the only logical way to avoid being victimized, it seemed, was to employ the same tactics. If you can't beat 'em, join 'em.

But it is precisely when dishonesty seems most appropriate, when it can be excused because of injustice, that it must be resisted. Christians who hold fast to Kingdom values, even suffering loss as a result, become living gospel witnesses. The politician who resists the urge to demean his opponent, even though he may lose the race; the CEO who fights to retain employees, though it may cost him millions in the short term; the spouse who forgives in spite of unfaithfulness—these show proven character.

It is said that a man's integrity is not proven until it is tested. His core values are not revealed until they are exposed. His faithful obedience to a godly set of values will cause people to stand up and take notice.

BOTTOM LINE

For a man of God, there is no greater opportunity to display faith in Christ than when he exemplifies honesty when it is least expected.

Moment of Strength: James 5:7-12

MISPLACED CONFIDENCE

We who worship by the Spirit of God are the ones who are truly circumcised. We rely on what Christ Jesus has done for us. We put no confidence in human effort.

Philippians 3:3

THE APOSTLE PAUL WAS a superstar in his previous life as Saul the Pharisee—all the right connections and credentials. Just listen to his qualifications and accomplishments:

> Indeed, if others have reason for confidence in their own efforts, I have even more! I was circumcised when I was eight days old. I am a pure-blooded citizen of Israel and a member of the tribe of Benjamin—a real Hebrew if there ever was one! I was a member of the Pharisees, who demand the strictest obedience to the Jewish law. I was so zealous that I harshly persecuted the church. And as for righteousness, I obeyed the law without fault.
> PHILIPPIANS 3:4-6

Paul was the man! But it didn't matter. And as far as God's Kingdom goes, it doesn't matter for us, either. Whether we have the right background, have been to all the right schools, have the right job and make the right amount of money, God doesn't measure success as the world does. He doesn't measure it "according to the flesh" (Romans 8:5, HCSB). And because God isn't impressed with what we have and what we can do in our own strength, we shouldn't be either.

Paul came to view success in a different way.

> I once thought these things were valuable, but now I consider them worthless because of what Christ has done. Yes, everything else is worthless when compared with the infinite value of knowing Christ Jesus my Lord. For his sake I have discarded everything else, counting it all as garbage, so that I could gain Christ.
> PHILIPPIANS 3:7-8

Where do you find your value? What do you value most?

BOTTOM LINE

Our culture lauds self-admiration, and it can seem so right. But it isn't, because it places self at the center rather than Christ. Focus your attention on Him.

Moment of Strength: Philippians 3

THE RIGHT KIND OF CONFIDENCE

Do not throw away this confident trust in the Lord.
Remember the great reward it brings you!
Hebrews 10:35

THOUGH THERE'S A DANGER OF placing too much confidence in ourselves, this doesn't mean we shouldn't be confident. The truth is, we have every right to be supremely confident in our position in Christ and in our future as secured by Him. In fact, to not be supremely confident is not humility; it is unbelief. It is to discount God's promises and live at a level far beneath what He's offered us. We often do that because we don't feel worthy and God's promises can sound too good to be true. But remember—this is Almighty God we're talking about! He doesn't offer stingy forgiveness or measly power or meager promises. He offers more than we could ever ask or think (Ephesians 3:20). We must take Him at His word and believe Him!

What are some things we can be confident about? Well, for starters, as Christians we are completely forgiven and accepted by God, both now and forever. Ephesians 3:12 says that "because of Christ and our faith in him, we can now come boldly and confidently into God's presence." Our sin is no longer a barrier between us. And this access, this relationship, will extend throughout eternity: "As we live in God, our love grows more perfect. So we will not be afraid on the day of judgment, but we can face him with confidence because we live like Jesus here in this world" (1 John 4:17).

We also have confidence in prayer: "We are confident that he hears us whenever we ask for anything that pleases him" (1 John 5:14). God wants us to be confident in Him.

BOTTOM LINE

The right kind of confidence—confidence in God and His promises—is not arrogant. It takes humility to believe that what God says is true is true.

Moment of Strength: Hebrews 3:6

THE FREEDOM OF FAITH

If the law could give us new life, we could be made right with God by obeying it.
But the Scriptures declare that we are all prisoners of sin, so
we receive God's promise of freedom only by believing in Jesus Christ.
Galatians 3:21-22

THE LAW IS GOOD, but it doesn't give life. It can't give life. It isn't meant to. Trying to please God simply by obeying laws, rules, and principles never works for long. Instead, it produces either pride or despair: pride if you feel as if you're doing pretty well, especially compared to other Christians; despair if you feel as if you're not measuring up to some external standard coming from God, others, or even yourself.

There's something in us (sin) that wants to earn its own way rather than receive grace. The simplicity of faith, of receiving a gift apart from anything we've done, will do, or ever could do, is an affront to our pride. The perception we have of ourselves as pretty good people doing the best we can must give way to the humble acknowledgment of our true condition as people captive to sin who can be set free only by the grace and mercy of God in Christ.

If you've struggled under the bonds of performance-oriented Christianity and legalistic rule-keeping, you know how liberating the gospel message can be. Often, Christians start off well but then gradually begin focusing more on what they're doing for Christ rather than what He's done for them. When that happens, their joy leaves the building. Only grace produces willing and true heart obedience that's good for the long haul. If joy is missing in your Christian life, go back to the gospel to recover it.

BOTTOM LINE

Your joy is linked to your understanding of the gospel. As you live under God's love, you will grow spiritually, and it won't be burdensome.

Moment of Strength: Galatians 3:19-26

MONEY, MONEY, MONEY

Wherever your treasure is, there the desires of your heart will also be.
Matthew 6:21

LEARNING HOW TO MANAGE MONEY can be one of the biggest challenges we face as adults. Day after day, month after month, questions arise about how to be good stewards of what we have. We wonder how much money is enough, what our priorities should be, and how much we should give to the church.

Struggling to stay solvent can become a routine part of life. Pay a little bit extra on this bill this month, then some on the next one next month. There may be enough to cover everything for the time being, but not much left over. There are regular expenses that we can predict, but then there always seem to be unexpected costs that come up.

Cutting back does not necessarily mean having to cut certain things out entirely. The movie you once impulsively purchased on DVD for $20, you now watch on OnDemand for $4. You used to eat out all the time, with barely a second thought to the cost. Now, you savor a once-a-week opportunity for a night out with your family.

It's all about being a good steward. There's a big difference between living in extravagance and simple contentment, and an even bigger one between comfort and poverty. What many of us think of as hardship is a life of unimaginable luxury for millions around the world. Be wise with what you've been given, and be thankful for it!

BOTTOM LINE

Making ends meet can be hard, so pray for the wisdom to set your priorities correctly.

Moment of Strength: Philippians 4:11-13

DON'T BE AFRAID

"Joseph, son of David," the angel said, "do not be afraid to take Mary as your wife. For the child within her was conceived by the Holy Spirit."
Matthew 1:20

AN ANGEL APPEARED TO Joseph in a dream and told him to not be afraid to take Mary as his wife, despite the fact that she was pregnant and the baby was not Joseph's. You can imagine how the news of her pregnancy could have caused some concerns about the viability of their relationship. After all, a marriage is supposed to be built on trust, and Mary getting pregnant before their marriage and without Joseph's involvement was not part of their plan. Joseph likely would have been tempted to be afraid of what others would think of Mary and him for going through with the marriage despite what appeared to be a moral indiscretion. But things were not as they seemed.

We cannot know God, love God, or obey God without faith. Hebrews 11:6 says, "It is impossible to please God without faith. Anyone who wants to come to him must believe that God exists and that he rewards those who sincerely seek him." Our faith is a gift from God (Ephesians 2:8), and it pleases Him for us to develop it. He wants us to trust Him.

Fear is the great enemy of faith. Living in fear is looking at circumstances as if God doesn't exist, as if everything depends on us. Fear is trying to control the uncontrollable. It shrinks our world and can cause us to be ineffective. But God's love casts out fear and gives us the faith we need to trust Him.

BOTTOM LINE

There's a battle going on in each of our lives between fear and faith. Over and over again, the Bible tells us to not be afraid. We can look to God instead.

Moment of Strength: 1 John 4:18

DON'T TRY TO FIX IT

"So I will prove to you that the Son of Man has the authority on earth to forgive sins." Then Jesus turned to the paralyzed man and said, "Stand up, pick up your mat, and go home!"

Mark 2:10-11

ACCORDING TO THE ART OF Manliness website, every man must own four essential power tools: a cordless drill, a reciprocating saw, an oscillating multi-tool, and a circular saw. (Can we all let loose a manly grunt?) The truth is, men love tools because we love to fix things. Just give us some power tools and a free afternoon and watch what we can accomplish.

Jesus could fix things too. He worked as a carpenter with His earthly father, Joseph. Jesus could probably build a wall, fix a chair, or hang a door. But Jesus didn't come to fix things; He came to transform them.

The Gospel of Mark describes a scene where four friends pulled off the roof of a house and lowered their paralyzed buddy down to where Jesus was teaching. Jesus saw the paralytic and said, "My child, your sins are forgiven" (Mark 2:5). What do you think the man's friends were thinking? *Hey, we just want him fixed so he can walk again. What does having his sins forgiven have to do with anything?*

But Jesus had a deeper purpose. He wanted this man's life to be transformed. That should be one of the goals of our marriages, too. When our eyes are focused on ourselves or on our wives, it's easy to see things that need to be fixed. However, when we fix our eyes on Jesus, we can be transformed to have a truer life and a better marriage.

BOTTOM LINE

Do you want to fix things or transform them? Follow Jesus' example and go deeper in your life and in your marriage. It's worth it.

Moment of Strength: Romans 12:2

ALL GUILTY

The person who keeps all of the laws except one is as guilty
as a person who has broken all of God's laws.

James 2:10

KEVIN ENJOYED HELPING his daughter memorize Bible verses for Sunday school. This week's verse was James 2:10.

"For the person who keeps all of the laws except one is as guilty as a person who has broken all of God's laws," his daughter read.

"Exactly right, sweetie," Kevin said as he read along.

Then his daughter asked something that caught him off guard. "Am I guilty, Daddy?"

Thinking quickly, Kevin answered, "Do you always obey Mommy and Daddy? Do you share and not fight with your brother and friends?"

Kevin's precious girl thought for a moment, then answered with tears in her eyes, "No."

"So you are guilty," Kevin said, hugging her. "But you can be forgiven. If you have Jesus in your heart and ask Him to forgive you, then you're not guilty anymore."

Kevin's daughter didn't pray to accept Christ that day, but this interaction showed Kevin that she was old enough to understand her need for a Savior. Through additional conversations, Kevin's daughter did make that life-changing decision. As fathers, it's our responsibility and honor to help introduce our children to Christ. We need to look for opportunities, cooperate with the Holy Spirit, and help make our kids' faith strong.

BOTTOM LINE

Do your children know Jesus personally? Make the effort to help your kids build a firm foundation on Christ.

Moment of Strength: Mark 10:14-15

MANAGE YOUR MONEY

All too quickly the message is crowded out by the worries of this life, the lure of wealth, and the desire for other things, so no fruit is produced.
Mark 4:19

MONEY IS LIKE SEX. We don't like to talk about it, but we want to have a whole lot of it. One of the most important things we can do to improve our finances—and even our love lives—is to talk about them with our wives. Although many couples talk about money, the conversations typically stay pretty basic: "Do we have enough to pay the bills?" "Is there enough in savings for soccer club?" "Why can't I buy that new titanium driver?"

When it comes to handling money, it is imperative that we have a plan. How much goes to savings? Who pays the bills? Who decides how money is spent? Experts say couples should decide together about making extra purchases—even small ones. Then each person feels some ownership over the finances.

Though it's good to talk about money in a marriage, we shouldn't allow the topic to consume us. Constant conversations can create undue stress. When Jesus told the parable of the sower, He said, "All too quickly the message is crowded out by the worries of this life and the lure of wealth, so no fruit is produced" (Matthew 13:22). Our main focus in life should be to spread God's Word, not to increase our wealth.

By keeping an eternal focus and having good communication about money, you'll be able to control your finances, instead of the other way around.

BOTTOM LINE

Have you talked this week about money? Make a financial plan and stick to it.

Moment of Strength: Proverbs 23:4-5

CHOICES

I have given you the choice between life and death, between blessings and
curses. Now I call on heaven and earth to witness the choice you make.
Oh, that you would choose life, so that you and your descendants might live!
You can make this choice by loving the LORD your God, obeying him, and
committing yourself firmly to him. This is the key to your life.
Deuteronomy 30:19-20

WHAT ARE SOME OF the right choices you've made? The girl you married? Disciplining and requiring respect from your children? Staying in a lower-paying job because it was best for your family? What rewarding consequences our right decisions bring!

Have you ever made any wrong choices? Taking a promotion you knew would keep you away from your family more without seeking God's will about it first? Experimenting with drinking or drugs as a teenager? Of course, those are big choices, but what about the choices we face daily—saying hurtful words in anger, staying in addictive lifestyles, or cheating on our expense account at work? Bad consequences will follow.

Look at the choices made by Joseph and David in the Bible. In Genesis 39, Joseph flees from the advances of his employer's wife. He later gains greater power and position because of his integrity. On the other hand, David commits adultery, and that terrible choice spirals down into deception and murder (2 Samuel 11). He pays a huge price in the end.

As today's Scripture advises, God gives us choices that have monumental consequences. It's up to us to make the right choices—integrity and character at home, at work, and in our walk with the Lord. There is nothing better than the joy and peace that come from obeying God.

BOTTOM LINE
Resolve today to prayerfully seek God's wisdom and guidance regarding every choice you face.

Moment of Strength: Genesis 39:1-19

OVERCOMING WORRY

Don't worry about anything, but in everything, through prayer and petition with thanksgiving, let your requests be made known to God.
Philippians 4:6, HCSB

DAVE STOOD AT THE MAILBOX and stared at the foreclosure notice that had finally arrived. To say he had been dreading this moment would be a huge understatement. Risky investments over the past few years had finally caught up with him, and now his family's future was in serious jeopardy. He was paralyzed by fear and ashamed that he had allowed things to get this bad. He knew that he should be turning to God, but how could he expect God to bail him out of his bad decisions?

The Gospel of Matthew records an incident with Jesus and His disciples on the Sea of Galilee in which Jesus confronts their fear and lack of faith. Because of its location, storms often arise quickly on the Sea of Galilee. In the middle of one of these sudden storms, the disciples, fearing for their lives, panicked and ran to Jesus, exclaiming, "Lord, save us! We're going to die!" Jesus, who had been asleep in the boat, said to them, "Why are you fearful, you of little faith?" (Matthew 8:25-26, HCSB).

Like the disciples, we often worry. In the middle of a storm—even one that we brought upon ourselves—we must remember that God has not abandoned us. Even though we face consequences for our own choices, He is right there with us. What storms are you facing today? Are you trusting God to deliver you? Are you releasing your fears to your Savior?

BOTTOM LINE

Worry is fear of the unknown. It comes when we try to control what we can't control. The antidote is to cast our worries upon the Lord and trust Him.

Moment of Strength: Matthew 6:34

TRUST IN THE LORD

Trust in the LORD with all your heart; do not depend on your own understanding. Seek his will in all you do, and he will show you which path to take.

Proverbs 3:5-6

PAUSE FOR A MOMENT AND REFLECT ON TODAY'S SCRIPTURE. What does it mean to "trust in the LORD with all your heart"? You've probably faced more than a few issues over the course of your life that seemed utterly hopeless until you turned them completely over to God. There's a huge difference between simply acknowledging God and truly trusting in Him.

Not relying on our own understanding can be incredibly difficult sometimes because there seem to be no clear answers for some questions. Why does someone we love have a life-threatening illness like cancer? What about world peace or the economy? If we're trying to figure it out on our own, we're going to be out of luck. We need to trust someone much greater and wiser than ourselves.

All of life is meant to be lived with and for God. The way you treat the waitstaff at a restaurant reflects on God. The same goes for how you react when you get cut off in traffic or when your favorite sports team loses the big game. Think about Him in all your ways, not just during church activities.

God is always there for you. The road you're called to walk may be difficult and lonely sometimes, but you have a sure guide who will help you overcome every obstacle—not because you're perfect, but because He is. The way of trust is the only way to experience true joy and peace.

BOTTOM LINE

Proverbs 3:5-6 is a game plan for your everyday life. Are there areas of your life where you need to stop striving and start trusting?

Moment of Strength: Psalm 37:3-6

THE GRACE OF GIVING

You know the generous grace of our Lord Jesus Christ. Though he was rich, yet for your sakes he became poor, so that by his poverty he could make you rich.

2 Corinthians 8:9

RADICAL GENEROSITY IS CONTAGIOUS. When others give sacrificially, it can inspire us to do the same, especially when they have less than we do. In 2 Corinthians 8, the apostle Paul is urging the Corinthian church to contribute to a fund-raising project for the Jerusalem church. In motivating them to give, Paul doesn't use guilt or manipulation. He simply tells a story. He calls attention to the generosity of a tiny group of believers in Macedonia who are dirt-poor. He even mentions that he tried to persuade them to keep their money, knowing that they needed it more than those in Jerusalem. However, they considered contributing to God's Kingdom work a privilege, even when living in extreme poverty.

What would inspire a group of people living in poverty to give beyond their ability? The answer: *grace*. The grace of Christ turns our understanding of the world upside down. It's easy to think you get more by grasping, but in the Kingdom, more comes through giving. The way that God wins the hearts of sinners isn't through guilt and fear but through generosity. In Jesus, God gives beyond our expectations. In Jesus, He broke the bank. He gave all that He had. The more we give, the more we participate in the life of God. The reason we can hold our material resources loosely is that, through Jesus, we have an endless supply of heavenly riches.

BOTTOM LINE

The motivation for giving generously, even in the midst of scarcity, is the grace of Jesus Christ. Ask Him to help you give from a generous heart.

Moment of Strength: 2 Corinthians 8:1-15

NAGGING WITH LOVE

*Speaking the truth in love, let us grow in every way
into Him who is the head—Christ.*
Ephesians 4:15, HCSB

RESEARCH OVER THE PAST 150 YEARS has shown that married men tend to enjoy better health and live longer than their single, divorced, or widowed peers. A good, loving marriage also helps to decrease stress and to alleviate loneliness and depression. One possible reason for why married men live longer is the "nagging" of their wives. Many men, once they hit their forties and fifties, don't exercise as much. They don't eat the way they should either. In such cases, being nagged by your wife can be good for your health.

Is it fun to be nagged? No. Is nagging good for us? It can be. We may not like it, but it can help us do what we should already be doing. Many men get in the habit of tuning out their wives' observations, but that's not the best response. Oftentimes, our wives nag us because they love us. And one way she may be speaking truth to you is by encouraging you to become more like Christ (Ephesians 4:15).

Research shows that nearly 70 percent of men rely on their wives as their primary social support. So if you're married, the main person who speaks into your life is probably your wife. The next time you feel nagged, look for the truth in her words. Sometimes we need to be reminded to do the right thing. Sometimes, the godly wife who loves you is trying to speak the truth into your life.

BOTTOM LINE

Instead of being annoyed by your wife's "nagging," look for what you can learn from it. It may help you become more like Jesus.

Moment of Strength: Ephesians 4:29

SPEAK UP

Speak up for those who cannot speak for themselves;
ensure justice for those being crushed.
Proverbs 31:8

THERE ARE PEOPLE ALL AROUND US who cannot speak up for themselves, and it's not just limited to the poor and needy. Sometimes, we seem to think that it's enough to drop a few bucks in the offering plate for world missions. That couldn't be further from the truth. There are all kinds of ways to stand up for all kinds of people.

Those you can speak up for may be halfway around the world, but they may also be just down the street. Maybe it's a cashier being given a hard time by a customer. Maybe it's a child who isn't the best athlete in the world playing on the same sports team as your son or daughter. Opportunities abound to help and encourage.

As He did in so many other ways, our Savior set forth a remarkable standard. When the disciples tried to shoo away a group of children, Jesus set the disciples straight very quickly, saying, "Leave the children alone, and don't try to keep them from coming to Me, because the kingdom of heaven is made up of people like this" (Matthew 19:14, HCSB).

In a lot of cases, the situation wouldn't have been given a second thought. The kids were in the way, so they had to go, right? Wrong. You come into contact with people every day who need that same kind of support in some way, even if it's nothing more than a kind word or a pat on the back.

BOTTOM LINE

There are people both near and far who cannot speak up for themselves. Ask God to show you ways and opportunities to speak up for them.

Moment of Strength: Isaiah 1:17

ALL NATIONS IN QUEENS?

Go and make disciples of all the nations, baptizing them in
the name of the Father and the Son and the Holy Spirit.
Matthew 28:19

YOU'VE HEARD SERMONS PREACHED, Sunday school lessons taught, and Bible studies focused on the great commission, that passage at the end of the Gospel of Matthew when Jesus commissions His followers to take the Good News around the world.

Hasn't that been done? Wouldn't you think that after more than two millennia, the church has at least come close to fulfilling that command from Jesus? Think again. According to statistics from the Joshua Project, there's a lot more work to be done. There's still a wide-open field ready for some who follow Jesus to sow seeds and others to harvest, sharing the gospel around the world.

Nathan Creitz is a church planter for the Southern Baptist Convention who moved to Queens, New York, in December 2011 to plant a church. Creitz says, "The word for 'nation' is better understood as an ethnic people group. Though we may not all go to all peoples, we are all responsible to bring the gospel to all unreached people. . . . One fifth of the people in our neighborhood are from unreached people groups."

Creitz challenges each man to do his part in fulfilling Jesus' command, but not necessarily by packing up and moving to the other side of the world. We can look for the nations represented in our own hometowns, even in our own neighborhoods. Your town may not have the ethnic diversity of Queens, but *somebody* from *somewhere* lives there. Reach out. In today's transient culture, there's no excuse for not being personally involved in the great commission.

BOTTOM LINE

What nationalities are represented in your hometown? What are you doing to take the gospel to these nations in your own backyard?

Moment of Strength: Matthew 28:18-20

THE HORIZONTAL DIMENSION

For the entire law is fulfilled in one statement:
Love your neighbor as yourself.
Galatians 5:14, HCSB

A LARGE HOLE HAD BEEN dug as part of the excavation at a construction site. A number of workers were in the hole removing dirt when the walls collapsed around them. Rescuers began running in from everywhere, but the foreman stood by and watched the scene with detachment. Suddenly a woman called out from the construction office trailer: "Jim, your brother is in the hole!" Instantly, the foreman ran to the collapsed hole, stripped off his coat, and began digging for dear life. Why? Because his brother was in mortal danger and he had to get him out.

Our neighbor is anyone in danger, in need, in pain, or in trouble. We bear a responsibility to help. In helping, we obey Jesus' command to love.

When asked what the greatest commandment was, Jesus gave not just one but two (see Matthew 22:36-40). The two are so integrally tied together that they almost function as one. Why? Because the essence of Christianity is love: loving God and loving people. Christ followers can't have one without the other. A vertical dimension and a horizontal dimension must both be present. Christianity always moves in two directions: toward God and toward people. One of the ways a believer demonstrates his love for God is by loving others. It is in loving God and people that we identify and mark ourselves as Christians.

BOTTOM LINE

Do you know someone who is in a hole—spiritually, emotionally, or relationally? Whom you can help rescue?

Moment of Strength: 1 Peter 4:8

THE FAITH REQUIREMENT

There was a man in Jerusalem whose name was Simeon.
This man was righteous and devout.

Luke 2:25, HCSB

TOO OFTEN WE WANT GOD'S RESOURCES, but we don't want His timing. We want His presence, but we don't want His patience. We are amateurs at waiting, yet we must wait. God is working. Waiting means we give God the benefit of the doubt and trust that He knows what He's doing.

Simeon must have wondered whether God would be true to His word. He had been promised to see the Messiah, but he was running out of years. His life was at the eleventh hour. God must have reminded him: "Your job is to trust . . . to wait . . . to accept My timing. That is all. You keep your heart right; I'll keep My promise."

Maybe you're at a point in your life when you wonder whether God will come through. Maybe you are about to give up hope that He will show up. Maybe you feel that time is passing you by. Maybe you want to run ahead of God. Maybe you want to give up on God.

The story of Simeon teaches us that God proves Himself faithful even when it seems as if nothing is happening. His timing is perfect. Our part is to trust—a confident, disciplined, patient waiting for His help and deliverance. God seeks to reveal Himself to us. He wants to meet us. And He will, but it will be on His timetable and in His way. So relax and trust, rather than worry and fret.

BOTTOM LINE

Are you waiting on God or are you running ahead of Him? He can be trusted. He is faithful. He will come through. Choose to wait patiently.

Moment of Strength: Psalm 9:10

WHEN GOD ASKS US TO WAIT

Simeon . . . was righteous and devout, looking forward to Israel's consolation, and the Holy Spirit was on him.

Luke 2:25, HCSB

WE ARE LIKE CHILDREN AT CHRISTMAS, eagerly anticipating the day to open presents. In our culture, the ability to wait patiently is not a common character trait. We're not patient people; we're taught early on to "make it happen."

Waiting may be the hardest single thing we are ever asked to do. Though we may not like it, waiting is a necessary part of the Christian life. What God does in us while we wait is as important as what we are waiting for. Waiting is not easy. It's the toll on the road that each of us must travel.

The Old Testament promised a coming Messiah. Israel had to wait—generation after generation, century after century. When the Messiah came, only those looking for Him recognized His coming. For one man in particular, waiting turned out to be a blessing.

We are told in Luke 2:26 that the Holy Spirit told Simeon he would not die until he saw the Messiah. So Simeon had been looking for, waiting for, the Christ. He recognized the Savior because, unlike many of God's people, he was acting in faith on the promises of God. Simeon's hope finally materialized; his dream turned into reality. Was it worth the wait? Simeon saw the baby Jesus, the Messiah. He got to hold the baby Jesus in his arms, and then he was content to die. Joy filled his heart.

BOTTOM LINE

Consider what God is doing while you wait for Him.

Moment of Strength: Psalm 130:5

FINDING JESUS

It had been revealed to [Simeon] by the Holy Spirit that
he would not see death before he saw the Lord's Messiah.

Luke 2:26, HCSB

THE GREAT SCIENTIST Blaise Pascal said we have a God-shaped vacuum inside us that only God can fill. We were created to know God, and nothing in this world can take His place in our lives. If we live for thirty, fifty, seventy, or ninety years and don't find God, it really doesn't matter what else we've done with our lives. If we don't find God, we have missed the very reason for our existence. If we miss out on knowing God, we will have missed the central reality of the universe. Compared to knowing the one who made us, everything else is superficial and ultimately unsatisfying.

Simeon spent many years of his life committed to the task of looking for the Messiah. His looking was not a casual observance, a passing glance, or a nonchalant peek. His looking was intentional. It was an honest, sincere waiting for the Savior. Though we don't know how long he waited between the time the Spirit spoke and the time Jesus was born, Simeon believed God and remained faithful to the hope that God's promise would be fulfilled.

Are you hungry for more spiritual truth? Do you want to experience more of the Savior? Many things can wait, but the search for more of God's presence, power, and love cannot wait. He has given us a constant longing in our hearts for more of Him, and we should follow that longing with all we've got.

BOTTOM LINE

Are you restless for the Savior? Are you desperate to know Him better? Seek Him. Pursue Him. You were made to know Him and love Him.

Moment of Strength: Matthew 7:7

LOOKING FOR JESUS

*Guided by the Spirit, [Simeon] entered the temple
complex. When the parents brought in the child Jesus . . .
Simeon took Him up in his arms, praised God, and said:
"Now, Master, You can dismiss Your slave in peace."*
Luke 2:27-29, HCSB

A SOUTH AFRICAN DISCOVERED one of the world's largest diamonds—the size of a small lemon. He wanted to ship it to the office of a London company as safely and quickly as possible. He sent a steel box with four men to protect it. When the steel box arrived, much to everyone's surprise the diamond wasn't there, but just a lump of coal. Three days later, by parcel post in an ordinary box, the diamond arrived in the London office. The South African figured that no one would pay any attention to an ordinary box.

Two thousand years ago, God came wrapped in an "ordinary box," in a way no one expected and in a place that was as remote and off the beaten path as one could imagine. Who would ever look for God there?

Simeon did. He looked for God and found Him in the most ordinary place. Jesus' parents presented Him at the Temple, as was customary, and with no fanfare. The only one who saw Him was a man looking for the Messiah, in the right place at the right time. Simeon was paying attention.

How many times have we looked for Jesus in the spectacular and missed Him in the ordinary? How often have we looked for Him among the elite and missed Him in a small child, or sought Him in ritual and missed Him in relationship? He is always present to us through His Spirit—it's we who miss Him because we're not looking.

BOTTOM LINE

Where are you looking for Jesus? Ask God to open your spiritual eyes to see Him at work around you.

Moment of Strength: Psalm 105:3-4

RISE UP!

Stand up in the presence of the elderly, and show respect for the aged.
Fear your God. I am the LORD.
Leviticus 19:32

IT MAY BE PART OF the Old Testament law, but it's still a valuable principle for life. One of the ways we show reverence for God is to honor our elders. And this takes us back to our parenting skills.

First, we model what we want our children to become. In this case, demonstrating care and concern for older people is important. Our children need to see that the value of a life is not dependent on how much a person can accomplish or how much money he or she makes. The elderly deserve our respect and love simply for being created in the image of God. Besides, we are not in a position to evaluate someone else's contributions to society. There's no limit to what someone can accomplish simply by praying.

Second, just as we strive to create a warm, safe environment of unconditional love for our children, we must do the same for our elders. It's easy to feel discouraged after your career is finished and your health begins to diminish. Insecurities can rise to the surface, and sometimes even personalities can change. We need God's help to love others well.

When we respect our elders and obey God's command to honor them, we teach our children about unconditional love. And our obedience pleases God and deepens our relationship with Him.

BOTTOM LINE

Honor your father and mother in their old age. It honors them and God, and sets a good example for your children.

Moment of Strength: Psalm 71:9

TRUE FRIENDS, THICK AND THIN

*How we thank God for you! Because of you we have
great joy as we enter God's presence.*
1 Thessalonians 3:9

JOE AND RICK HAVE BEEN best friends since high school. They have laughed together more times than they can count, and Joe has been a rock of support for Rick when he really needed some help. As far as Rick is concerned, Joe is a lifelong, I'd-take-a-bullet-for-him kind of friend.

Another family, the Knights, took Rick in at a very difficult time in his life and gave him a place to stay for several months when he had no place else to turn. He became an unofficial Knight, complete with a Christmas stocking like the rest of the family! He will never forget their kindness.

God placed Joe and the Knights in Rick's life for a reason. He knew exactly the kind of support Rick would need over the course of his life and when he would need it. Like the apostle Paul's expression of gratitude for the church in Thessalonica in today's verse, how could Rick ever thank God fully for these kinds of friends?

Take a moment to consider the folks who have crossed your path over the course of your life. You've probably formed incredibly strong bonds with at least a few of them. They're not there by accident. They've been placed in your life by a kind and loving God who knows we need all the love and support we can get.

BOTTOM LINE

You probably have friends who will stick with you through thick and thin, no matter what. Take a moment to thank God for such a precious gift.

Moment of Strength: Proverbs 18:24

THE PRESENT OF BEING DAD

Whatever is good and perfect is a gift coming down to us from
God our Father, who created all the lights in the heavens.

James 1:17

A FEW YEARS AGO, children in Great Britain were asked what they wanted for Christmas. A new baby brother or sister topped the list. Close behind came a real-life reindeer. But the tenth-most-requested gift was a shocker: a *dad*. (A *mum* placed twenty-third.)

Your kids might not always say it, and as they enter their teen years they might not act like it, but they appreciate your role in their lives. This survey proves that children desire a father figure. They need a provider and mentor. They long for somebody to play with, learn from, and act like. You can be their hero as you seek to show them that Jesus is the true hero that you're following.

Being a dad is a gift. It's a gift we can give to our children for both the present and the future. But at its deepest level, fatherhood is a gift that God gives us. We're reminded in the Bible that children are a "reward from him" (Psalm 127:3). James 1:17 tells us, "Whatever is good and perfect is a gift coming down to us from God our Father, who created all the lights in the heavens." To get the most out of a gift, we have to use it. So open and enjoy the gift of being dad.

Spend time with your children. Be present. Don't take for granted the years you have together. They need you far more than a pet horse or a car (which finished third and fourth on the list), so strive by God's grace to be a gift to them.

BOTTOM LINE

Being a father is a gift from God. Treat it that way, and you'll be the best present your children ever receive.

Moment of Strength: 1 Thessalonians 2:11-12

HERE TO HEAR

LORD, you know the hopes of the helpless.
Surely you will hear their cries and comfort them.
Psalm 10:17

THE MESSAGE OF CHRISTMAS IS simple and eternal. Jesus says, "I am here." Four hundred years of silence between God and His people—beginning with the closing of the Old Testament (Malachi 4:5-6) and lasting until the coming of John the Baptist—had finally come to an end. In sending His Son, God the Father proclaimed to the world, "I hear you, and I am now with you. I am Emmanuel—God with you."

Notice two things about the way God hears us. First, He listens with the purpose of strengthening our hearts. He hears what we say, He feels what we feel (Hebrews 4:15), and He doesn't cut us off as we pour out our hearts to Him. Second, He listens carefully. He doesn't miss one word or one tear.

Here's the principle for Christian husbands: If the man is to be to his wife as Jesus is to His church (Ephesians 5:21-33), then the husband must listen to his wife in the same manner—that is, unconditionally, without prejudging what she says, without cutting her off in midsentence. He must listen carefully and help her see that her cares and concerns are his own.

This is a Christmas gift to give to your wife 365 days a year. It's a gift she will treasure far more than baubles and beads. It's the gift of listening—when she knows that you are "here to hear." It's a gift that will keep on giving for the rest of your days.

BOTTOM LINE

Thank God that He listens to you, and ask Him to put the power of listening to work in your marriage.

Moment of Strength: James 1:19

JOY TO THE WORLD

You will have great joy and gladness, and many will rejoice at his birth.
Luke 1:14

SOME THINGS ARE better sung than spoken. Here are the lyrics to the second verse of the beautiful and well-loved hymn "Joy to the World":

> *Joy to the earth, the Savior reigns!*
> *Let men their songs employ*
> *While fields and floods, rocks, hills, and plains*
> *Repeat the sounding joy,*
> *Repeat the sounding joy,*
> *Repeat, repeat, the sounding joy.*

The Savior's birth is meant to bring joy—something this weary world desperately needs. Joy is something that many Christians desperately need, too, but sadly lack all too often. The truth is, if our faith does not give us out-of-this-world joy, then we're seriously missing something. God wants us to have joy—to both feel it and express it. The world needs more joyful Christians. Nothing is a greater witness to the truth of the gospel and the goodness of God than joyful Christians. It is attractive to a watching world. It makes Jesus look good. It brings Him glory for His people to be filled with joy.

It takes time to appreciate the wonders of Christmas. Before long, we'll be right back into the rush of a new year, and the glory of Christmas will quietly recede into the background without much lingering effect—unless, that is, we learn to slow down, ponder, and give thanks. Pray that God by His Spirit would continue to pour joy into your heart throughout the year and not just during the Christmas season.

BOTTOM LINE

Joy comes when we focus on Jesus. Ask God to fill you with joy by His Spirit this Christmas season and throughout the year.

Moment of Strength: Luke 2:9-11

IMPOSSIBLY TRUE

And she will have a son, and you are to name him Jesus,
for he will save his people from their sins.

Matthew 1:21

THE IDEA OF A VIRGIN GIVING birth to the Son of God who would later die for the sins of the world may be a familiar part of our creed, but it should be no less astonishing to us than the first time we heard about it. *Christmas is a miracle.* It is Almighty God, "[who] made heaven and earth" (Psalm 146:6), reaching down into our completely hopeless situation and rescuing us in the humblest, yet most dramatic, way.

We forget that we are not in control. We didn't create ourselves, and we can't save ourselves. Everything depends on God. Christmas reminds us of that fact. God came to earth to rescue us. This is a stunning truth that can easily be taken for granted. What should our response be to such an incredible occurrence? Deep gratitude: "Thank God for this gift too wonderful for words" (2 Corinthians 9:15).

Christmas reminds us that nothing is ever hopeless with God. You may feel as if you have some hopeless circumstances in your life that you are powerless to do anything about. You may have even been praying about these things for some time, and so far nothing has changed. There just doesn't seem to be an answer. The truth is that from a human perspective, circumstances can look pretty hopeless sometimes. But that doesn't mean they *are* hopeless. God can do the miraculous. Christmas is proof of that. Keep hoping and praying.

BOTTOM LINE

Allow the miracle of Christmas to change how you think about the world and your life. Even when things look bad, God is still able to comfort us and sustain us.

Moment of Strength: Luke 1:37

JOY UNCEASING

*Satisfy us each morning with your unfailing love, so
we may sing for joy to the end of our lives.*

Psalm 90:14

THE REMOTE-CONTROLLED monster truck was the coolest Christmas present ever! That truck could cover the entire church parking lot in no time, making jumps that boggled the imagination. The church had a waist-high sawdust pile that made for a perfect ramp. Sure, it was dirty and messy, but that's kind of the point when it comes to boys and their toys.

The fun never seemed to last long enough, though. The truck batteries ran out. The controller batteries ran out. All those fantastic leaps and jumps over the sawdust pile and barrel rolls in the parking lot meant that truck parts broke. The nearest hobby shop was an hour away, so repairs sometimes had to wait for a week or more.

Here's the point of all this talk about a silly remote-controlled truck: It's temporary in nature. When it comes to a daily walk with Christ, however, the joy never ends. He is there for us twenty-four hours a day, seven days a week, 365 days a year. The satisfaction to be found in a relationship with Christ was, is, and always will be fulfilling.

Most of all, eternal life is just that—eternal, never-ending, unceasing. Mere words aren't enough to express the wonderful forever experience that heaven is going to be. No more stress. No more tears. No more pain. Just being in the presence of God will bring fullness of joy like never before.

BOTTOM LINE

Hobbies, no matter what they might be, are only temporary. Life with Christ is forever.

Moment of Strength: Psalm 103:1-5

WE NEED OTHERS

*Confess your sins to each other and pray for each
other so that you may be healed.*

James 5:16

MARK WAS TERRIFIED. For as long as he could remember, he had pretended to have it all together and had hidden his secrets behind a mask of spiritual activity: teaching Sunday school, leading a men's Bible study, and serving as a deacon. But his perfectionism had worn him out, and he was tired of the facade. Today he was going to come clean and tell his small group about his struggle with pornography and his recent emotional affair.

Instead of rejecting him or throwing him out of the group as he had feared they might, each man embraced him and told him how much they respected his courage. Mark was shocked as the other men began to open up about their own struggles and failures. It quickly turned into one of the most intimate and meaningful meetings they had experienced in years.

Like Mark, we often strive to be the kind of men who are self-sufficient and do not need the help of others, including God. Like Mark, we pretend to be strong. But this individualism has severe consequences. We are left to face our fears and insecurities alone. We were not designed to live isolated, self-sufficient lives. We need each other and were designed for authentic community.

In what ways are you hiding behind a mask of spiritual activity? Are you experiencing real community with other men?

BOTTOM LINE

God wants to bring us to a place where we can accept our need for others.

Moment of Strength: Proverbs 15:22

WRESTLING HONESTLY WITH GOD

My life is poured out like water, and all my bones are out of joint.
My heart is like wax, melting within me.

Psalm 22:14

STEVE MANAGED A SMILE and a convincing "I'm fine" when his friend Bob asked how he was doing. But the truth was, he was far from fine. He was in a commission-only job, and it had been four months since he had gotten paid. In a matter of days, the bank was going to take his home. He was terrified and felt like a failure as a husband and a father. And if he were to be honest, he was also angry and felt as if God had abandoned him when he needed Him the most.

Like Steve, we can often feel like failures when life isn't working out the way we planned. It is easy to envision "good" Christians as those whose faith is unwavering and who can smile no matter the circumstance. It is often hard to envision good Christians struggling with fear, doubt, anger, or sadness. But the psalmists were honest with their doubts and struggles and felt the freedom to come to God with their questions and heartache. Scripture is full of examples of men and women who struggled honestly with life's brokenness.

Do you feel the freedom to wrestle honestly with God when your circumstances are less than desirable? What situations are you attempting to deal with on your own because you feel God might be disappointed with you? Take your fears and worries to your heavenly Father. He loves you, and He wants to help you.

BOTTOM LINE

People of real faith struggle honestly with the brokenness of life. We can get help from God and others only if we're honest and ask for it.

Moment of Strength: Psalm 13:1-2

OVERCOMING SHAME

Don't be afraid; there is no more disgrace for you.
Isaiah 54:4

WE OFTEN HEAR THE WORDS *guilt* and *shame* used interchangeably, but there is a huge difference between them. Guilt is what we feel when we've made a mistake; shame is the core belief that we *are* a mistake. True guilt plays a vital role in healthy repentance because it allows us to see exactly how we have fallen short and missed the mark. Shame, on the other hand, traps us in a perpetual cycle of fear and self-loathing that leads us to one conclusion: God is disappointed with us.

This experience causes us to be afraid and to want to cover up. We strive to look good on the outside and may go to great lengths not to allow others the opportunity to get to know us.

But the more we hide our shame, the more we hinder the deep healing that God wants to bring about. Our shame diminishes as we reveal our true selves to those who love us and accept us rather than disgrace us. This is not easy, because we don't expect to be loved or accepted. What a wonderful moment of grace when God says, "Do not be afraid, for you will not be put to shame" (Isaiah 54:4, HCSB). We are free to open our hearts to God and find love and acceptance and not shame. The thing is, He knows absolutely everything about us and loves us anyway. We have to take His word on this, not our own thinking or life experience. What shame have you been covering up that needs to be uncovered this week?

BOTTOM LINE

It is God's desire to heal our deep wounds of shame. Risk opening up and allowing Him into those painful places.

Moment of Strength: Joshua 1:9

THE CIVILITY PROJECT

Let your conversation be gracious and attractive so that
you will have the right response for everyone.
Colossians 4:6

EVEN AMONG CHRISTIANS, the topic of civility may produce little more than eye rolls and groans. This is the digital age, after all. Every voice deserves a platform, and everyone's opinion is considered worthy, regardless of its merit or proximity to truth. Your morning scroll through your Twitter feed tells you everything you need to know about the level of vitriol in the public square. And yet followers of Christ are called to something higher—to speak with grace in an increasingly uncivil society thick with the rising cacophony of vulgarity and boorishness.

When writing to the believers in Colossae, Paul urged them to mark their speech with grace, especially when engaging with "outsiders" (Colossians 4:5-6, HCSB). Some Christians confuse grace-tinged speech with a lack of conviction, as if civility and conviction can't coexist. But not only can they coexist; they are allies in the battle of ideas, both in private engagement and in the public square.

God is concerned not only with what we say and believe, but with how we articulate it. Our tongues should reflect the difference between light and darkness, and they should adorn the gospel well, rather than adopting the base rhetoric of the world. In an increasingly verbal world, with every word we speak, type, or text, we must ask: *Does this bring glory to God?* If not, we shouldn't say it.

BOTTOM LINE

Grace epitomizes the speech of a gospel-centered man. How are you doing in that area?

Moment of Strength: Proverbs 8:8

WHAT'S NEXT?

For the LORD God is our sun and our shield. He gives us grace and glory.
The LORD will withhold no good thing from those who do what is right.

Psalm 84:11

EVERY MAN HAS A special interest in *something*. For some, it's sports—be it baseball, football, hockey, or NASCAR. Other men hunt and fish. It might be a particular book that's a real page-turner, or maybe it's something as simple as a night out with your wife or quiet time at home with the family.

One of the most fun things in life is to be looking forward to something. There's a keen sense of anticipation that for a lot of folks is like being a kid at Christmas again. For the briefest of moments, such eager expectation can be a great escape from the everyday pressures of living in today's busy world, which is filled with responsibilities and stress.

As enjoyable as our interests may be, however, they pale in comparison to our ultimate hope in Jesus Christ. A day is coming when we will stand face-to-face with Him, free from the trials and pains of this world. No more sleepless nights, sickness, or suffering. No more regret or longing.

Let that soak in for a few moments. Our hobbies are fun, yes, but in the end, they're only temporary. A thousand years from now, it simply won't matter how the Steelers did this year or how many home runs you hit in your church softball league. The hope of eternal life with Jesus puts everything in perspective. If we lose sight of that, we will try to get more out of our hobbies than they can provide.

BOTTOM LINE

Our interests can be a lot of fun, but the enjoyment we find in them will be nothing compared to the day we meet Jesus face-to-face. Put your hope in that.

Moment of Strength: Psalm 84

NOTES

JANUARY

6   *Economists David Blanchflower and Andrew Oswald* . . . David G. Blanchflower and Andrew J. Oswald, "Well-Being over Time in Britain and the USA," *Journal of Public Economics*, 88 (2004) 1359–86, www.dartmouth.edu/~blnchflr/papers /jpube.pdf.

9   *A scene from the 1999 movie* October Sky . . . *October Sky*, directed by Joe Johnston (Universal Pictures, 1999).

    Like those people who missed their chance . . . see Greg Daugherty, "Seven Famous People Who Missed the Titanic," *Smithsonian*, March 1, 2012, www .smithsonianmag.com/history/seven-famous-people-who-missed-the-titanic -101902418.

12   *a 2006 Gallup poll* . . . Scott Todd, *Hope Rising: How Christians Can End Extreme Poverty in This Generation* (Nashville: Nelson Books, 2014), 144–47.

13   *A piano tuner doesn't tune one piano* . . . A. W. Tozer, *The Pursuit of God* (Abbotsford, WI: Aneko Press, 2015), 79–80.

24   *Many people were so upset* . . . Associated Press, "Bullied Bus Driver Fund Has More Than $700,000," *Columbia Daily Tribune*, July 22, 2012, www.columbia tribune.com/wire/bullied-bus-driver-fund-has-more-than/article_74f0956c-f3a7 -511f-b569-5b26b4bc006a.html.

25   *"What comes into our minds"* and *"For this reason the gravest question"* . . . A. W. Tozer, *The Knowledge of the Holy* (New York: HarperCollins 1961), 1. Italics added.

26   *the ratio of high school students* . . . "Student-to-School-Counselor Ratio 2013–2014," The American School Counselor Association, https://www .schoolcounselor.org/asca/media/asca/home/Ratios13-14.pdf, accessed June 13, 2017.

27   *For a thirty-second commercial* . . . Thomas Duffy, "Super Bowl Ads 2017: Latest Info on Cost of 2017 Super Bowl Commercials," Bleacher Report, February 5, 2017, http://bleacherreport.com/articles/2691154-super-bowl-ads-2017-latest-info -on-cost-of-2017-super-bowl-commercial.

    Time *magazine* . . . Alex Fitzpatrick, et. al., "The 25 Most Influential Super Bowl Ads of All Time," *Time*, January 31, 2017, http://time.com/4653281/super-bowl-ads -commercials-most-influential-time.

FEBRUARY

3 *"Man is born broken"* . . . Eugene O'Neill, *Selected Letters of Eugene O'Neill*, ed. Travis Bogard and Jackson R. Bryer (New York: Proscenium, 1994), 264.

10 *Great companies pinpointed* . . . Jim Collins, *Good to Great* (New York: HarperCollins, 2001), chapter 6.

12 *"God loves you just the way you are"* . . . Max Lucado, *Just Like Jesus* (Nashville: Nelson, 2012), 4.

15 *When Michael Aamodt published* . . . Ellen McCarthy, "Study Breaks Down Divorce Rates by Occupation," *Washington Post*, September 19, 2010, www .washingtonpost.com/wp-dyn/content/article/2010/09/16/AR2010091607509 .html.

MARCH

9 *"Aim at Heaven"* . . . C. S. Lewis, *Mere Christianity* (New York: HarperCollins, 2001), 135.

12 *"Someone at the table"* and *"Being a good example"* . . . Randy Alcorn, "The One Surprising Thing My Daughter Remembered Most about My Parenting," *Church Leaders*, November 20, 2015, http://churchleaders.com/youth/youth-leaders -articles/266502-the-one-surprising-thing-my-daughter-remembered-most-about -my-parenting.html.

25 *"Your reactions reveal"* . . . Mark Batterson, *Primal: A Quest for the Lost Soul of Christianity* (Colorado Springs: Multnomah, 2009), 22.

30 *"Honey, I forgot to duck"* . . . Jacob Weisberg, *Ronald Reagan* (New York: Times Books, Henry Holt, 2016), 71.

APRIL

6 He may not be "safe" . . . adapted from C. S. Lewis, *The Lion, the Witch and the Wardrobe* (New York: HarperCollins, 2000), 79–80.

17 *A study at San Diego State University* . . . Kathleen Doheny, "Choose Dark Chocolate for Health Benefits," WebMD, April 24, 2012, www.webmd.com/diet /news/20120424/pick-dark-chocolate-health-benefits#1.

MAY

5 *Tattoos have come a long way* . . . Jennifer Viegas, "Oetzi Iceman's Tattoos Came from Fireplace," *NBC News*, July 17, 2009, http://www.nbcnews.com/id/31965532 /ns/technology_and_science-science/#.WQka1BPyuUk.

8 *"live on a good compliment two weeks"* . . . Samuel L. Clemens, letter to Gertrude Natkin, March 2, 1906, in *Mark Twain's Aquarium: The Samuel Clemens Angelfish Correspondence, 1905–1910*, ed. John Cooley (Athens: University of Georgia Press, 2009), 16.

16 *"I realized early that my strength"* . . . Shane Hamman, interview with Jesse Florea, April 19, 2008.

JUNE

4 *In 2010, professors at Boston College* . . . Prof. Brad Harrington, Fred Van Deusen, and Prof. Jamie Ladge, *The New Dad: Exploring Fatherhood within a Career Context,*

June 2010, www.bc.edu/content/dam/files/centers/cwf/research/publications/research reports/The%20New%20Dad%202010_Exploring%20Fatherhood%20within%20a%20 Career%20Context, accessed May 2, 2017.

9   *"people who believe the unrealistic [romantic] portrayals"* . . . Jeremy L. Osborn, "When TV and Marriage Meet: A Social Exchange Analysis of the Impact of Television Viewing on Marital Satisfaction and Commitment," *Science Daily*, September 11, 2012, www.sciencedaily.com/releases/2012/09/120918121322.htm.

18 *Mark says that when he coaches parents* . . . Mark Gregston, "The Value of a Question," *Heartlight Ministries*, January 20, 2014, www.heartlightministries. org/2014/01/question.

19 *"She gives you authority"* . . . Meg Meeker, *Strong Fathers, Strong Daughters: 10 Secrets Every Father Should Know* (Washington, DC: Regnery, 2013), 28–29.

21 *"The place God calls you to"* . . . Frederick Buechner, *Wishful Thinking: A Theological ABC* (New York: Harper & Row, 1973).

22 "Why did you attend a small, obscure university" . . . Black Education Television interview with Jerry Rice, quoted in *1001 Quotes, Illustrations, and Humorous Stories for Preachers, Teachers, and Writers*, eds. Edward K. Rowell and *Leadership* (Grand Rapids, MI: Baker, 2008), 333.

    86 percent of new converts . . . Elmer Towns, *Winning the Winnable: Friendship Evangelism* (Lynchburg, VA: Church Leadership Institute, 1986).

25 *"Any one can get angry"* Aristotle, *The Nicomachean Ethics*, book II, sec. 9, trans. W. D. Ross, http://classics.mit.edu/Aristotle/nicomachaen.2.ii.html, accessed May 2, 2017.

JULY

10 *"There is not a square inch"* . . . Abraham Kuyper, *Abraham Kuyper: A Centennial Reader*, ed. James D. Bratt (Grand Rapids: Eerdmans, 1998), 461.

18 *"Men today are facing incredible adversity"* Phil Waldrep, interview by Teddy James, "Gridiron Conference Urges Men to Stand Strong," *AFA Journal* (May 2013), www.afajournal.org/2013/May/052013gridiron.html.

AUGUST

4 *"Never give in, never, never, never"* . . . Winston Churchill, speech at Harrow School, October 29, 1941, www.winstonchurchill.org/resources/speeches/1941 -1945-war-leader/103-never-give-in.

6 *"the ape that gibbers"* . . . Frederick Buechner, *Godric* (San Francisco: HarperCollins, 1980), 153.

    "Lust is taking a complete, complex human" . . . Bill Hybels with Kevin and Sherry Harney, *Living in God's Power: Finding God's Strength for Life's Challenges* (Grand Rapids: Zondervan, 1998), 47.

    "We are not masters of our own feeling" . . . François Fénelon, "On the Prospect of Death in Old Age," in *The Spiritual Letters of Archbishop Fénelon: Letters to Women*, trans. H. L. Sidney Lear (London: Longmans, Green, 1877), 174. Italics in the original.

7 *"Talk to a man about himself"* . . . Benjamin Disraeli, quoted in David Graham, *The Philosophy of Benjamin Disraeli* (CreateSpace, 2014), 18.

11 *"Freedom is 'the absence'"* . . . Merriam-Webster's 11th Collegiate Dictionary, s.v. "freedom," www.merriam-webster.com/dictionary/freedom, accessed May 2, 2017.

28 *"There are only two kinds of people"* C. S. Lewis, *The Great Divorce* (New York: HarperCollins, 2001), 75.

SEPTEMBER

11 *"How much pain have cost us"* . . . Thomas Jefferson, in *The Writings of Thomas Jefferson: Memoir, Correspondence, and Miscellanies from the Papers of Thomas Jefferson,* ed. Thomas Jefferson Randolph, volume IV, letter dated April 8, 1816 from Thomas Jefferson to John Adams (Charlottesville VA: F. Carr, 1829), 271.

   "Drag your thoughts away" . . . Mark Twain, *The American Claimant: And Other Stories and Sketches* (New York: Harper & Brothers, 1898), 135.

13 *"I was the child"* . . . "South Carolina Executes Man Who Strangled Prison Inmate," *Reuters,* May 6, 2011, www.reuters.com/article/us-execution-south -carolina-idUSTRE7456SK20110506.

14 *"I took a pack of cigarettes"* . . . Tommy Lasorda, in Ron Fimrite, "He Goes Where the In Crowd Goes," *Sports Illustrated,* January 30, 1984, www.si.com /vault/1984/01/30/540986/he-goes-where-the-in-crowd-goes.

16 *First, modify your environment* . . . Adapted from Robert Epstein, "Change Your Bad Habits to Good," *Reader's Digest,* October 1998.

18 *"Wikipedia is the best thing ever"* . . . Michael Scott, in "The Negotiation," on *The Office,* season 3, episode 18, first aired April 5, 2007. Created by Greg Daniels, Ricky Gervais, and Stephen Merchant. Written by Greg Daniels, directed by Jeffrey Blitz.

19 *"Women may really push"* . . . "Males Believe Discussing Problems Is a Waste of Time, MU Study Shows," MU News Bureau, August 22, 2011, http://munews .missouri.edu/news-releases/2011/0822-males-believe-discussing-problems-is-a -waste-of-time-mu-study-shows.

20 *competition, camaraderie, and community* . . . "Community Basketball League Stresses Three C's," momsTEAM, June 13, 2011, www.momsteam.com/sports /community-basketball-league-stresses-three-cs.

OCTOBER

7 *"Pick it up!"* . . . Jim Paul, *You Dropped It, You Pick It Up!* (Baton Rouge, LA: Ed's Publishing, 1983).

31 *More than $8 billion* . . . "Halloween Fast Facts," *CNN,* October 17, 2016, www .cnn.com/2013/06/13/us/halloween-fast-facts/index.html.

NOVEMBER

13 *"Possibly the greatest malaise"* . . . William McNamara, "Wasting Time Creatively," recording of a talk given at an unknown time and place (Sedona, AZ: Spiritual Life Institute).

17 *a ten-pack of chewing gum* . . . "UPC: The Transformation of Retail," *IBM,* www-03 .ibm.com/ibm/history/ibm100/us/en/icons/upc/transform, accessed May 2, 2017.

DECEMBER

5 *four essential power tools* . . . Marc Lyman, "Four Essential Power Tools," *The Art of Manliness*, July 29, 2011, www.artofmanliness.com/2011/07/29 /four-essential-power-tools.

12 *married men tend to enjoy* . . . "Marriage and Men's Health," *Harvard Health*, July 2010, www.health.harvard.edu/newsletter_article/marriage-and-mens-health.

nearly 70 percent of men . . . Ibid.

14 *According to statistics from the Joshua Project* . . . "Global Statistics: All People Groups by Reachedness Status," Joshua Project, accessed April 27, 2017, https:// joshuaproject.net/people_groups/statistics.

"The word for 'nation'" . . . Nathan Creitz, "Know Jesus and Make Him Known (Matthew 28:18-20)," sermon at City Life Church, Ridgewood, NY, January 14, 2015, http://citylifechurchnyc.com/know-jesus-make-known-matthew-2818-20.

22 *the tenth-most-requested gift* . . . Hannah Furness, "A 'Dad' Is Tenth Most Popular Christmas List Request for Children," *The Telegraph*, December 24, 2012, www.telegraph.co.uk/topics/christmas/9764688/A-dad-is-tenth-most -popular-Christmas-list-request-for-children.html.

ABOUT WALK THRU THE BIBLE

Walk Thru the Bible ignites passion for God's Word through innovative live events, inspiring biblical resources, and a global impact that changes lives worldwide . . . including yours.

Known for innovative methods and high-quality resources, we serve the whole body of Christ across denominational, cultural, and national lines. We partner with the local church worldwide to fulfill its mission, communicating the truths of God's Word in a way that makes the Bible readily accessible to anyone. Through our strong global network, we are strategically positioned to address the church's greatest need: developing mature, committed, and spiritually reproducing believers.

Our live events and small group curricula are taught in more than 50 languages by more than 80,000 people in more than 130 countries. More than 100 million devotionals have been packaged into daily magazines, books, and other publications that reach over five million people each year.

Wherever you are on your journey, we can help.

Walk Thru the Bible
www.walkthru.org
1.800.361.6131

It's both /and

{
biblical *and* fun
spiritual *and* innovative
inspiring *and* surprising

"**Walk Thru the Bible** provided our families with a fantastic journey through the Old Testament . . . filled with laughter, inspiring teaching, and unforgettable lessons about our Creator."
—Dave K. Smith
Executive Pastor, Willow Creek Community Church
Crystal Lake Campus

It's your move. Start here.*

* **ot LIVE** is designed for any size church.
Learn more at **www.walkthru.org**

Follow up **ot LIVE** with our exclusive 6-week
God's Grand Story churchwide Bible engagement campaign.
Learn more at **thegrandstory.org**